Converting a Nation

Studies in European Culture and History
edited by
Eric D. Weitz and Jack Zipes
University of Minnesota

Since the fall of the Berlin Wall and the collapse of communism, the very meaning of Europe has been opened up and is in the process of being redefined. European states and societies are wrestling with the expansion of NATO and the European Union and with new streams of immigration, while a renewed and reinvigorated cultural engagement has emerged between East and West. But the fast-paced transformations of the last fifteen years also have deeper historical roots. The reconfiguring of contemporary Europe is entwined with the cataclysmic events of the twentieth century, two world wars and the Holocaust, and with the processes of modernity that, since the eighteenth century, have shaped Europe and its engagement with the rest of the world.

Studies in European Culture and History is dedicated to publishing books that explore major issues in Europe's past and present from a wide variety of disciplinary perspectives. The works in the series are interdisciplinary; they focus on culture and society and deal with significant developments in Western and Eastern Europe from the eighteenth century to the present within a social historical context. With its broad span of topics, geography, and chronology, the series aims to publish the most interesting and innovative work on modern Europe.

Published by Palgrave Macmillan:

Fascism and Neofascism: Critical Writings on the Radical Right in Europe
by Eric Weitz

Fictive Theories: Towards a Deconstructive and Utopian Political Imagination
by Susan McManus

German-Jewish Literature in the Wake of the Holocaust: Grete Weil, Ruth Klüger, and the Politics of Address
by Pascale Bos

Turkish Turn in Contemporary German Literature: Toward a New Critical Grammar of Migration
by Leslie Adelson

Terror and the Sublime in Art and Critical Theory: From Auschwitz to Hiroshima to September 11
by Gene Ray

Transformations of the New Germany
edited by Ruth Starkman

Caught by Politics: Hitler Exiles and American Visual Culture
edited by Sabine Eckmann and Lutz Koepnick

Legacies of Modernism: Art and Politics in Northern Europe, 1890-1950
edited by Patrizia C. McBride, Richard W. McCormick, and Monika Zagar

Police Forces: A Cultural History of an Institution
edited by Klaus Mladek

Richard Wagner for the New Millennium: Essays in Music and Culture
edited by Matthew Bribitzer-Stull, Alex Lubet, and Gottfried Wagner

Representing Masculinity: Male Citizenship in Modern Western Culture
edited by Stefan Dudink, Anna Clark, and Karen Hagemann

Remembering the Occupation in French Film: National Identity in Postwar Europe
by Leah D. Hewitt

"Gypsies" in European Literature and Culture
edited by Valentina Glajar and Domnica Radulescu

Converting a Nation

A Modern Inquisition and the Unification of Italy

Ariella Lang

palgrave
macmillan

CONVERTING A NATION

First published in 2008 by PALGRAVE MACMILLAN® in the US—a division of St. Martin's Press LLC, 175 Fifth Avenue, New York, NY 10010.

Where this book is distributed in the UK, Europe and the rest of the world, this is by Palgrave Macmillan, a division of Macmillan Publishers Limited, registered in England, company number 785998, of Houndmills, Basingstoke, Hampshire RG21 6XS.

Palgrave Macmillan is the global academic imprint of the above companies and has companies and representatives throughout the world.

ISBN-13: 978-0-230-60672-2
ISBN-10: 0-230-60672-5

Library of Congress Cataloging-in-Publication Data is available from the Library of Congress.

A catalogue record of the book is available from the British Library.

Design by Scribe Inc.

First edition: October 2008

10 9 8 7 6 5 4 3 2 1

Printed in the United States of America.

For Alex

Contents

Acknowledgments

I am indebted to a great many friends, colleagues and teachers who helped me at all stages in the writing of this book, from clarifying the ideas I was interested in pursuing to refining the final manuscript. I wish to thank Teodolinda Barolini, Victoria De Grazia, Andrea Malaguti, Nelson Moe, Silvana Patriarca, and Luciano Rebay, who read this book or parts of it at different stages, and whose insightfulness and advice helped me define, and redefine, the scope of my research. I also benefited enormously from the discussion group that Victoria De Grazia organized during my graduate student days at Columbia University; the dialogues we had were illuminating and have remained with me. Nelson Moe deserves special thanks: his careful reading and constructive criticism made me think harder and write better, and he has been an invaluable mentor and friend. Early conversations with Robert Amdur, Anthony Marks, and Franco Moretti were important as I navigated new territory and considered different approaches in the initial stages of the project. David Kertzer generously met with me before I entered the web of Italian and Vatican archives, which can be an overwhelming and confusing place indeed without such guidance. For reading countless pages and offering both practical and scholarly criticism, as well as welcome interruptions, I thank Miriam Halpern, Rebecca Mechanic, and Carin McLain. Jessica Lang generously read many drafts and sat through many a conversation about my project; her perceptive insights and editing skills were more beneficial than she knows. I am also grateful to the writing group she organized and to its participants for their helpful feedback and constant prodding. Thanks as well to Carmen, Franco, Mario, and Roberto Cigliano for their warm hospitality in Rome; my research would not have been nearly as fruitful or enjoyable without them. My parents, Berel and Helen Lang, have read these pages numerous times, submitting my work to their own rigorous standards of scholarship. They have taught me the value of serious inquiry, and I am grateful for their constant encouragement. My daughters, Michela and Nina, provided me with a respite from the solitary process of writing, and their passion for books served as a constant reminder of the true value of literature. Gabriel's arrival at the end of this process is proof that, while conclusions are satisfying, beginnings are even more inspiring.

Finally, I thank my husband, Alexander Kornfeld, partner in all things that matter. He has seen this book through from its earliest stages, putting up with months of commuting, listening tirelessly to the stories I discovered in the archives, reading drafts of chapters, and providing enthusiasm for the project that I would never have been able to sustain on my own. His confidence in me gave me courage, and his curiosity, encouragement, and generosity made this book possible.

I am grateful to the editors of this series, Jack Zipes and Eric Weitz, for their enthusiasm with regard to this project, and to Farideh Koohi-Kamali, Julia Cohen, Brigitte Shul, and Daniel Constantino for the guidance they provided at the press. Research for this study was funded in part by a Columbia University travel fellowship and by a fellowship from the American Association of University Women. In Italy I found valuable documents at numerous Vatican archives, including the Archivio del Vicariato di Roma, the Archivio della Congregazione per la Dottrina della Fede, and the Archivio Segreto Vaticano. The Archivio di Stato di Bologna and the Archivio di Stato di Firenze were also extraordinarily useful, and the community members running the Archivio della Comunità Ebraica di Livorno generously shared their important materials with me. I would also like to acknowledge an edited collection and a journal in which early versions of two chapters appeared: "The Politics of Conversion: Jews and Inquisition Law in Nineteenth Century Italy," *The Roman Inquisition, the Index and the Jews*, ed. Stephan Wendehorst (Boston: Brill, 2005); "The Politics and Poetics of Vatican Holocaust Discourse," *Judaism* 52.3–4 (2003).

Introduction

In the first half of the nineteenth century, Italy, as the emerging nation-state closest to the Church's own seat of power, produced a sense of vulnerability within the Vatican by threatening the power and values it represented. For its part, the presence of the Vatican on Italian soil was, according to many scholars, a key factor in the weak, indeed fragmented, sense of national identity among Italians. This presence thus raises a number of issues, the most prominent of which include the relationship of Catholic officialdom to secular Italian ideology—particularly as the latter became more distinct from Catholic policy—and the more general problem of the situation of minority religions in the context of Catholic culture on the peninsula. These topics have not been thoroughly studied, either individually or as an interrelated set; more specifically, scholarship concerning this period fails to consider an analysis of the situation and the peculiar difficulties facing minority populations as a means for better understanding the community at large—and its "majority problems."

The present study addresses this failure by examining these issues in terms of religious rule and secular politics within a sharply defined timeframe. I begin at the reestablishment of the Papal States in 1814, when Catholic officialdom was reasserted in a way that defined much of the culture on the Italian peninsula, and end in 1864, when Pope Pius IX issued his famous *Syllabus of Errors*, a list of the errors, according to the Church, produced by modern advances in the political, social and scientific worlds—a list that acknowledges the Church's view of Italian culture and its direction during the preceding fifty years. I argue that the larger issues at the heart of Italian culture within this period can to a significant extent be understood, or at least identified, by investigating critical problems such as the relationship between the Vatican hierarchy, clergy, and laity; the politicization of Catholicism; and the interaction between minority cultures and Church authority.

Although these problems are in fact amply documented, the documents have been largely overlooked; indeed, the character of the documentation itself has contributed to its neglect. I rely on a wide range of sources that include clerical correspondence, diaries, newspapers, novels, and the largely untapped resources of the recently opened Inquisition Archives in Rome. As I argue, taken individually these sources provide important evidence concerning the difficult and complicated relation of religious and secular interests. More specifically, each draws in its own way on the theme of conversion as a motif meant to improve the citizenry and counter, or at least slow, the changes that come with unification. Taken together these sources reveal a fuller tapestry of cultural pressures, exchanges, and compromises.

My approach, then, is interdisciplinary insofar as it rests on the use of distinctly different kinds of sources. I employ these different genres for several reasons. First, each kind of writing is shaped by the consequences that the French Revolution and subsequent Restoration produced on the Italian peninsula. Within this larger framework, each has its own story to tell, its own motives to reveal. Reading novels in relation to Inquisition trials and newspaper stories, I argue, locates the fictive texts in their historical context and so reveals the importance of the interaction between the historic context of the work and the interpretation of the work itself. In addition, this interdisciplinary approach enables me to provide a fuller examination of the status and treatment of minority religions on the peninsula—an analysis that, in turn, yields a better understanding of the community at large, the Church's developing political voice, and its relationship with non-Catholic and secular culture. In other words, by exploring the theme of conversion as it occurs in different literary contexts, my study offers a multifaceted approach to understanding the relations between the Vatican and the modernizing nation-state in nineteenth-century Italy. The first half of the nineteenth century, after all, is the period when a national Italian identity was being constructed, a project that itself weaves together the fictive and the historical in an attempt to create a unified vision.

The Church's officially mandated efforts at enforcing a certain identity are illustrated in a variety of Vatican-supported literature, from trial documentation to novels to journal articles. Such literature responds to Vatican anxieties regarding individuals and minority groups who are gaining a civil and political voice in the period under examination, not to mention more access to Christian society; it thus reflects the Church's attempts to censure and control how these individuals participated and identified with general, that is, Christian, society. The experiences of these individuals nonetheless resurface in a variety of ways, from challenges to the juridical process, for example, to personal letters and appeals, to coded language that tries to evade detection, just to name a few. In so doing, these individuals attempt to narrate an identity that differs from or stands in opposition to the voice of Catholic officialdom, creating an important subnarrative to the conversion stories examined herein.

Thus my investigation into the phenomenon and theme of conversion leads to a study of literary, legal, and social works that cross traditional disciplinary boundaries and genre classification and that are not often placed next to one another for study. The way in which these works resonate with one another and the crucial role they all play in this period of transformation confirm the extent to which concerns of national definition and belonging to a larger community cross traditional lines of study. Indeed, the texts belong together precisely because of their common cultural significance. The authors and subjects of the conversion narratives to be examined—and all the texts examined can be defined as such, regardless of genre or discipline—were engaged in imagining, defining, or redefining a community. This work contemplates the consequences and results of this engagement.

Through an examination of these sources, I propose an account of how the process of conversion, both voluntary and forced, affected the construction of national identity in nineteenth-century Italy. The narratives provided by Inquisition trials, novels, and newspaper stories are in an important sense independent and so provide a wide range of evidence ranging from the legal to the literary and the cultural; at the same time, this evidence can be examined systematically and can be considered as bearing on the specific cultural issues surrounding nationhood and national and religious identity. I propose that Vatican supporters advocated conversion because they wished to ensure that the newly emerging nation-state remained culturally and religiously Catholic. "The wish is father to the deed," and by identifying this motive I also bring into sharp focus a number of elements of nineteenth-century Italian culture.

My claim that conversion plays an important role during this time is evidenced by the variety of sources, from theology to fiction, that grapple with this topic. Indeed, such evidence also links these sources to an important common theme: the issue of conversion is in each case prominent.

The conversion stories analyzed here differ from one another in a variety of ways: some pertain to real people, others are entirely fictional; some stories take the form of journal articles and letters, others of short stories and novels; they depict religious conversion from different traditions—Protestantism, Judaism, and lapsed Catholics of the Roman Catholic tradition. But these differences should not obscure—indeed they highlight—an important shared characteristic: both singly and as a group these stories bear witness to and so can provide the modern reader with a keen sense of the difficulties of forging a national identity. This narration of the problematic relations between the Vatican and the modernizing Italian nation-state is particularly significant as it occurs at a time when the construction of Italian national citizenship and its Catholic inflections were being invoked, contested, and reimagined. Ultimately, then, my goal in this work is to establish, analyze, and ultimately account for these difficulties.

My inquiry is divided into three parts: trials of the Inquisition, nineteenth-century fictional narratives, and the development of a Catholic press. In Part I (Chapters 1 and 2), I examine a number of Inquisition trials. All these trials, and certainly the two that I consider at greatest length, center on the issue of coercive conversions from Judaism to Catholicism. The issue of conversion in this context is significant because it reflects a dynamic between the clergy and the people, whether Catholic or Jewish, living under the jurisdiction of the Papal States. The trials, all occurring in the first quarter of the nineteenth century, reflect growing Vatican concern for public opinion, as well as changes in Vatican diplomacy, both indicators of the politicization of ecclesiastical policies. Indeed, this period marks a time of considerable change on the peninsula as well, and thus these trials deserve to be closely examined both for the rhetoric they employ and the politics they espouse: taken together, they simultaneously provide a detailed sense of communal Italian cultural politics during this period and a commentary on the tension produced by the Vatican enforcement of Inquisition law in the context of the increasing strength of secular law elsewhere on the peninsula. These trials are particularly significant because they have come to light only recently, with the opening of the Vatican's Inquisition archives in 1998; indeed, the opening of the Sant'Uffizio archives provides my project with its point of departure, and in Chapter 1 I examine the issue of conversion as it is taken up in trials in the Papal States as a form of "cultural politics" that reflects more broadly the dynamic between the Church and individuals living under its jurisdiction. Legal narratives, I argue, and the rhetoric they employ, are an integral aspect of the society in which they appear, and this examination of such narratives seeks to explore precisely the relation between law and culture through a close reading of the poetic and social elements revealed in the documentation surrounding these trials. In other words, I seek to understand how these stories give the contemporary reader access to a better cultural understanding of the concerns of the Vatican and the means by which they sought to deflect the onset of modernization.

The detailed exploration in Chapter 2 of two conversion stories seeks to understand and explore Christian and Jewish identity in the Papal States, and how (regional) Italian identity fit in with the strong religious undercurrent of daily life in this period. I suggest that Inquisition trials provide a combination of elements—cultural, psychological and behavioral—that the Church employs to sustain itself. By exploring these trials, I mean not only to evaluate the circumstances of the people whom we meet within specific cases but to understand aspects of nineteenth-century culture in the Papal States more generally and the ways in which the legal process reveals and reflects the culture that it shapes. Through its ruling, reasoning, and rhetoric, the Vatican played a central role in shaping attitudes that encouraged religious intolerance; indeed, through the law the Vatican sought to rewrite the Jew as a convert to Catholicism, and thus as a conquest of the Church. The remaining Jews, and their community at large, were portrayed as a separate, dangerous entity to be shunned at all costs. By going to such efforts to condone and enforce conversions, Vatican legal narratives display a method by which papal supporters sought to define Italian identity in Catholic terms.

Studying a small religious community within the larger population may seem an indirect approach for establishing the character of Italian nationality during, and after, the Risorgimento. Unification, after all, is marked not only by tensions between secular and religious identity but also by a movement from more regional affiliations, including those of religion, profession, and family, to an allegiance with a greater nation that itself combines the secular and the religious. However, by exploring both the cultural identity of a person or small group, their relation to a community, and the ways in which this identity overlaps or conflicts with a newly formed national identity, we can discover recognizable political affiliations on a national level. Thus I examine how, on the one hand, national culture defines a concept of personhood and, on the other, the discrepancies between this idea of personhood and how the language of selfhood was expressed by the individual and groups brought under investigation. The Jewish community wished to retain its rights as a minority, that is, as a "local" community, which coincided with a religious identity, while retaining membership in the larger community. In this sense, the relationship between Italians as the majority and Jews as a religious minority exemplifies the problem of unification in a country where nationhood and religious identity are profoundly intertwined. Examining the stories and experiences of individuals within the Jewish community exposes these difficulties in both forms, as members of one group struggle to maintain their religious identity while trying to become members of the new secular nation-state. I propose considering and examining Italian national identity by looking through a narrative lens, one that marks the struggle involved in the displacement and replacement of regional and religious affiliations with a national and secular identity. This reformulation lies at the heart of any study of how nationality is defined, since the difficulties encountered by the Jews not only are specific to their community but also address these problems within the political, legal, and social framework of the society at large.

In Part II (Chapters 3 and 4) I discuss two nineteenth-century novels, Alessandro Manzoni's *The Betrothed* (*I Promessi Sposi*) and Antonio Bresciani's *The Jew of Verona* (*L'Ebreo di Verona*). In a desire to return to tradition and belief, and to establish Catholic ideals firmly in the new generations of Italians, these narratives represent the conversion of lapsed Catholics, Protestants, and Jews. That these works are entirely fictional extends the trope of conversion to an entirely different representational field. And yet these novels, I argue, provide readers access to cultural truth. That is, they reflect social and national concerns of the period in which they were written and are here read, analyzed, and interpreted within their historical context. Thus, like the trials that I examine as works defined by their political and poetic essence, here too I understand Manzoni's and Bresciani's texts as works defined by their relationship, and that of their authors, to society.

In Chapter 3 I explore the conversion stories of Manzoni's novel as reflective of the author's vision of a unified Italy anchored to and guided by Christian values. This vision rests on and so reflects the author's political identity as a liberal conservative and his view of a modern nation eschewing the excesses of the French Revolution. Most importantly, his vision is the result of his own conversion to Catholicism, and so we find in this novel a representation of the same issue raised by historical accounts of conversion. Here, however, the voice of the author is also the voice of the convert, rather than a historical account that is presumably "third person." Manzoni's views and experiences are reflected in the Catholic awakening of the novel's principal characters, Padre

Cristoforo, the *Innominato* (the Unnamed), and, as I argue, the young protagonist, Renzo.

In Chapter 4 I analyze Antonio Bresciani's best-selling novel, *The Jew of Verona*, which has largely been overlooked in contemporary criticism. With his novel, Bresciani popularizes ideas that were already present among reactionary thinkers of the religious right. Indeed, reflecting the differences between liberal and reactionary Catholicism, Manzoni and Bresciani differ significantly from one another. And yet both men envision a modern Italy that is essentially Catholic, and Bresciani, similar to Manzoni, uses conversion in his widely popular novel to promote a collective, Catholic existence that can be defined as a national identity. The startling aspect of the novel, however, is the way its author uses the tools of the modernizing nation, such as the need for a Catholic press, to reassert traditional Catholic cultural, political, and rreligious ideals. Thus far, this system of interaction and publication had empowered revolutionary fervor to the detriment of Vatican supporters. By recognizing the significance of a wider reading public, Bresciani helps the Vatican grapple with issues surrounding the circulation of information and ideas. I understand Bresciani's awareness of the power of circulation, which can be found in both the serial form in which his novel was published and within the drama of the novel itself, to suggest that the circulation of ideas and information can work together to strengthen a national, Italian Catholic culture.

In Part III (Chapter 5), which represents the third section of this study, I explore the development of the Catholic press as a phenomenon that significantly contributed to the politicization of Italian Catholic identity. The themes that recur juridically and fictionally find yet another outlet in this venue. The title of the leading journal, *Civiltà Cattolica*, itself underscores the oft-expressed Catholic belief that Christianity was at the heart of European civilization and thus should continue to play an integral role in the political life of the country. *Civiltà Cattolica*, together with other journals, regularly reported on Jewish and Protestant converts to Catholicism. The very regularity of these stories in the press bears witness to the cultural phenomenon that we find across the board. Stories of Protestants returning to the fold, stories of Jews recognizing the error of their ways, and stories of straying Catholics dedicating themselves anew to their faith, allowed papal supporters to demonstrate the strength and conquests of Catholicism, the very universality proclaimed by the name itself, despite the revolutionary changes in European politics. The celebrated conversion of the Protestant minister Carl Haller, for example, was considered a "vindication" for the upheaval brought about by the Protestant Reformation and French Revolution.

In conclusion, I argue that accounts of conversions, whether narrated through trials, novels, or newspapers, not only provided a means for expressing prevailing Catholic political opinions of the time but also reflected the radicalization of the reactionary attitudes of the ecclesiastical hierarchy throughout the first half of the nineteenth century. While newspaper stories differ in quality and style from novels and trial literature, all developed in step with the nation-state and were in this sense devices through which the Church sought to define a political and religious identity for Italians. Narratives of conversion to Catholicism allowed papal supporters to tell a story of national conquest and to advocate a society that upheld the legal, social, and religious tenets of Christianity. In a vehement, albeit ultimately futile, rejection of modernization, and modern conceptions of nationhood in particular, these stories embodied the Vatican's quest to ensure that the future Italian state and its citizenry remained the promised land and chosen people of the Catholic Church. And finally, as I explore in the epilogue to this work, the papal preoccupation with conversion and the language and attitudes of the Church that Catholic officials, writers, and journalists endorsed in the nineteenth century prefigured attitudes that continued to express themselves, though in a very different context, through the twentieth century and up to the present day.

Part I

Trials

Chapter 1

Reading between the Lines

Inquisition Texts and Catholic Conquests

In the memoirs that Bartolommeo Cardinal Pacca penned in 1828, the former Vatican secretary of state recorded the story of a pontificate that survived a turbulent time of transition. At the beginning of Pope Pius VII's twenty-three-year pontificate, which began in 1800 and encompassed Pacca's tenure, the pope had been interested in stabilizing the turbulent relationship between the Papal States and Napoleonic France. The emperor appeared, at least initially, equally eager to maintain a close relationship with the pope. The pope was angered, however, by Napoleon's intimation that the security of the Papal States depended upon the Vatican's accommodation of Napoleon's demands regarding religious matters; he stated in no uncertain terms that he would not conflate temporal and spiritual issues. Napoleon's failed efforts to make the pope accede to his wishes and his general belief that the Vatican greatly limited his powers led the French emperor to make good on his threats. In 1809 he invaded the Papal States. Pius VII immediately responded by excommunicating Napoleon, but this move did nothing to thwart the emperor, who annexed the Papal States to his empire and ordered a general in his army to take the pope prisoner. The Pope was supposedly carried out of Rome with no more than a *papetto*, equivalent to a ten-cent coin, in his purse.[1] He was taken first to Avignon and later to Savona, and in February 1810, he was imprisoned in Fontainebleau, where the conditions of his captivity were a good deal harsher than they had been. Here, exhausted, ill, and under enormous pressure, the pope signed a draft of a concordat that Napoleon had helped write. The concordat largely satisfied the emperor's demands regarding the relationship between the Catholic Church and the French Empire, and Napoleon immediately declared the signed draft public and binding.

Papal supporters from France, Germany, and Italy received news of the concordat with shock and dismay, recorded Pacca: "One cannot describe the sinister impression, and the terrible effect produced by the publication of this Concordat . . . the good Catholics of Paris were inconsolable. . . . In the rest of France no one believed it. . . . The same occurred in Germany, and in Italy."[2] Most striking about Pacca's description was the reception of this news in the capital city of the Papal States—Rome: "In Rome, then, news of the same new Concordat was received among laughs and hisses, and many, upon hearing the articles, went about repeating that expression that one uses in Rome when one believes something has occurred that is not only false, but impossible: *If this is true, let us go immediately to the Ghetto and make ourselves Jews.*"[3] The concordat's demotion of papal powers was such that Roman Catholics expressed their surprise by aligning themselves with arguably the most oppressed—and certainly among the most controlled—communities in the country. "Let us go to the Ghetto" and "make ourselves Jews" suggests that the restrictions invoked by this second concordat, perhaps recalling the condition of papal Jews, placed Catholics in an improbable, indeed unthinkable position—as impossible as imagining themselves as Jews.

Pacca's anecdote of the commotion that news of the concordat brought to Rome describes, in essence, an inverted story of conversion. The inversion of the conversionary act, the transition from Catholic to Jew rather than vice versa, denotes the absurdity of the action, making the maxim reflect not simply a falsehood but an impossibility. And, while Pacca often cites entire letters from leaders and government officials, the recounting of a maxim marks the only moment in his memoirs where Pacca attempts to cite the voice of common Romans. Thus Pacca's quotation is also significant because of its narrative value: while Jews made up a tiny percentage of the inhabitants of the Papal States, this reference reflects their pervasive presence in the imagination of the general populace.[4] In addition, if the expression was indeed as popular as Pacca appears to suggest, it reveals just how broadly the theme of conversion had entered the popular culture of nineteenth-century Rome. But even if Cardinal Pacca's claim was exaggerated, even if the saying was not as prevalent as he believed, his citation demonstrated the need within the Church hierarchy to perpetuate the government's vision of the status—both religious and political—of the Jewish community. That is, if this inverted story of conversion signified the ultimate impossibility, then by implication the traditional conversion story, the passage from Judaism to Catholicism, from the ghetto to the larger context of Rome, was an extremely plausible—indeed, acceptable—one.

The cardinal's use of and reference to this motto made it part of the official reaction to the events that occurred during Pius's exile. I use the term "official" here in relation to the fact that these are the stories of a political authority that wielded power over, and even determined the rights and privileges of, the inhabitants of the lands of the Papal States. The trials discussed in the following two chapters should be considered legal narratives in the same vein: they are the work of the Inquisition tribunal and its adherents, of Vatican clergyman and local church leaders. They are official documents detailing stories against individuals whose crime hinges upon rejecting conversion to Catholicism; they occurred at a time when, I will argue, the Vatican's recognition of its weakening power led to a redoubling of its efforts to impose a Catholic identity upon its own subjects. In other words, the actions of the converted Jews in these trials reflect Vatican anxiety at the possibility of disingenuous citizens that cross the border from the peripheral, outsider community of the ghetto into the larger, imagined community of the Church. The official nature of these different narratives should not suggest that they are static, however—quite the contrary: they respond to the pressures, threats, and issues that absorbed the powers of the Vatican at the time they were written.[5] These stories thus articulate the vision that the Vatican had of itself, both as a religious and temporal power, and of its relationship to other states in post–French Revolution Europe.

More specifically, Catholic leaders considered the French Revolution and the current state of political affairs in Europe to be an extension of the divisiveness that the Protestant Reformation had initially produced. Like the Protestants of earlier centuries, secular, atheist, and non-Christian forces were blamed for the revolutionary spirit and process of modernization that was gaining momentum. This conviction led many papal supporters to believe that Christian unity was more necessary than ever before. In the words of Viscount De Bonald, "The divisions among Christianity did nothing but open the door to the hostile errors of every religion revealed, and they consider[ed] Christianity as a besieged fortress, attacked on every side, and for which it is necessary, under pain of death, that the inhabitants unite for a common defense."[6] Pius VII adhered fully to this philosophy of unity, and conversion became a means to achieve this end. That is, through the radical rupture demanded of converts, and by means of extraordinary pressure on the Jewish community to convert, Pius sought a return to what he and others remembered as the faithful, unified society of an earlier era—a return to what appeared in retrospect to be the order of the Old Regime, and the religious devotion and practice of the past.

The Inquisition Tribunal wished to confirm the legitimacy of its courts, and by so doing establish the fundamental relevance of Catholic identity to the general populace and neighboring governments. This endeavor, which was meant to respond to and counter the ideals of the New Order, signaled the Vatican's entrance into the political arena surrounding the question of Italian Unification and nationhood. Thus, aside from telling the story of Jewish conversion to Catholicism, the official documents of the Inquisition tribunal sought to prove the justice of these actions, just as the Inquisition law that was in effect throughout the Papal States during this period attempted to ensure the growth, prosperity, and longevity of a Catholic society by enforcing the temporal and religious power of the Vatican.

In this sense, the laws that dictated the rules of society within the Papal States should be considered an important expression of ideological developments among Vatican leaders, since, like any government, the Vatican sought through its laws and trials to imbue in its citizenry, as Robin West writes, a belief in the "legitimacy of the social structures of empowerment and disempowerment that constitute the larger society of which the legal system is only a part."[7] In other words, whereas Massimo D'Azeglio would speak of the task of "making Italians" in postunification Italy,[8] for the Vatican the trope of conversion and the symbol of the convert became a means for it to pursue the "making of Catholics" in an era when issues of Christian doctrine and the hegemony of Christianity were at stake.[9] In the trials that follow we see one avenue, that of the law, the Church employed as it sought to assert Catholic identity across its lands and even beyond its geographical borders. It will be evident that the notion of conversion is not simply about the clash of authority, even at the level of the legal institution; it presents a historical, textual and metaphoric moment in an ongoing discussion of what it meant to be a subject or inhabitant in a rapidly changing local and national landscape.

As a reflection of the dynamic between representatives of the Church and the people living under the jurisdiction of the Papal States, between Church culture and the populace, the issue of conversion that is taken up in the trials examined here falls into the category of what today would be called "cultural politics." In his seminal work on the subject, Richard Weisberg uses the term "poethics" to define the relationship between literature and jurisprudence. As Weisberg explains, "Rhetoric *is* the argument, and the perceived rightness or wrongness of the conclusion may be as much based on the style and form of the argument as on the extrinsic application to it of the observer's notion of what the law of the case 'should have been.'"[10] Weisberg correctly suggests that legal narratives represent a genre in which the style of a legal decision affects its legal meaning, and, by extension, the meaning it conveys to the larger society. Examining law as literature proposes using legal rulings and trials as a means to reveal a culture, just as it suggests that the documents being examined are linked to the social structure of the society in which they appear, enabling modern readers to understand the relationship between the documents at hand, their authors, and the society in which they were constructed. My examination of legal narratives is thus both a political and poetic study; the trials overseen and directed by the Vatican legal system deserve to be closely examined both for the rhetoric they employ and the politics they espouse, and I seek to examine the texts surrounding several Inquisition trials as a space defined by the relationship between literature and society.[11]

Such an examination requires first considering the rhetoric of a judicial opinion by examining how judges, lawyers, and prosecutors construct stories and images to achieve their goals.[12] The legal narratives analyzed here reflect the narrator's desire to tell his story from a certain perspective, "to seduce and subjugate the listener, to implicate him in the thrust of a desire that never can quite speak its name."[13] This relationship between narrator and listener is particularly true for trial literature, in which both sides are trying to portray facts and tell a story that proves their claims. One must therefore ask several questions of these narratives: What did Vatican representatives expect or desire? What does their story aim to say and do, and what does it seek to conceal? Can the attitudes of oppression and inequality within the society of the Papal States be traced to the operations of the courts? As Robert Ferguson states, "The surface narrative of a courtroom transcript is not unlike the consciousness of an individual; both offer the official record of what passes for explanation, and both know themselves to be under distinct pressure from other levels of explanation that need to be contained."[14] In the trials that the Vatican conducted in its Holy Tribunal, Vatican leaders ask their readers to judge the story as they judge it, and, as I argue, to enforce the power of a Catholic citizenry in Italy. I seek therefore to explore the relationship between reader and storyteller—in this case legal and diplomatic representatives of the Vatican—in order to understand the shape of their stories and the reasons behind their narration. In particular, I examine what I call the rhetoric of persuasion, or the language with which the courts convince themselves and their followers of the legitimacy of their actions and the logic of their rulings. I suggest that Inquisition trials provide a combination of elements—cultural, psychological, and behavioral—that the Church employs to sustain itself. By exploring a number of these trials, and two in depth, I mean not only to evaluate the specific circumstances of the people whom we meet within the cases detailed below but to understand aspects of nineteenth-century culture in the Papal States more generally and the ways in which the legal process reveals and reflects the culture that it shapes.

Thus a large part of the following two chapters is a discussion of the stories themselves, which the Inquisition tribunal so often constructed as part of the legal process. The trials I have chosen span the time period between 1814 and 1825, a period of considerable changes around the peninsula. Publications buried long ago can be found inside the recently opened Inquisition Archives, detailing papal views on current events and new legislative actions; letters and diaries, heretofore unread, provide a window into the daily lives and views of numerous ecclesiastical leaders, and trial documentation tells the story of a government seeking to maintain its power and defend its legitimacy.[15]

Together with letters, poems, and other documents regarding the case, each conversion story presents a mixture of trial and narrative, or as Natalie Zemon Davis writes of her work on Martin Guerre, the stories combine legal text with literary tale.[16] They therefore provide a new framework within which to understand the position the Vatican held with regard to Jews in the nineteenth century. More generally, however, these trials point to the tension that arises from the fact that, from a legal standpoint, Jews were different from other subjects of the Papal States. Indeed, while they had been granted citizenship elsewhere on the peninsula and in Europe, juridical differentiation between Jews and Catholics in the Papal States comes into play most starkly when their legal status and nationality is questioned, as was so often the case under Inquisition law.

Before I continue with the conversion stories that are the main subject of this section, it will be useful to consider the law and language that the Vatican employed in the testimony and trials that decided the fate—legal, religious, and social—of numerous Jews. Inquisition law, originally instituted by Pope Paul III in 1542, demanded that Jews live separated from the general community, in a walled-off section of the city known as the ghetto.[17] Different religious practices thus produced a physical border that relegated the Jewish community to the margins of papal society. John Hawley summarizes precisely the alterity marked by the Jew and the ghetto when, in his discussion of conversion, he writes that the border that marks individual religious differences, "quickly extends to one's community, and soon becomes quite literally a geography of difference—us here and you over there."[18] The only way to cross the border represented by the ghetto walls was to convert to Catholicism, a process that, in the Papal States, occurred in a church edifice known as the House of the Catechumens. Every papal city that housed a Jewish community also contained a House of the Catechumens. The Catechumens thus represented a significant landmark—the gateway between the confined area where Jews were forced to live, and life outside the ghetto where, upon accepting the tenets of the Catholic religion, converted Jews were permitted to reside. If one considers the ghetto to be a "moral geography"[19] that denoted marginalization and degradation, crossing from the ghetto into Christian society not only resulted in the physical transfer of one's body from the geography of alterity to the geography of inclusiveness but suggested a form of expansion and conquest on the part of the Vatican that was both cultural and religious.[20]

Vatican officials described an individual's arrival at the Catechumens in several ways when documenting stories of conversion. If the newcomer presented himself voluntarily at the Catechumens—and leaders of the Jewish community often disputed Vatican claims regarding the voluntary nature of these conversions—then the document would read that the individual "came spontaneously to this Pious House of the Catechumens," or that he "presented himself voluntarily at this Pious House of the Catechumens." Often the Catechumens was simply referred to as "the Pious House" in legal documentation. Either way, even from these few words, readers are aware of the official nature of these presentations: the House of Catechumens was a holy place only for those who approved and supported its role in society. Not surprisingly, Jewish community members were prohibited from interfering with the voluntary conversion of other Jews. Breaking this rule had dire consequences for any Jew "who dared": "If any Jew of either sex dares to dissuade or impede by any means the conversion of another Jew or a Catechumen Jew to the Holy Faith, or if he makes the other Jew defer even for the briefest period, he will immediately incur a punishment of imprisonment and the confiscation of all of his property. . . . Instead of prison, Jewish women will be punished by whipping and exile, and in other more serious abuses, according to the circumstances of the crime."[21] Thus the Vatican tried to ensure that Jews who had an inclination to convert would not be impeded or pressured by family, friends, or community leaders—whom Vatican officials viewed as audacious because of these efforts—to remain within the Jewish community. Similarly, converted Jews were forbidden from maintaining any contacts with Jewish friends or family, a measure meant to limit the possibility of a convert returning to his former life. The strictly enforced separation defined the extraordinary sense of rupture the Vatican demanded of Jews who would join the Catholic community.

However, while an entrant to the House of Catechumens was required to discontinue contact with any Jews, he was promised help beginning a new life outside of the oppressive walls of the ghetto: the rector of the Catechumens would help find him a new job, and a network of Christian benefactors whom he would not otherwise have known would often help him economically as well. For example, Salvatore Tivoli, one of the men whose story we will examine below, took the baptized name Labani, an anagram for the name of his benefactor, Bishop Albani. Together, Albani and the rector of the Catechumens, Don Filippo Colonna, secured a job for the young man, which may have been one of the reasons that initially drew him to the Catechumens. Other young men turned to the Catechumens if their position within ghetto society precluded their chances for marriage.[22] Women, who generally left the ghetto more rarely and whose social circles would have insulated them from the world outside of the ghetto walls, came to the Catechumens less frequently. Given that they had few, if any, contacts with the outside world, a life outside the ghetto was unimaginable to most. Jewish men, however, many of whom were merchants and small businessmen, traveled often and regularly had contact with life outside the ghetto walls. Many found Christian society a tempting alternative to the social and economic restrictions placed on Jews. Thus, while some individuals may have converted because of a change in their religious beliefs, the Catechumens overwhelmingly attracted young men who were trying to escape poverty and begin a new life without the restrictions imposed upon the Jewish community.

With the onset of the nineteenth century, the number of Jewish conversions to Catholicism had decreased from preceding centuries. Pius VII, who became pope in 1800, was (at least early in his reign) more liberal than his predecessor, Pius VI, and his initial inclinations to reconcile the Vatican with the New Order appeared, to a certain degree, to perpetuate the decline in efforts at proselytization. Pius's humiliating deportation from Rome, however, and his subsequent exile—which Pacca described so strikingly—changed these attitudes dramatically. When in 1815, at the Congress of Vienna, the powers that had defeated

Napoleon agreed that the Papal States be restored and that the pope could return to Rome, Pius had become an adamant opponent to the liberalism vaunted by the French occupation. Reflecting this change of heart, and signaling the reactionary turn politics was taking within the Vatican, Pius VII reinforced and reissued several decrees, including the aforementioned punishment for those who impeded "voluntary" conversion. The result was a resuscitation of the culture of conversion. This revival was particularly energetic because, while Jews represented a very small percentage of the overall population of the Papal States, their liberation and emancipation under Napoleonic rule irked conservative papal leaders, who viewed these steps as symbols of the New Order. As a result, among the first Napoleonic reforms abolished and among the first edicts reissued were those regarding the Jews of the Papal States.

Thus, while in Tuscany any person belonging to the *nazione ebrea* (Jewish nation) received almost full civil rights, in the Papal States an edict was pronounced declaring a return to the laws of 1770 insofar as they pertained to the Jews—enactments that began falling into place before the Congress of Vienna had even finished meeting.[23] The aforementioned Cardinal Pacca, who became acting secretary of state when the secretary, Ercole Cardinal Consalvi, was abroad, ordered that the ghetto doors, which had been destroyed by Napoleon's troops, be rebuilt and that the Jews once again return to the ghetto. Also as a result of this edict, Jews had once again to wear a sign upon their clothing identifying them as Jews; Jewish students were expelled from the university, and Jews were blocked from entering certain professions. The legislation, which regulated everything from daily life to the local economy and deliberately separated non-Catholic individuals or communities from society at large, suggests that Vatican officials did not consider assimilation without conversion as a desirable outcome; if a Jew did not convert, he was to be separated as much as possible from the general community. Thus, for example, Jews were not allowed to sell Christians meat they had slaughtered; they were allowed to buy only limited quantities of milk, and they were not allowed to sell that which they did not use. Christians were similarly forbidden from buying items from Jews. In an attempt to further separate the two communities, Jews and Christians were discouraged from socializing together or employing one another; Christian servants, wet nurses, and doctors were punished for working for or treating Jews, and Jews were punished for hiring them.[24]

These edicts reflected the sense of vulnerability that the French Revolution and subsequent Napoleonic invasions had produced within the Vatican. Such reactionary and anti-Jewish sentiments were by no means monolithic, however; despite the defeats the Vatican had suffered, and the humiliating exile of its leader, a number of voices within the clergy proposed that the Vatican consider changing its policies and abandon its support for medieval social and political structures. Foremost among these voices was the pope's secretary of state, Ercole Consalvi. Unfortunately, Consalvi did not have the power to single-handedly change Vatican policies, nor did he find support among the right-wing *zelanti* (zealous ones), as the conservative wing of the Vatican clergy came to be known. While all these men were exiled as a result of the French invasion of the peninsula in 1798, and again in 1809, the experience proved to have a different effect on Consalvi than it had on other clergymen who suffered the same fate: rather than pledge hard-line conservatism when the pope regained his seat of power in Rome, Consalvi set to work trying to convince fellow Vatican officials that the Church had to accept some of the changes wrought by modern times if it wanted to survive. Despite Consalvi's great diplomatic skills, and his success as the Vatican representative at the Congress of Vienna—during which he succeeded in winning back almost all the lands formerly under Vatican control—he failed to cut a popular figure among the Vatican hierarchy.[25] Consalvi's fellow cardinals, and Pius himself, did not view their return to Rome as the time to adapt to a new political and social dynamic in Europe; indeed, just the opposite. As a result, the *zelanti*, who were gaining the upper hand in internal Vatican politics, immediately undid the reforms Napoleon had initiated, and tried to return the Papal States to its former standing in the days of the Old Regime.

Not only did the pervasive reactionary attitudes of Vatican officials result in a return to the anti-Jewish laws of the eighteenth century; the pope also expressed his desire to return to the legal conditions of the past century with his 1814 bull known as *Sollicitudo omnium Ecclesiarum (The Care of All the Churches)*. Among other things, the bull ordered the complete restoration of the Society of Jesus in the Papal States. The Society of Jesus, or Jesuit order, had been suppressed since 1773, upon the orders of Pope Clement XIV.[26] Its readmittance is particularly relevant to this discussion, since the Jesuits, who toed a reactionary line in the battle against laicism, were the founders of the original House of Catechumens in the sixteenth century.[27] They had been among the leaders of the Counter-Reformation, and their prominent role in this earlier battle, as well as their identification as active converters, appeared particularly attractive to Pius VII. Indeed, the battle against secularization and the ideals of the French Revolution, often posed in Catholic texts as a drastic opposition between Christian and secular forces, was similar to the course the Holy See had pursued in its battles against Enlightenment thinkers years before.[28] Pius's welcome of the Society may well have been a further attempt to distance himself from Napoleon, who banned the order in France and hated its members to such a degree that he ordered French newspapers never to print the word "Jesuit" again.[29] The Society, which had also once been deemed a threat to the monarchical power of the Bourbon Restoration, now appeared to be very much in step with that which the Vatican viewed as its battle against the revolutionary, non-Christian fervor spreading across Europe.[30]

Many Vatican supporters took pride in the reestablishment of the Society of Jesus and in the renewal of anti-Jewish edicts. After all, the original laws were established well before the French Revolution and before the French invasion of the Papal States; they marked a time when papal authority appeared, at least in retrospect, to go largely unchallenged. In one letter that a Vatican official at the Sant'Uffizio sent the Father Inquisitor, the former wrote that the memory of these times should be recalled and hopefully reinstated with no modifications whatsoever, because, as he wrote, these laws were written in times "in which the Church did not suffer from any crisis, and happily enjoyed the most perfect tranquility."[31] These words confirm several significant themes of the Vatican in this period. First, they express nostalgia for a return to a Christian regime and an aversion to all that appeared as a compromise of this earlier era.[32] The writer thus expresses a desire, ubiquitous in the early nineteenth century, that medieval Christianity be a model for the measure of Christian presence that would ideally be present in society. As Giovanni Miccoli notes, both liberal and reactionary papal supporters dreamt of a papacy that would return to this medieval structure and have "its end and its destiny . . . not only in the salvation of souls and in the conservation of Catholic truth, but in the good government of Christian society."[33] During the Restoration, Vatican supporters thus desired a government in which spiritual leadership was connected to public institutions and government. In addition, there was a general belief, harkening back to the ideology of the Old Regime, that only religious unity could guarantee civil union.[34] This belief tapped into the desire to counter the spread of secularization by conquering those who symbolized the opposite of Christian piety and ideology, and the means for such conquest, for the "salvation of souls," as Miccoli characterizes the sentiment, was clear: conversion to Catholicism.

Thus there is a significant correlation between the reactionary attitudes reflected by the reinstatement of anti-Jewish edicts and the accompanying mobilization of Catholic forces to fight revolutionary and de-Christianizing forces. Not surprisingly, these elements had significant consequences for Rome's House of the Catechumens, which was hardly immune to the political environment surrounding it. The conversion statistics of the period reflect the consequences of Pius's legislation: during the second decade of the nineteenth century, the Catechumens saw the greatest number of Jewish converts since before the French Revolution. The number more than doubled in the years immediately following the defeat of Napoleon.[35] In 1814, for example, the baptismal registry at Rome's House of the Catechumens recorded nineteen baptisms, seventeen of which involved Jews, in contrast to four the year before and one the year before that. The next year, the book contains records of twenty baptisms, and by 1816 this number had doubled to forty baptisms, thirty-eight of which involved Jews.[36] These statistics provide further evidence that, with the reestablishment of the papal government in 1815, the Vatican sought to respond to the Napoleonic period with conquests of a religious ilk. As Ermanno Loevinson writes, papal policy "did nothing other than follow its misoneistic tendency by considering from the perspective of conversion the revolutionary and Napoleonic period as a disagreeable period, the traces of which they had to make disappear."[37] Furthermore, while the ecclesiastical and civil authorities of the Papal States may have concentrated on different issues and had different agendas, they collaborated on the issue and importance of conversion as a means to reassert Catholic religious and political power in the region. That opposition to this means of reasserting Catholic hegemony was easily overridden—if not completely dismissed, as seen in Consalvi's unsuccessful efforts to curb the reactionary attitudes of the Vatican hierarchy—further reflects the central role that Catholicism and conversion to Catholicism played in this time of political upheaval.

While voluntary conversion was undoubtedly preferable, the pressure on a convert's family members to follow that individual's example, and the secret conversion of children by a Christian, were not discouraged. Indeed, throughout the first half of the nineteenth century, Church policy enforced a rule that any Jew entering the Catechumens had to offer to the Church all of his dependents, and any attempt to dissuade an individual from offering his family to the Church was viewed as a crime: "When a Jew is offered to the Church to be baptized," proclaimed the edict regarding the Jews, "the Jews cannot disturb or commit any injury whatsoever towards the person making the offer or towards the offered, particularly while they remain in the Ghetto, under the gravest pecuniary or corporal punishments as deemed appropriate."[38] Often these individuals, generally the wives and children of the convert, were not with the converting Jew when he entered the House of Catechumens. As a result, the rector of the Catechumens would order the papal police—the Papal States still had a police force—to go to the ghetto and gather up the "offering." "Extraction" was the term that Vatican officials used to describe the action of entering the ghetto and arresting the family members of a baptized Jew. Rather than "voluntarily" or "spontaneously" presenting themselves at the Catechumens, these Jews were brought there by papal police. Generally, papal forces entered the ghetto at night to retrieve the family members of a convert; doing so lessened the possibility and extent of protests and violence on the part of the ghetto's other inhabitants. The Manganetti affair, discussed in the next chapter, represents one case where papal police entered the ghetto during the day to retrieve the family of a new convert; the protests and violence this action provoked contrast strikingly to more typical "extractions." Between 1814 and 1818, for example, police entered the Roman ghetto twenty-two times, entering at night in order to lessen any resistance, to "extract" Jews and bring them to the Catechumens.[39]

This "*offerta* [offering]," the text generally read, "was extracted from the ghetto in expectation of the offering made of the Catechumen Jew." The phrase is suspiciously complacent; the passive voice of the words "was extracted" not only distances the actions from the individuals responsible for carrying them out but negates the violence and force with which this act was conducted. As we will see below, Ricca and Salvatore Tivoli, despite the fact that Ricca was eight months pregnant, chose to flee Livorno rather than submit willingly to papal forces. Furthermore, the word *offerta*, "offering," which Vatican officials used to refer to the person, generally a Jewish woman or child, being volunteered for conversion, is also the word used to refer to financial donations to the Church. That one reference is used for both human and monetary "gifts" reflects an identification of both as objects of acquisition: both enrich the Church, and both are handed over as a means to further the objectives of the Church. The two men at either end of this spectrum, the converted "offerer" and the Catholic "acceptor" are in a similar position as well: both are empowered by the gift, the former because it proves genuineness of his change in faith and raises his status as a convert, and the latter because his latest "conquest" extends Church control and proves his own piety and faithfulness.

Once the relatives of a converted Jew arrived at the House of the Catechumens, they were treated like all other occupants of the

Catechumens: family members were separated from one another, and they were denied contact with family and friends from outside the Catechumens for a period of three weeks. During this time, they were subjected to lectures, taken to church services, taught the rudiments of Catholic practice, and often left in isolation to ponder the choice before them. These choices were painfully clear: either the family members could submit to conversion themselves or they must give up ever seeing their children, who, if young enough, would be baptized within a matter of days. These children would be raised by a wet nurse and often were educated for a life of service to the Church. Six year-old Edgardo Mortara, for example, who was secretly converted by a family servant and whose family refused to follow suit, was taken from his parents and raised in the Catechumens; he ultimately became a priest.[40] Needless to say, these "offerings" also had to consider that refusing to convert would mean never again seeing the individual who was responsible for bringing them to the House of Catechumens in the first place. Such a separation generally had economic implications, since it usually signified a loss of the head of the family and hence the family's main breadwinner; it also led to legal marital separation, since, if a spouse refused to convert, the Church sanctioned a divorce between this individual and the person who underwent baptism.

In one such case, a twelve-year-old Roman Jewish boy, Isacco Biondi, "presented himself" at the "Pious House" for conversion. According to practice, Rector Filippo Colonna refused to permit the Biondi parents to visit their son; rather, he used the boy's baptism to try to convince the boy's mother and father to convert as well. The rector's attempts to convince the couple were particularly ardent, since they had a five-year-old daughter, Perla, and another child on the way: "And on such an occasion the aforementioned [rector] did not miss the chance to insinuate to the woman [Isacco Biondi's mother, that is] that she should want to follow the example of her son; to these insinuations she always responded, 'Who knows, maybe with enough time I will do it.'" While it appeared that the couple had no intention of converting, both Isacco's mother and later the boy's father told the rector that they would consider the action as a means of quieting the man and enabling them to see their son. Two weeks after this conversation, however, the wife died in childbirth. While Don Filippo failed to convince the father to convert, he wanted "at least the acquisition of the indicated Perla." He thus secured written testimonies from individuals who heard his conversation with Perla's mother and the promises of the girl's father. Only after he was armed with this testimony did the rector send papal forces into the ghetto on a cold January night in

1816 to remove the five-year-old from her father's home. [41] It appears that the papal government, in order not to be accused of abusing Vatican power, devoted money and resources to a hearing, rather than simply entering the ghetto and taking little Perla by force.

From a practical standpoint, there were signs that the return to earlier anti-Jewish laws was difficult to enforce. In the trial of Giuseppe Manganetti, discussed below, his wife daringly fled the Papal States with her two children rather than being offered to the Church. Other laws also seemed difficult to enforce. In the papal city of Pesaro, for example, one papal supporter wrote the office of the Sant'Uffizio to complain that the taste of freedom provided by the pope's exile had rendered the Jews uncooperative and many refused to follow the reinstated edicts. Before Napoleon's invasion of the Papal States, wrote this Pesarese inhabitant, the law dictated that Jews were forbidden to leave their homes from Holy Thursday until the morning of the following Saturday. When all previous laws were taken up again in 1815, however, the Jews, accustomed to their newfound liberty, were "spiteful" and uncooperative, and, as a result, he writes, "The edict remains ineffectual."[42] Easter often included special laws restricting Jews' movement because of their participation in the crime of deicide.[43] In this letter, the author portrays the sanctity of the Easter holiday as being at risk because of Jewish delinquency—a complaint that recalls accusations of deicide and recalcitrance that resulted in Jesus' death. Complaints such as these not only reflect the disgruntlement of the author; they also provide evidence of the widely accepted view that revolution, the French occupation, and efforts at religious equality threatened the Catholic culture of the Papal States.

Another form of resistance can be seen in those who withstood the pressures of confinement within the Catechumens. Indeed, despite the vast repercussions facing those who were being offered—and others who were either brought by force to the House of Catechumens or came of their own will and had a change of heart—records demonstrate a significant number of Jewish men and women who refused baptism. The words in Vatican documents denouncing Jews who refused to convert are unequivocal: "still persisting in his obstinacy, he was sent back to the ghetto." That individual, branded as unchangeable, was thus deemed a disgrace who could only be sent back to the ghetto. And while this phrase changed somewhat depending on the case, the Jew who refused baptism was generally depicted as "*ostinato* (obstinate)," an adjective saved for nonbelievers and political revolutionaries. The term recalls medieval stereotypes that depicted the blindness and intractability of the Jew in accepting Christianity. That is, the Jew's obstinate nature was often portrayed as waywardness—the sign of and the reason for his betrayal of Christ. The immoral Jew, identified with Judas, was portrayed as the Antichrist, and as such he was connected to the desecration of holy icons and the host.[44] Thus, in Inquisition texts, Jews and their so-called Jewish obstinacy were a reminder to readers of a people who refused to recognize the truth of Catholic ideology; it was used to emphasize the oft-held belief that Jews who refused to convert sought to challenge Catholic hegemony with their rejection of Jesus Christ and his teachings.

One example of such a documented case can be seen with the story of Angelo Tagliacozzi. Tagliacozzi, a 40-year-old Roman Jew, "came spontaneously to this Pious House" on August 30, 1814. He left a pregnant wife and four children in the ghetto, whom "he gave immediately (as is customary according to the pontifical constitution and the decrees of the Holy Inquisition) as an offering to the [Catholic] religion." Thus it appears, according to Vatican documentation at least, that Angelo came to the House of Catechumens of his own free will. As was the practice—indeed, the law—of that time, Angelo's desire to convert enabled and empowered papal police to enter the ghetto and bring his dependants to the House of Catechumens as well. Angelo's wife and children were removed from the ghetto on the very day that he presented himself at the House of Catechumens. After seven months, on March 25, 1815, Angelo was baptized, and took the name Filippo Carlo Maria Neri, his new first name honoring the rector of the Catechumens, Filippo Colonna, for his role in the act of conversion.

However, Angelo Tagliacozzi's wife was clearly not interested in converting—at least not at first. The wife, "after being obstinate for a period of about fifteen days,"[45] agreed to convert. Most likely her "obstinacy" was overcome by the fact she was pregnant with the couple's fifth child who, the rector records, was born at two o'clock in the morning on February 1. Because the woman was pregnant when the papal police brought her to the Catechumens, the usual waiting period of three weeks, after which time "obstinate" Jews were released and returned to the ghetto, was ignored. Angelo Tagliacozzi's wife would have been kept at the House of Catechumens until she gave birth. In this case that meant that the woman was a virtual prisoner for five months. Any child born at the Catechumens was taken from the mother and immediately baptized, and no argument the mother might have proffered could have changed that procedure. Thus it appears that after fifteen days, the thought of losing all five of her children convinced the woman to convert, and she was baptized together with her husband on March 25, 1815.

"Perfidy" was the other term regularly used to describe Jews and the Jewish community. The Inquisition archives contain numerous trials and letters that attest to the perfidy of the Jews. Significantly, the archives also contain letters from lay inhabitants of the Papal States who make use of this vocabulary. Much like their leaders, inhabitants of the Papal States sent letters to the father Inquisitor of Rome complaining of the disproportionate wealth of Jews and of the excessive socializing between Jews and Christians. Others complained that too much freedom had enabled the Jews to own too many goods and an abundance of property, making it impossible to distinguish Jew from nobleman. The fact that the terminology extended from the official voice of the Vatican to the populace reflects how widely the net of reactionary sentiment had been cast. One such letter, addressed to the Sant'Uffizio and written by an inhabitant of Pesaro, connected the evils of the French government and those of the Jewish communities of the Papal States by describing both as "perfidious" threats to Christianity.[46] In the Middle Ages, the terms *perfidy* and *perfidious* referred to the theological definition of a nonbeliever. While the term was used in Catholic liturgy through the early twentieth century, in a nontheological context it came to signal a moral condemnation of Jews. Here this vocabulary, like the term *obstinate*, once again recalled a people associated with revolution and the rejection of Catholic belief and rule. The slippage between the theological and nontheological uses of the term is emphasized by the fact that it had become part of common parlance, used by the general population and not reserved for the clergy. As Maria Paiano explains, the Church, "even in its official language could . . . express a negative judgment with regard to them that went beyond a simple reflection of their 'lack of faith' with respect to the faith that Christians professed."[47] That this theological vocabulary had been adopted by the larger community reflects the success with which the Vatican has spread its official view of the threat Jews posed to the Catholic community.

Pius VII's anti-Jewish laws also contributed to a Vatican policy of uncompromising intransigency with regard to the Papal State's secular neighbors. While in earlier centuries the balance of power between the Papal States and its neighbors had often led the Inquisition tribunal to bargain over the future of individual suspects, this flexibility ended after Napoleon's invasion.[48] As a result, for example, in September 1815 the Austrian Minister Ludwig von Lebzeltern sent a letter to the Vatican secretary of state regarding the Jews who inhabited the lands that the Congress of Vienna had recently restored to the papacy. In it he requested that these Jews be given greater independence, in particular asking that they be allowed to own property and to enter into various professions prohibited them thus far. In a long response to these requests, Pius VII denied the request. Exhibiting dislike for change and a nostalgia for the past, Pius explained that it was generally unnecessary to amend the law of the land.[49] Given that the Vatican depended upon Austria for military protection, a request from that country could not, on the one hand, be taken lightly; on the other hand, the pressure implicit in Lebzeltern's letter undoubtedly irritated Pius. As his response suggests, the use of French Revolution ideals to challenge the jurisdiction of Inquisition law made papal representatives unwilling to practice any system of rapprochement.

This intransigence can be seen in the case of Angelo Sacerdoti, whose wife, in a rare role reversal, converted and offered up their four children to the Church. Rather than allow the Vatican to take his children, Angelo left the Papal States, bringing his children first to Trieste, and later to his parents in Modena. In the end, the Duke of Modena became involved in the case and, much to the Vatican's satisfaction, permitted the Vatican custody of the children. Before arriving at the Catechumens in Rome, the children had been on the run for three years, and during this time, the rector writes with dismay, "they were impiously educated by rabbis; thus all four have become extremely obstinate, and the oldest boy in particular vomits horrendous blasphemy upon hearing that the coming of our redeemer has already occurred." Comparing the children to lions, the rector goes on to note that upon separating the children from each other and from their father, he successfully convinced three of them to convert. The oldest boy was declared "obstinate" and was released from the Catechumens, as was his father. Nonetheless, the Vatican deemed the case a success, as the rector suggested when he summed up the case, writing that "the Pious House of the Catechumens is satisfied, its esteem unscathed."[50]

Also as a result of the newly instated edicts, papal police arrested a seventeen-year-old Jewish woman and sent her to the Catechumens in March 1815. Reale Zarfati was caught outside the Catechumens, where it was illegal for Jews to congregate or loiter. Once again, a law was in place that tried to ensure that the Jewish community could do little to block individuals from seeking conversion: "no Jew of either sex, from any state, or of any condition, can go to or approach within the space of thirty *canne* from the Houses of the Catechumens, nor the Monastery of the Most Holy Annunciation in Rome; he cannot go in person or by means of an intermediary person, under the penalty of 300 *scudi*, imprisonment, and other corporal punishments to be determined."[51] While the law bespeaks a punishment in the form of a fine or imprisonment, the zealous Don Filippo had another form of punishment in mind for Zarfati: he ordered the young woman to be brought to the Catechumens, "and having made her undergo various interrogations, it appeared that the Jewish woman gave excellent hopes that she could embrace the Catholic Religion."[52] The rector's record of Reale Zarfati's stay at the House of Catechumens gives readers an idea of what one potential convert went through upon entry into the Catechumens. The young woman was made to attend daily lectures and receive religious instruction for twelve days. At first things seemed to be going well: The girl "did not refuse to go to the Church of the Most Holy Madonna of the Mountains to hear public catechisms." However, after four or five days of these activities, the young woman suddenly refused to continue her Catholic reeducation. After twelve more days of noncooperation, the rector declared her "obstinate."[53] Don Filippo gave up on his hopes of converting the young woman and ordered that she be returned to the ghetto, charging the ghetto inhabitants for the expenses that she incurred while at the House of Catechumens.

Another revealing view of the proceedings endured within the Catechumens can be found in a diary of a young Jewish woman who was sent to the Catechumens in 1749, returned to the Jewish community, and wrote of her experience.[54] This work, however, is told by the Jewish woman who succeeded in rejecting Catholicism despite the pressures upon her. In contrast, Zarfati's story is told by her captor. The authority with which Don Filippo writes this official story, his articulation of the status of the Jews with whom he interacts, exposes his vision of how they should be treated. As a result the text, vocabulary and wording are crucial: as readers we can only guess what Don Filippo meant by the term "excellent hopes," and it is difficult to interpret what he meant when he stated that the woman "did not refuse" to attend Church and listen to lectures. Were these activities indeed presented as options, and did Reale Zarfati actively agree to them? What kind of pressures did the rector place upon her? It is hard to imagine that a legitimate set of choices was given to the young Jewish woman. The rector's description of catechism lectures and the woman's church attendance, his use of the negative "did not refuse" rather than an active verb to describe the woman's acquiescence to these activities, expose what were deemed legitimate forms of pressure to "help" a Jewish inhabitant of the Catechumens choose the Christian way of life; anything that would appear to undermine the judicial procedure used for obtaining converts would obviously not be referred to openly.

Indeed, as we will see in the final trial discussed herein, the Manganetti affair, when the Vatican was accused of forcing conversions and holding Jews against their will, they vociferously denied the claims, presenting the conversionary process as legitimate and humane—a reflection of the society to which Catholicism had given rise. Thus Colonna's awkward and vague grammatical constructions and his neutral descriptions of the woman's reeducation reflect an aspect of official narrative that we will repeatedly encounter: putting the facts into legal context sterilizes them, making them lose the severity of their meaning. The language is so factual and colorless that readers of the time—or listeners, as the case may be—can easily overlook the trauma of the situation. This poetic neutralization in turn influences both the political and moral beliefs of the audience exposed to them.[55] And, while the audiences one speaks about with regard to trial narratives is limited to lawyers, judges, prosecutors, and defendants, this forum is significant because these official views are ultimately conveyed to the society at large. In other words, because the facts are stated in terms favorable to the victor—that is, those in power—the legal system itself perpetuates a source of bias that is inevitably reflected in the culture of the society more generally. As Richard Delgado writes, such narratives allow the individual or group in power to define and express a reality "in which its own superior position is seen as natural."[56] In legitimizing his work, the rector furthers the goals of the Catechumens and enforces the current social order. Thus the official stories related in these legal narratives remind readers of the relationship between Catholic ideology and the non-Catholic culture it dominates.

CHAPTER 2

REWRITING THE JEW IN RESTORATION ITALY

THE STORIES OF SALVATORE TIVOLI AND SAMUELLE CAVALIERI

In the years following the fall of Napoleon, the Vatican found itself embroiled in two particularly striking cases of conversion: the first, known as the Labani affair, involved a young Roman Jew named Salvatore Tivoli, who converted to Catholicism in 1804 at the age of twenty-three, taking the name Giuseppe Labani. According to Rome's baptismal registry, he was one of only twelve individuals to convert that year.[1] Since conversion entailed cutting ties completely with the Jewish community, the rector of the Catechumens, Don Filippo Colonna, hired Tivoli as a cook until the young man could find accommodation and a job outside of the ghetto.[2] About a year after his conversion, however, Tivoli had a change of heart, renounced his newly adopted religion and sought to return to Judaism. He could not return to the Jewish community in Rome, since under Inquisition law apostasy was a crime for which one would be imprisoned.[3] Forced to flee the Papal States altogether, Tivoli sailed to Turkey, where he settled among the Jewish community of Adrianopolis. In 1808, however, Tuscany was annexed to the French empire. For Tivoli, this change of government meant that he could finally return to one part of the Italian peninsula without fear of being arrested. He moved to the Tuscan city of Livorno that same year, where his mother, brother, and sister had been residing since shortly after his conversion.[4] In short order, he established himself as a shopkeeper in the city's ghetto, married a Jewish woman by the name of

Rebecca "Ricca" Astrologo, and, when the Vatican finally caught up with him, was about to become a father. The Vatican, mired in the political upheaval of a French invasion of the Papal States, found itself forced into diplomacy with its secular neighbor in order to procure his arrest and the custody of his soon-to-be-born child. His conversion and subsequent apostasy ultimately resulted in an Inquisition trial against the young man that lasted from 1814 to 1822.

A second case to which the Vatican devoted great time and energy, and the other trial explored herein, occurred in the papal city of Ferrara. Giuseppe Manganetti, a Jewish resident of Ferrara's ghetto, converted to Christianity in 1821, taking the name Samuelle Cavalieri.[5] He brought his eldest son, aged eight, with him to Ferrara's local House of Catechumens but left his younger two children, aged two and three respectively, at home. It became the Church's objective to gain custody of these children and their mother, who was pregnant with the couple's fourth child. To do so they raided the children's school, as well as several homes belonging to family members. Within the close and closed walls of the ghetto, however, news of the pending raids traveled fast. In an astonishing display of temerity, Jewish friends whisked Cavalieri's wife and children away under the noses of the papal police who had come to arrest them. The difficulties that local papal officials encountered within the ghetto, and the complicity of numerous Jews in aiding the escape of those sought, led to the involvement of the central House of the Catechumens and the Rome Inquisition tribunal, which conducted a trial to gain custody of Cavalieri's children that lasted from 1821 to 1823.

Both the Labani Affair and the story of Samuelle Cavalieri's conversion provide a window into the relationship between the legal and religious authority of the Papal States and the Jewish minority who lived under this rule. As we will see, the testimony of the rector of the Catechumens in both stories reveals an official vision of conversion as a kind of conquest not dissimilar to the territorial conquest of secular powers.[6] Like territorial expansion, conversion proved the dominance of the Catholic religion both as a religious and cultural system. In addition, the ideology of conversion lies at the center of Vatican attempts to counter the territorial conquests of other powers and the secularization that generally accompanied such victories. While the Church lacked the power to expand its geographical borders, expanding the Christian community was one response it could execute. The Vatican, interested in reinforcing its bonds to Western civilization and in promoting Catholicism in newly conquered colonies in Africa and elsewhere, had a particular interest in the Italian peninsula, which was the center of its power and the symbol of Catholic hegemony. Conquest through conversion was a response that returned the Church to the center of conceptions of community and nation, and the Vatican used conversion as a force that crossed regional borders, propelling Catholicism forward as a national identification for inhabitants of the Italian peninsula.

In addition, both stories relate the conversions of relatively young men who, if we are to believe Inquisition sources, presented themselves voluntarily at the House of the Catechumens for conversion. Whether their actions were a product of conviction or a result of more practical needs (economic, amorous, and so on) is not clear, but the Vatican's supposition that the two men came voluntarily reflects the environment that empowered and legitimated Inquisition law, one that was enforced through the language of the Inquisition tribunal and the legal power the Vatican wielded over its subjects and, to a certain degree, over Catholic citizens of neighboring territories as well. Yet the question of what constitutes legitimacy for the institution of the Inquisition and why Vatican authorities and the Inquisition tribunal sought to outline their lawsuits and conversions in a juridical framework remains pressing throughout both cases. Why and from whom was the Vatican seeking legitimacy? One answer is that Vatican leaders were interested in maintaining and solidifying support on the peninsula. To do so, the Inquisition tribunal held carefully recorded trials, called witnesses, and wrote up the proceedings for the record. While these documents were not available for public consumption, they help us understand the environment within the Vatican hierarchy, as well as the daily routine of Jewish ghetto life before the involvement of the papal police.

Furthermore, the rulings and sentiments that prevailed in cases such as these had a ripple effect: while only a relatively small number of officials might testify in any one case, and the ruling itself only affected a handful of Jews, the culture that prompted the case to begin with, and the reactionary culture that was then strengthened by the outcome of these cases, had, I argue, a significant impact on how the Jewish community was treated and how the Vatican viewed itself with regard to minority religions and the secular governments that were beginning to prevail in Western Europe. That is, Vatican officials used its legal system and official correspondence to promote its interests and, ultimately, to gain the sympathy of lay Catholic communities, particularly those of neighboring governments and the general populace.[7] The convergence of religion and ecclesiastical politics meant that while these trials were only seen by a limited number of people, their policies and attitudes were far reaching and encouraged the dialectic the Church initiated centuries earlier between Christian piety and anti-Semitism.[8]

For example, Rector Colonna, when he learned that Tivoli had resurfaced in the Jewish community of nearby Livorno and was soon to be a father, began pondering retribution—or justice, as he viewed the punishment awaiting Tivoli in the Papal States. Colonna, referring to Tivoli disparagingly as "the apostate," kept a record of the young man's whereabouts in the hopes that he would return to Rome, where papal authorities could arrest and prosecute him.[9] When it became clear that Tivoli would avoid Rome at all costs, Colonna and the Vatican leadership sought to persuade the Tuscan government to allow their child to be baptized and placed in papal hands. While the Vatican's demand for custody of the child and her parents provoked a flurry of diplomatic activity and a trial that we will examine below, the Vatican's aggressive diplomacy regarding the baptism of the child paid off: the governor of Tuscany ruled in the Vatican's favor, stating that he found justified the Vatican's desire "that the baby be baptized, reared in our holy religion."[10] That the governor described Catholicism as "our holy religion" suggests that his personal connection to Catholicism—a connection that Vatican officials tried to exploit—was a factor as he ruled in the Church's favor on a matter of religious identity. The baby was secretly baptized and given the name Fortunata, "fortunate one," reflecting the Vatican's view of having won the right to raise her in the Catholic tradition.

Don Colonna, and papal authorities more generally, sought a legal reckoning as an attempt to further prove the legitimacy of the papal government to supporters as well as to neighboring governments. Indeed, one reason Colonna paid such close attention to Tivoli's movements was precisely because Tivoli was taking advantage of the changes and civil emancipation of Jews in Tuscany. That is, the Church perceived the secularization that the French Revolution championed, and the civil emancipation of Jews that accompanied this antiecclesiastical mantra, as the last push of de-Christianizing forces. From the Church's perspective, the civil emancipation of Jews that the French Revolution brought about confirmed the belief in a connection between Jewish emancipation, revolution, and the general de-Christianization of society. Tivoli, who succeeded in returning to the peninsula precisely as a result of Jewish emancipation in Tuscany, therefore represented an individual case reflective of this greater problem, particularly because his "escape" to Tuscany forced the Vatican into the unhappy position of negotiating with neighboring Tuscany rather than imposing its own law immediately. His trial also involved questions of belonging: the Inquisition trial held regarding the case sought to condemn Tivoli and to determine whether he, his family, and his Jewish in-laws were Tuscan citizens, and hence untouchable by papal law, or Papal subjects, in which case they could be prosecuted to the full extent and power that the Inquisition tribunal held.[11]

The great lengths to which the Vatican and the Inquisition courts went to punish Tivoli and his family suggest that apostasy symbolized much more than the return of a single man to his Jewish roots; the apostate and his so-called Jewish "accomplices" represented to the Vatican the alterity and subversion of the Jewish community more generally. Ironically, however, while the Vatican opposed the democratization and liberalism that many governments around it were adopting, the Holy See had to maintain diplomatic relations with these same governments if it was to remain an active player in the political future of the Italian peninsula. As a result, in an era when questions of citizenship and civil rights were receiving more attention than ever before, the Vatican had to treat the inhabitants of its lands, even those who were denied civil rights, with a certain degree of care.

Herein lies one of the curious paradoxes of the Vatican in the context of the modernizing state: while the Vatican's leaders promoted and supported political and social policies that were conservative and antirevolutionary, they were not, at the same time, completely opposed to the development of the nation-state that was occurring across much of Europe. That is, leading Vatican officials recognized that to maintain its political clout on the map of European politics and among Europe's Catholic population, the Holy See could not wholly reject or ignore the revolutionary influences that were spreading across the continent. Politically, the Vatican not only had to engage with its neighbors, it had to negotiate and compromise with them. This multipronged battle reflects the politicization of Vatican Inquisition policies, just as it proves the hegemonic logic with which it sought to control social and cultural policy in the Papal States and, when possible, beyond its borders.

In the case of Samuelle Cavalieri, the rector of Ferrara's House of the Catechumens had to prove to the government officials of neighboring Mantua, where Cavalieri's wife had fled with their children, that inhabitants of the House of Catechumens converted of their own free will and that the procedures employed to encourage baptism were not coercive. Of course, the rector was motivated to prove just that, since the baptisms he oversaw were only valid if they reflected the honest desire of those they converted. Political aims also colored the rector's insistence: to accuse the rector of overstepping his bounds by impinging on an individual's personal liberty would be to suggest that the religious and temporal power of the Vatican conflicted with modernizing conceptions of government and the role of the papal government toward the people it governed. The Vatican, aware of the need to establish its relevance in a rapidly changing era, viewed such accusations as both a political and religious challenge to the legitimacy of its courts and government. In response, Vatican leaders sought to portray the Holy See's legal system as a just institution that reflected more generally the morality of the Vatican government, the seat of the Catholic Church. At the same time, however, gaining custody of Cavalieri's children, like bringing Tivoli to justice and reconverting the young man, demonstrated the power of the Papal States and the continuity of Catholicism; it countered the various actions, from emancipation to territorial conquest, that Napoleon's troops had brought about and thus was a means of substantiating legislation that was viewed as a central ingredient to the ideology of Catholic reconquest.

The Cavalieri case differs from the Labani Affair in that it was not a fight against an apostate Jew; Cavalieri converted willingly, made *offerte* (offerings) of his wife and children, and appears never to have later questioned his actions. Rather, the case stands out because of how aggressively Cavalieri's wife and the Jewish community of Ferrara fought the actions of ecclesiastical leaders and papal representatives. After Cavalieri converted, papal police planned to go to Ferrara's Jewish school to remove Cavalieri's two other children in the afternoon and to Cavalieri's father-in-law's home to collect the man's wife, who spent the afternoon with her father. In and of itself, this course of action was already unusual. Generally, to ensure that they encountered no obstacles or resistance, these forces would call at houses late at night or in the early hours of the morning. Pietro Tabacchi, the rector of Ferrara's local House of Catechumens, explained, however, that the papal police went to collect the children and their mother in the afternoon hours at Cavalieri's request, as the new convert feared that an unexpected knock in the middle of the night might make his wife lose the child she carried.

The plan did not go smoothly, but the testimony of papal officials regarding the incident gives readers a good sense of how these raids were carried out (or meant to be). The rector ordered two policemen to guard the entrance to Cavalieri's father-in-law's house to ensure that no one left the premises. He and one other policeman, accompanied by the custodian of Ferrara's prison, Pietro Piccoli, then went to the school where the Cavalieri children spent their day. The schoolteacher, initially denying that the children were present, finally acknowledged that they were under her supervision but refused to turn them over. Meanwhile, as news of the rector's presence quickly passed through the ghetto, a large crowd of Ferrarese Jews gathered at the school. When the papal policemen stationed outside the father-in-law's residence saw the Jews flocking to the school, they too came to the scene, leaving their post unguarded. The rector immediately sent the two back to their station, but his orders meant that very few reinforcements remained with the papal representatives at the school, and the situation quickly grew out of control. Both the rector and Piccoli later testified that the Jews gathering at the school spoke to each other in Hebrew, clearly improvising a plan. Indeed, Piccoli became suspicious of one man in particular, who was yelling instructions to the schoolteacher. Piccoli confronted the man, and a struggle ensued, which ended only when Piccoli found himself lying flat on the ground as the children were simultaneously whisked away:

> The number of violent Jews with the most audacious temerity was growing; some were pushing the painted door in order to enter, and the others broke down the door from the inside in order to open it. They broke down the door with such force that as I tried to keep to the door of the room closed, I was knocked to the ground, falling on my back. And with my fall, the door remained open and I saw numerous Jews riotously take away from that place Cavaglieri's two children who were sought. . . . At the moment when I was thrown to the ground, I saw the porter Laudadio Rietti snatch from the hands of the schoolteacher first one and then the other of the two children and pass them into the hands of other Jews who were at the entrance of the door.[12]

Piccoli's words describe his outrage at the disrespect proffered him as he was thrown to the ground. They also reflect his indignation and surprise at the "audacious," "violent," and "riotous" response on the part of the Jews. Indeed, in the lawsuit that the Inquisition tribunal filed against the Jewish community for the crime of kidnapping and hiding the children and their mother, Vatican lawyers emphasized the legal jurisdiction and thus the political power of the Church, underscoring its political and religious hegemony. While the formality of the trial was executed to demonstrate to foreign governments the legitimacy of the governing power of the Vatican, the language of the trial was also directed at reminding the non-Catholic community of their dependence on the legal decision-making of the controlling authority.

The rector and Piccoli attested that because of the Jews' ability to communicate with one another in Hebrew, they were essentially able to improvise an escape for the children and foil the policemen's plans. We do not know what was said, of course, and neither did Vatican officials, which was precisely the problem. The importance of language as a cultural marker cannot be overemphasized: that the Jews used a private language to communicate among themselves, to plan and carry out acts that the Church could only view as subversive, underscores their difference, their nonbelonging—from the Church's perspective—to a larger community.

Escaping from the tumult of the Jewish day school, Rector Tabacchi went to Cavalieri's father-in-law's house to claim the new convert's wife as an offering. When he arrived, the policemen outside assured him that no one had come or gone from the house. But when the rector knocked on the door, no one answered. He then entered the house of his own accord, only to discover that Cavalieri's wife was not there: "I knocked at that door and since it was open I entered into that house, and I made the most thorough of searches. I was unable to find Cavaglieri's wife who was supposed to be in that house. And the people that I did find in the house assured me that she had indeed been there, but that she had already left that very place about an hour and a half earlier."[13] Jewish community members had sneaked a message to Cavalieri's wife that she needed to escape. Indeed, searching for her within the walls of the ghetto proved futile. Piccoli later testified that he heard from one source that the woman escaped the ghetto dressed as a man and from another that she had assumed the identity of the wife of a prominent member of the community and used that woman's passport to escape the confines of the ghetto and to leave the Papal States altogether. Either way, papal attempts to bring Cavalieri's family to the Catechumens failed, and the rector immediately ordered the arrest of the schoolteacher and others who were present in the schoolroom and aided in the escape of the Cavalieri children.

In total, six of the Jews who had gathered at the school were arrested, including the schoolteacher, for their role in the struggle. The Jews were accused of violating natural and civil law, of teaching their community members to use force against the Church, and thus of violating the most sacred rights of the Church. While only six Jews were arrested, the criminal trial indicted the city's entire Jewish community, which, the suit claimed, "led to the substantial subversion of natural and civil laws to inculcate episcopal authority and jurisdiction, and violated the most sacred and unchangeable rights of the church."[14] The distinction between believer and nonbeliever, between Christian and non-Christian, is underscored in this text. The differentiation between the Italian-speaking Vatican forces and the Hebrew-speaking Jewish community members, the rector's description of his escape, and of the fracas that the Jews made, all compounded the anti-Jewish stereotypes that were already expressed quite openly in Church writings of the time and were evident in the writings surrounding the Labani affair as well. In the Cavalieri case, the Vatican viewed the overt repudiation of the law of the land on the part of the Jewish community as proof that the Jews were anti-Christian rabble rousers, and the lawsuit cited above taps into these stereotypes regarding the Jewish population and their supposed penchant for revolution, upheaval, and anti-Christian behavior.

In his description of the crime committed, Ferrara's Cardinal Lorenzoni specifies the crimes committed against the Cavalieri children and connects them to the crimes of the Jews of Ferrara more generally:

> The *kidnapping* and precipitous flight of two young children, these are, most eminent Prince, the enormous crimes for which the Israelite nation has rendered itself impudently guilty in the face of ecclesiastical Authority and in the face of the very government, teaching by example and with fact the most pernicious [idea] of these times—teaching, I say, to the populace to make use of force against force: these are the crimes that the Jews of Ferrara triumphantly bear today with impunity, and for which they have resorted to a fraudulent supplication to the Holy Father, and sounding also directly to the holy supreme tribunal of the Sant'Uffizio, and even to the secretary of state with the aim of avoiding with false and specious pretexts and with insolent threats of the most serious punishments, that all the laws have wisely decreed against these most egregious attempts.[15]

As we will see in the Labani affair, Lorenzoni seems less concerned with the fate of Cavalieri's wife than that of his children. Interestingly, the cardinal does not deny the force that Vatican officials used when attempting their "extraction." The issue, rather, is the Jews' use of "force against force" and the dangerous example this provides the general populace. In addition, Cardinal Lorenzoni disputes the legitimacy of the legal recourse the Jews have taken, describing their protest to the pope and the Inquisition Tribunal as a "fraudulent supplication," a sign of Jewish falsity and a means simply to avoid punishment. Finally, the cardinal warns that if the Holy See does not reign in the Jews of Ferrara, the possibility of severe political upheaval threatens all the Papal States.

The kidnapping of the Cavalieri children is the basis of this belief, but the cardinal also claims to have wind of an attempt—nothing less than a conspiracy—by the Jews to shut down the Inquisition tribunal. The Jews, writes Cardinal Lorenzoni, "even dare to feign publicly that they will silence the Tribunals with their money."[16] The rebellion at the schoolhouse and the subsequent "kidnapping" of the Cavalieri children foiled the normative extraction procedures of Inquisition law. Not only did this tumultuous Jewish response tap into stereotypical accusations of Jews as fomenters of rebellion, but with his last accusation Lorenzoni was taking matters one step further, suggesting that Jews were threatening the very existence of the entire Inquisitorial legal system.

In a letter filled with similar rhetoric, the Archbishop of Ferrara goes even further, claiming that the belligerence of Ferrara's Jews is a dire sign that presaged greater turmoil and revolution: "And if there were in this province only one seed of revolution scattered in light of the recent political events, there is no doubt that they [the Jews] would be the principal leaders, and the proudest sustainers of the revolutionary party, just as they have done in the past."[17] Both statements connect Jewish inhabitants of the Papal States to the larger revolutions sweeping Europe in this time period, and both reflect papal fears that the Cavalieri kidnapping would feed into this revolutionary fervor. Like Cardinal Lorenzoni, the Archbishop of Ferrara accuses the Jewish community of violently kidnapping the two children, and informs the secretary of the Inquisition offices of the "undeniable, notorious kidnapping of the two dear Cavalieri children carried out in an educational school of this Ghetto by the Jews."[18] With these words, the archbishop rekindles another stereotype often associated with the Jews. His description of a "notorious" kidnapping executed by the Jews contrasts with his description of Cavalieri's two "dear" children. In other words, the clergyman attributes a violent act to the Jews, and a sense of love and value to the Church's newest members. The latter thus appears to be motivated by benevolence, while the Jews resort to violence.

The Roman rector's planned arrest of Tivoli also met with some unexpected snags. Although Colonna had received news of Tivoli's arrival in Livorno, a series of political developments in the Papal States prevented him from traveling to Tuscany and tracking down "the apostate" himself. In 1809, as the rector explains in his diary, papal defenders were busy fighting off the French invasion of the pontifical state. Napoleon's forces proved unstoppable, however, and French forces occupied the Papal States. After Pius VII was carried off to Avignon, the general arrested and deported Rome's priests and clergymen, including the rector of the Catechumens, to the island of Corsica; the year was 1812.

While the rector's detainment in Corsica foiled his plans to arrest Tivoli—at least for the time being—he did not desist from his proselytization efforts. In his diary, the rector recounts his successful conversion of a gendarme for the French army by the name of Jochanan, who was assigned the job of guarding one of the groups of priests held captive. Rumors spread among the clerical prisoners that Jochanan was a Jew. The possibility of being guarded by a nonbeliever compelled the rector to speak to his captor more frequently about Catholicism, and eventually, to Colonna's great delight, Jochanan admitted his Jewishness, and asked to be educated in the Church traditions and baptized.

Before the conversion could be carried out, however, Colonna was transferred to another location on the island of Corsica. The trip between the two prisons was particularly difficult because of the antipapal supporters that the clergymen met on the way. The young Jewish gendarme showed his good intentions and faithfulness by shielding the rector and other priests from the insults hurled at them: "Throughout the extremely painful voyage of the night of June 2 that we were forced to make from Bastia to S. Fiorenzo in the midst of insults, rudeness, and even blows both from the gendarmes and the colonial soldiers, for his part the Jew sought to help the priests with his compassionate and good offices; and having discerned this, the bitter enemy brigadier . . . strongly reprimanded him for his actions and had him placed in prison for thirteen days upon returning to Bastia."[19] This difficult moment is a turning point in the story of Jochanan. The hardships that the clergymen suffered reminded the rector further of the threat nonbelievers and antipapal thinkers posed toward the Vatican and its supporters. In addition, it marked a clear instance where the political implications of the French Revolution clashed unmistakably with the world of the papal hierarchy—where a military force tried to undermine Catholic leaders in their tracks. Finally, Colonna depicts a significant series of contrasts with this description: whereas most of the gendarmes humiliated the clergymen, Jochanan tried to help them. Just as the priests suffered insults and jeering, so too the Jew, who had recently declared his allegiance to Catholicism, suffered at the hands of the French. As a result, the gendarme suffers an impingement on his own freedom, in some sense sharing in the religious persecution that the clergymen endured. Indeed, Jochanan's fellow French soldiers viewed his attempts to help the clergymen as treasonous, and the Jewish gendarme was himself punished upon his return to his post. This shared persecution makes Colonna identify Jochanan, a French gendarme, simply as "the Jew" rather than the "enemy," the word used to describe other French officials.

The rector thus creates divisions that are not national, but religious: believers and papal supporters are juxtaposed with nonbelievers, who humiliated the pope's representatives in their demonstration of support for Napoleonic government. Colonna's memory of the encounter reflects his belief that the struggle between Pope and revolution was a struggle between good and evil, between the city of God and the city of shadows.[20] Despite being a Jew, Jochanan fell into the category of believers, both because of his aid to the clergymen he guarded and because of his intention to convert to Catholicism. To this end, he constantly asked Colonna to baptize him at the earliest possible opportunity. Napoleon's defeat in 1814 provided the perfect context for this new conquest. One day, despite the continual surveillance of a particularly menacing brigadier, Jochanan managed to speak with the rector, who had recently learned that he was to be freed. Since converting Jochanan was a risky business in French-controlled territory, Colonna instructed the Jewish gendarme to make his way to Rome's House of the Catechumens—the same place from which Tivoli had run away—and the rector would meet him there upon his release from prison.[21] In April 1814, the rector was freed and returned immediately to Rome. In mid-May of that year Jochanan arrived in Rome. The following day, he entered the Catechumens, and after four months of instruction was baptized "with the name of Agostino Leonardo Pacifico Benedetto Maria Rovalari."[22]

It was not unusual for clergymen to try to convert soldiers that passed near their churches or through their towns. Indeed, the archives contain numerous accounts of soldiers and other itinerant groups such as slaves and artisans, most of whom were Protestant and Muslim, whom they tried to convert.[23] The rector's story of Jochanan is particularly striking, however, for several reasons, most importantly because the successful conversion of the gendarme occurred shortly after Tivoli returned to the peninsula. Thus it provides an ideal foil to the saga of the apostate: Tivoli's return to the peninsula was made possible only by the conquest of Napoleonic troops. Jochanan's conversion, performed upon the rector's victorious return to Rome, no less, countered, I would argue, the earlier, failed conversion. Indeed, in his narration of this story, the rector successfully reasserts his religious authority, despite being held captive. Thus the story portrays a reversal in power between captor and captive; the clergymen depend on Jochanan's protection from aggressively anti-Catholic forces, but in his desire to convert, Jochanan becomes dependent on the rector for religious salvation. As such Jochanan's story provides the ultimate narrative of conquest: the "subversive" help he provides the clergymen and his subsequent conversion counter Napoleon's attempts at territorial expansion. The imprisoned rector is resourceful enough even to raise money among the clergymen to pay for Jochanan's voyage to Rome, and thus political imprisonment becomes a source of religious victory that, particularly in the rector's narrative, reflects the endurance of Catholicism and the continued relevance of its leaders. His successful attempt to convert the soldier points to a conversion narrative within the larger framework of the Labani affair, and this second conversion story reflects the rector's persistence in encouraging Catholic practice and identity and in ensuring the endurance of the Vatican's powers.

Colonna's return to Rome was made possible by Napoleon's defeat. A year after Colonna and other exiled ecclesiastical leaders were freed from their imprisonment in Corsica, Pius VII returned to the restored Papal States. While Cardinal Consalvi may have returned from exile convinced that the Vatican had to adjust to the times, many clergymen, Rector Colonna among them, believed that Pius's reactionary politics were necessary and warranted. Not surprisingly, Rector Colonna immediately returned to his unfinished business. Indeed after his imprisonment he appeared more ardent then ever in his desire to reassert the power of papal Rome and bring Tivoli to justice. To this end, in 1814 Colonna set out for Livorno shortly after being freed "to obtain the arrest of the apostate and invoke the consequences that could result from his apostasy."[24]

We see an interesting parallel in the stories of Colonna and Tivoli's exile: both are exiled because of their decision to practice beliefs that are not sanctioned by the political leaders in control, both are persecuted because of their beliefs; both return to the peninsula after a period in exile, Tivoli from Turkey and Colonna from Corsica; and, most importantly, the experience of exile appears to strengthen each man's resolve to practice his chosen religion. Tivoli, who faces imprisonment should he return to Rome, does not consider a return to Catholicism a possibility, since his family and his livelihood lie completely within the Jewish community of Livorno. Similarly, the experience of exile appears to make Colonna even more determined to capture Tivoli for his crime of apostasy, and to continue his proselytizing work.

When the rector arrived in Livorno, he learned that Tivoli had become a shopkeeper, selling cloth for a living, and that he had married a woman from the Jewish community. His wife, Rebecca "Ricca" dell'Astrologo, was eight months pregnant with the couple's first child at the time of the rector's arrival. Armed with this information, the rector's plan changed: aside from Tivoli's arrest and deportation to Rome, he sought the arrest of his wife and custody of the couple's soon-to-be-born child, who, according to Inquisition law, should be raised Catholic. Colonna's efforts were supported by the Vatican and by its representative in Livorno, Consul Gaetano Marchiò, who expressed great interest in the case and in ensuring that the child be baptized. To this end, the consul assured his superior, Cardinal Pacca, that the Vatican's representatives were redoubling their efforts "in order to hasten the arrest of Salvadore Tivoli and Ricca Astrologo, and to take into possession their child."[25] Letters such as this one flowed between Marchiò and Pacca, demonstrating the great interest generated by this single act of apostasy. In a letter that predated the trial, Pacca himself declared that he had never heard of a case similar to the Labani affair, and thus he suggested that the Vatican push hard to achieve a favorable end to the story.[26] So important was this case that it was one of the few cases recorded by the Sant'Uffizio records of a baptism in the nineteenth century that produced a full trial by the tribunal of the Holy Inquisition.

One reason that Vatican representatives went after the apostate Tivoli so energetically was European Christendom's view of apostates. The Spanish Inquisition, which had occurred centuries earlier in medieval Spain, was not instituted to persecute Jews, since theoretically they had all either converted to Christianity or been expelled from Spain in 1492. Rather, the Inquisition was aimed at discovering any apostates among the Jews who had converted to Catholicism.[27] The prevailing sentiment that these heretics could not be completely eradicated ultimately led to the establishment of blood laws, which were meant to distinguish between individuals with Jewish heritage and those of "pure" Christian descent. The Vatican never imposed this racially based lineage in the Papal States, but there existed a shared fear that the apostate presented in both these Inquisitions. As James Shapiro writes, the Spanish Inquisition and the subsequent blood laws were introduced because of "the threat to Iberian hegemony and identity posed by the counterfeit Christian."[28] Tivoli posed a similar threat to papal interests: by pretending to be Christian, but simultaneously maintaining his allegiance to Judaism and the Jewish community, he jeopardized the society of "true" Catholics and, for the Church, he threatened the Catholic-ness that they sought as a defining characteristic of the general public of the Papal States and beyond.

Indeed, in Inquisition Italy, at a time when the very power of the Church was in question, the apostate represented the ultimate traitor. Tivoli's unsanctioned return to the Jewish community reflected the most dangerous perversion of the baptismal procedure that a convert could carry out. A convert who returned to the Jewish community proved himself a Jew unable to assimilate into Christian society. As a failed product of the Catechumens, he undermined the workings of that institution, not to mention challenging the competency of the rector. Crossing the border from Jew to Christian had been encouraged; returning to the Jewish community, however, marked a treasonous violation of the line that divided Jews from Christians—a contraction of the Catholic community rather than the expansion that conversion symbolized. In a sense, it marked an enactment of the popular saying that Cardinal Pacca cited in his memoirs: *"If this is true, let us go immediately to the Ghetto and make ourselves Jews."* Tivoli had executed the forbidden act of an inverted conversion, something that, in the popular and official imagination, was considered an unimaginable impossibility. Local Jewish loyalties were unacceptable in the struggle to define and maintain the Catholic identity of the larger community. As a result, conversion in this direction was not simply discouraged, it was illegal, and all the more so in an era when the Vatican sought to strengthen the weakening position of Catholic identity in the Papal States and on the peninsula more generally.

Another reason for the interest the case generated lies in the fact that the Holy See was faced with a diplomatic dilemma regarding the arrest of Tivoli and his wife. Not only did the couple reside outside papal territory, but, contrary to Vatican officials' assertions, they claimed to be Tuscan citizens and consequently out of legal reach for the Vatican. Consul Marchiò, well aware of the challenges of seeking the Tivoli couple's arrest in Tuscany, warned the rector of Rome's Catechumens that without the support of the secular Tuscan government and its police forces, no arrests could be carried out. Confronted with the territorial boundaries of Inquisition law, Vatican officials therefore found it necessary to enlist the support of officials in a secular government. In a communication with the Tuscan government, Marchiò accordingly asked that the president of the *Buon Governo* issue a warrant for the couple's arrest. Although he was well aware of the limitations of his own power, his letter reflects his expectation that Tuscan officials would cooperate fully. As Vatican requests to the Tuscan government for the arrest of the Tivoli couple multiplied, they became more aggressive, reflecting papal displeasure at having to ask permission in a case that it viewed as an internal, judicial matter. To add insult to injury, the Vatican felt that the Tuscan government was not treating its requests with the urgency they demanded. Such feelings led Marchiò to complain to Monsignor Rivarola, the apostolic delegate in Rome, that the Tuscan government had not matched Vatican interest in the case. The Tuscan government, he wrote, did not "believe in supporting at all" issues of religious importance pertaining to the "solicitude and zeal by which we [live]."[29] Marchiò's words expressed how unthinkable it was from the Vatican's perspective that the Church's authority and requests would be thus ignored, and even challenged, by a government uninterested in spiritual transgressions.

Most significantly, the Vatican stance regarding both the Tivoli and Cavalieri trials, its interest in public opinion, and its emphasis on the inherently Christian nature of civilized society led to the development of a political voice for Catholic leadership on the peninsula. Indeed, in this context, a fundamental similarity between the two cases cannot be ignored: while the Vatican initiated its trials based upon the actions of two grown men, their judicial efforts became more extreme and more ardently pursued when the question of these men's children's religious affiliation was at stake. The reason for this particular attention is precisely the result of the precarious position in which the Vatican found itself. That is, by advocating Catholic identity and belief in a new, younger generation, the Vatican sought to maintain a grip on the power that appeared to be slipping away within the political arena. The Catholic identity that the Vatican advocated through its inquisitorial activities thus needs to be understood within the specific context of preunification Italy. Beyond the question of how to organize a political ideology that would resonate in a rapidly changing country, the Catholic Church felt it necessary to develop an initiative on the Italian peninsula that reflected the reactionary religious beliefs of many ecclesiastical leaders. In sum, they sought to provide the stimulus for a return to a Christian Italian—indeed, European—cultural and social renewal.

Actions such as those of the Ferrarese Jewish community when papal officials came to collect Cavalieri's wife and children enforced the reactionary mentality developing among Vatican leaders. And these actions did not end after the rebellion at the Jewish school, nor with the disappearance of the children and Cavalieri's wife; rebellious tones formed part of the correspondence between Ferrara's Jewish community and the Vatican—correspondence that the Inquisition archives contain regarding the case. In particular, two anonymously written documents arrived at the Inquisition Tribunal regarding the attempted "extraction" of Cavalieri's family. The texts provide an unofficial narrative, a perspective that Vatican officials attempted to silence in their official portrayal of the events at hand. In this sense, the Inquisition trial served a double purpose, to gain custody of the Cavalieri *offerte* and to reiterate the power of papal law and Catholic identity more generally. As John Brannigan writes, "Power can only define itself in relation to subversion, to what is alien or other, and at the heart of power is therefore the production and subsequent containment of subversion."[30] As we see here,

Vatican officials were intent on maintaining their power over the Jewish community, and they sought to do so in a variety of ways: they were able to filter out the voice, and hence the experiences, of the disempowered Jews by replacing the correspondence these Jews sent the tribunal with legal documentation that makes no attempt to explore their experience; they placed on trial numerous inhabitants of Ferrara's ghetto; they perpetuated stereotypes of the Jewish community as a threat to the well-being of society at large; and finally they sought to win over public opinion regarding its treatment of Jews.

The first of these documents was written with cutout letters from newspapers that were then glued to paper—much like a ransom note—and read as follows:

> SHIT FOR the God of Christians
> Guillotine for the Catechumen Jews
> To the lantern the ministers
> who encourage idolatry[31]

The words, angry and forceful, begin with extremely violent imagery: the first phrase blasphemes the name of God, the symbol of lightness, with shit—a powerfully visual image of darkness. The second suggests that Jews who choose to follow the Christian religion should be guillotined for doing so. Mention of the guillotine could not have been lost on papal readers, since it was the corporal punishment introduced into common usage during the French Revolution to exact bloody justice and retribution. Here, instead, this revolutionary symbol of justice is used against Jews who seek baptism, who in a sense seek to empower the Vatican and its clergymen. The concluding two sentences continue this violent imagery. In particular, the light of the lanterns in the third phrase contrasts with the darkness of shit and death envisioned in the first two lines. However, the author inverts this divine light, which God's representatives on earth carry with them. Instead of leading to salvation, as would be seemly of light carried by clergymen, this light leads to hell, and to the darkness of idolatry. Finally, the reader cannot forget the physical appearance of the note. It was presented anonymously, but the letters were clearly cut out of printed materials, most likely newspapers. Thus the author(s) appear to have literally made meaning from public documents, manipulating them for their own purpose. The message's anonymity gives it the sense that it comes from a wider public, one of readers; the printed letters become the appropriated message of this new public.

The other piece of writing contained in the documents of the Cavalieri affair is a poem, labeled a sonnet, which openly lauds the French Revolution and prays for the release and revival of Napoleon from his imprisonment:

> "The Subjects of the Pontifical State"
>
> Scandalized by bestial government
> Which gnaws and afflicts us everywhere,
> We are forced to hope that Bonaparte
> Returns from Sant Elena or from Hell.
>
> If we are condemned to eternal evil
> From the profane or holy scriptures,
> At least he rules us who employed the art
> Of having as his aim omnipotence of mockery.
> So that therefore we can say, if this law
> The heavens, entangled in disdain, [. . .] and in the feud that governs and rules us
>
> But that under the escort of gospel
> Having become a wolf the pastor devours the flock
> Such impiety makes us remain as ice.[32]

The poem does not follow the structure of a traditional sonnet in its rhyme, verse, or meter. Despite this roughness—indeed, because of it—the message that the poem relays is significant. First, it appears that the heading is intended as more of a dedication than a title: the author is a subject of the Papal States, and he is addressing another subject. The true subjects of the poem, however, are the Papal States themselves, and not the land's inhabitants.

The sonnet begins by expressing the frustration of a minority controlled by a "bestial government" that not only simply fails to represent its interests but also consumes and afflicts this people. The government, of course, was a religious one, and as such it claimed a moral superiority to the secular governments that were rising elsewhere in Europe. And yet this vision of a people being consumed by a bestial government conveys a sexual and morally corrupt image. The concluding two lines of the first quatrain reinforce this message. By mentioning the name of Napoleon, the author(s) refer to the French Revolution and to Napoleon's invasion and control of the peninsula, which had just recently ended. Napoleon is hardly portrayed in heroic terms, however; he is described as returning either from hell or from imprisonment on Sant'Elena, and the two places appear equally degraded in this context. Nonetheless, writes the author, the subjects of the Papal States are compelled to pray for Napoleon's return, since the present government has made life so unbearable. Thus, the present "bestial" government, at whose epicenter lies the papacy, condemns the state's inhabitants to eternal evil. Rather than be garnished with language describing the holy mission of this government, the author bluntly suggests that the Church is a morally compromised government. In contrast, Bonaparte has proved to be an upstanding leader: he has freed oppressed subjects of the Papal States from "derision," and thus these individuals stand with him. In political terms, the writer (or writers) appears to be suggesting that, as a result of the difficulties in which the papal government has placed the Jewish community, Jews are left with nothing but to hope that Napoleon will return from his exile to become once again a leader of Europe and a conqueror of the peninsula.

Jewish support of Napoleon comes as no surprise: the French Revolution—while Napoleon exerted control over parts of the peninsula—led to the abolition of many discriminatory laws against Italian Jews. As far back as 1796, the Jews of Ferrara were emancipated with a decree that stated that "the Jews of Ferrara shall enjoy the same rights as the other citizens of this Legation."[33] Despite this statement, however, the constitution of the Italian Republic, which was adopted on January 26, 1802 (and signed by Bonaparte himself), affirmed that even if inhabitants of the land may be free to practice any religion, "The apostolic Roman Catholic religion is the religion of the State."[34] As a result, not only was Catholicism the official religion of the state, but it had legal jurisdiction and control over all inhabitants, a reality that the writer of this poem clearly hoped to remedy.

In the second quatrain, the writer explains how papal rule results in the damnation of these inhabitants to "eternal evil." The person who should rule the land, the writer suggests, does so not because of mastery over secular or religious texts and documents but because he understands the law and the rules of government. The problems of religious government are outlined in the final sestet, in which the poet portrays the gospel as a shield and the pastor as eating his flock instead of protecting it. With this vision, the poem returns to the theme of the first quatrain: it is not simply the Vatican government that is bestial but its religious leaders as well. Thus the sestet resonates with the idea reflected in the poem's opening—or rather, of the animal-like nature of the "bestial" government and of the clergy, seen here as a wolf devouring its flock. Bonaparte will come back from hell to save the unsung subjects of the Papal States, and the great impiety practiced by the clergy makes them stand where Bonaparte had been, in hell. This reversal of the fortunes of these two powers is emphasized by the author's Dante-esque allusion to "ice." In his concluding line, the poet writes that the clergy and their impiety have forced the subjects of the Papal States to remain frozen. Not only is the writer suggesting that the papal government is unable to move forward, as the times demand, but he recalls the lowest circle of Dante's hell. The inertia and immobility of Dante's hell is the reality that the papal temporal government re-creates.

The verbs of the poem, particularly those in the first quatrain and the sestet, lend an immediate and unrefined sense of power to the message. Verbs of motion and emotion such as "scandalized," "afflicts," and "devours," lend themselves to the unambiguous and condemnatory tone of the text. Finally, if one examines the rhyme words of the sonnet, one discovers that the theme of the poem is re-created yet again: *inferno, governo, eterno, scherno* ("infernal," "government," "eternal," "scorn") make up one sequence, suggesting that there is a link between eternal hell, disdain, and the present government. "Bonaparte," on the other hand, rhymes with *ogni parte*, or "everywhere," reflecting the authors hope of this leader's omnipotence and dominion. Finally, and perhaps most devastatingly insulting for papal authorities, the Gospel, *vangelo*, rhymes with *gelo*, the cold ice of hell, the present state of the Papal State's unemancipated subjects.

Certainly, poems such as those deposited in the Inquisition archives did nothing to endear the Jewish community to the Vatican or the Inquisition tribunal. No direct response on the part of the Vatican or its local representatives to such texts exists, but clearly the two documents described here only reinforced the association that many believed existed between anti-Christian revolutionaries and Jews within the Papal States. Furthermore, if the Inquisition tribunal marked an attempt at sculpting a greater Catholic identity among inhabitants of the Papal States, in the sense of a recognizable, legal affiliation between the land's government and its Catholic inhabitants, then these poems represent the other, nondominant voice: the cultural identity of a community that shares certain beliefs and symbols that are articulated by their contrast to any sense of national belonging.[35]

The story of Ricca and Salvatore Tivoli produced similarly riveting questions of citizenship and belonging. Upon hearing that the police were searching for them, Ricca and Salvatore went into hiding, which meant that the Vatican now required even greater efforts and cooperation from the Tuscan police force, who continued to have little interest in the case. Fuming at his inability to locate and arrest the fugitive couple, Marchiò demanded first that the Tuscan government dismiss a Jewish member of Livorno's police force, Abramo Jacob Marace, suggesting that the couple had been able to elude the police thus far because Marace had helped his fellow "nationals" rather than enforce state law.[36] His argument that the Jewish man's presence compromised the integrity of the police force reflected the suspicion the Vatican felt toward the Jewish community more generally and the desire of Vatican representatives to discourage integration between Jews and Catholics. Marace's superior, A. Setrini, was displeased at being forced to suspend the Jewish policeman, and wrote the Tuscan president of Marace's qualifications. He argued that Marace's Jewishness was not a threat to law enforcement; rather, he wrote, it was as an asset to have a Jewish member on the police force: "You will see that this man was employed for about six years with the police bureau, and that it was essentially useful because of his personal knowledge of his nationals."[37] Though he differentiated Jews from the general populace with his use of the term "nationals," Setrini's advocacy of the man's qualifications and his view of the man's Jewishness as an asset rather than a threat both suggest that he understood the Jewish community to be separate on a cultural level but nonetheless part of the greater Livornese community. In contrast, Marchiò's claim that a Jewish policeman had greater allegiance to the Jewish community than to the larger community he was assigned to protect points to the consul's perception of the Jewish community as a separate entity. Despite Setrini's misgivings, however, and despite Livorno's history of tolerating interaction between the Jewish and Catholic communities, the Vatican Consul's political pull took precedence, and the governor of Livorno reluctantly complied with Marchiò's request to dismiss the officer.

The stereotype of Jewish subversion that emerges from Marchiò's accusation falls in step with the work of the well-known author Giovanni Battista Gherardo D'Arco, who reflects these views in the late eighteenth century in his well-known work *On the Influence of the Ghetto on the State*. The work depicts Jews as harmful to the state because their allegiance to other Jews surpasses state borders and is more valuable to Jews than the state.[38] Another author of the day, Francesco Gambini, similarly argued that the national "character" of the Jewish community rendered Jews incapable of being considered citizens in their country of residence. This fact justified closing Jews into ghettos, prohibiting Jews from traveling in the countryside, and forbidding them from having contact with non-Jews, about which Gambini appeared particularly fearful.[39] While there is no religious or theological basis to Gambini's arguments, both his views and those of D'Arco seem particularly relevant to Marchiò's comments against Marace and the Vatican mindset he represented, which opposed any kind of assimilation and viewed Marace's participation in the general society as a threat rather than an advantage.

Marchiò's second demand pertained to the arrest of Salvatore and Ricca's immediate family members, all of whom, he claimed, were papal subjects who had broken papal law by aiding an apostate:

> It is known that Astrologo's parents, together with three other close relatives of theirs, were responsible for making the aforementioned delinquent subjects [Ricca Astrologo and Salvatore Tivoli] flee the following night. This led us to ask the Governor that same day for the arrest of these individuals as accomplices in the attempted escape of the repeated guilty parties, all the more so since it is reasonable to assume that these individuals must have known the residence of the couple . . . such means [i.e., arrest] shall make them confess where the aforementioned daughter and relatives are hiding and we shall arrive at the desired aim.[40]

Marchiò's request for the arrest of the couple's families made clear his intentions to intimidate them into cooperating with the Vatican's search for the Tivoli couple. Also significant is the rationale behind his desire to arrest them: despite the fact that he is writing to a Vatican colleague in the letter cited above—not an enemy government official—Marchiò fails to relate how he knows that Astrologo's parents were responsible for the couple's flight. Rather, he uses the vague, passive construction "it is known," suggesting that this claim is an assumption on his part. His attempt to convince his readers of the legitimacy of the arrests is made more questionable by his awkwardly worded argument that if the family members were responsible for the couple's escape, then "it is reasonable to assume that" they know where the couple was hiding before fleeing. And finally, his true intentions come through in his last sentence, in which he suggests that arrest will convince Ricca's relatives to reveal where the couple is hiding.

Both Marchiò's rather unconvincing explanations and a general reticence on the part of Tuscan officials appear to contribute to the lack of reaction on the part of the Livornese government in response to the former's calls for the relatives' arrests. Frustrated once again by the Tuscan government's slow response to issues that were deemed urgent in Rome, the consul ignored protocol and communicated his request directly to a member of Livorno's police force. On June 5, following what must have been a forcefully worded request, police inspector Ramorino arrested the Tivoli-Astrologo family members without the consent or knowledge of his superiors. The consul's actions, and his belief that Tuscan leaders were not taking the Vatican's requests seriously, were indicative of the general mood change within the Vatican at this time. Feeling victimized by the French Revolution, and having lost power and status among other temporal rulers, the Vatican turned to a hard-line policy of intransigence that also affected its judicial policy: while in past decades there were examples that indicated both toleration and hostility on the part of the Inquisition tribunal, Vatican officials like Marchiò now tried to wield their power without offering much compromise in return. Lauding Ramorino to the president of the Tuscan government, Marchiò wrote that the policeman's actions made him feel "the strength of the friendly and religious relationships that exist between the august persons of the Holy Father and of King Ferdinand III."[41] By adhering to papal requests the Tuscan government had found itself a friend and ally, though Marchiò offered little relief from the political pressure he employed to achieve the arrests of the wanted suspects.

Marchiò's orders to the Tuscan police were particularly remarkable because he so egregiously overstepped his powers as consul. Indeed, his actions angered numerous Tuscan officials and heightened sympathy for the Jews whom he had targeted. In a flurry of letters written about the arrests, Tuscan officials refused to uphold the consul's actions. In fact, they went so far as to rule that until the Vatican could prove that the family members were indeed subjects of the Papal States, they would not be held in prison. Thus the Tuscan government ruled in favor of the Jews as a result of the rights Jews held in Tuscany and also as a message to the Vatican not to tamper with the duchy's political system. Reflecting this belief, an attorney for the Tuscan government wrote the duchy's leader, voicing concern that the consul's arrest orders had been an abuse of the Church's power. He requested that the Tuscan president free the arrested individuals, warning that their arrests threatened natural and civil law: "The Signor Consul abused the name of Your Eminence with Commissary Ramorino regarding the detention of the four people indicated in the said report . . . it might appear scandalous [not to liberate them] as well as contrary to all civil and natural laws."[42] Addressing the President of Tuscany's Buon Governo in similar terms, head of police Setrini wrote that the consul had subjected these individuals to torture by arresting them. He too described Marchiò's insistence regarding the urgency of the arrest of their family members as stepping beyond the bounds of his position as consul:

> Signor Marchiò was involved to the point that he did not examine the choice of means. He managed to surprise the good faith of the Inspector, making him believe that the arrest of the four closest relatives of the persons sought had been authorized, thus presenting the scandalous example of submitting them to a type of torture in order to force them to reveal the place where the Tivoli couple was hiding. . . . To uncover the true aim of the relatives' arrest, the Signor Vice-consul wanted to make it believed that they were implicated in the crime of the Tivoli couple. The nature of the crime is not noted: but if this crime was committed in the Papal States, it appears that the complicity of at least three of the relatives is excluded since they have a domicile quite far from there, in Livorno. . . . [The Vice-consul] demonstrated in addition that he wished to act in terms that were hardly measured. . . . I believed it my duty to warn Your Eminence of all this, because the most prompt delegation of Signor Marchiò left some sinister impressions regarding the execution of measures that could interest his government.[43]

Setrini's letter suggested that the consul had manipulated, even tricked, the policeman into making the arrests. His anger at the unauthorized actions and at the "torture" of the arrested individuals resulted from the very different legal proceedings that were the norm in Tuscany. Furthermore, because he viewed the vice-consul's zeal as unwarranted, and because the crime occurred in Rome, far from the Livorno homes of these Jews, he readily declared that the arrested individuals were innocent of any complicity. And finally, his last words of the "sinister impressions" that Marchiò's actions had left upon Tuscan government officials suggest an implicit warning that the Vatican government had overstepped its bounds and that future relations between the two states were at risk as a result.

Similarly, Livorno's governor expressed his concern that the consul's zeal had far exceeded proper political boundaries. In his letter to the president, he wrote that Marchiò had requested the family members' arrests with "a horrible insistence" and that he feared the vice consul's zeal "is born from a desire to eat these poor people."[44] This striking image of devouring a group of disempowered individuals suggests a sense of revulsion over the lengths the Vatican was willing to go to find the apostate Tivoli and his pregnant wife. But more than that, Spanocchi's graphic imagery turned the table on an accusation generally made against Jews, who were frequently denounced for ritual murders and consuming the blood of Christians—especially Christian children—for ritual purposes. Here, instead of the Jew being the cannibal and the Christian being the victim, the Christian leader was the cannibal and the Jew was the victim. Spanocchi's criticism of Marchiò could not have been harsher.

Taken together, these leaders argued that the consul's orders were not merely a threat to the civil rights of a handful of Jews living in Livorno; rather, they threatened Tuscan sovereignty and territorial jurisdiction, and as a result the consul's requests and actions were revoked. Upon receiving these various letters, the Tuscan gonfaloniere, himself perturbed by Consul Marchiò's actions, instructed the governor to free the imprisoned Jews, to warn Marchiò that only the Tuscan government could order such a communication, and to suspend Inspector Ramorino for failing to pass the consul's request through proper channels.[45] How, he exclaimed, could Marchiò's request for the arrest of "four Livornese individuals and Tuscan subjects" have been executed without going through the proper channels? Noteworthy too in the gonfaloniere's letter is his reference to four "Tuscan subjects" and "Livornese individuals." Religion was not an identifying characteristic in the Tuscan's letter; political belonging was, and this Tuscan leader identified the Tivoli-Astrologo family members by their citizenship rather than by their creed.

At the time of the Cavalieri affair, the Vatican was very much aware of the modernist sentiments it was fighting against, as shown in the way it conducted this trial and by the two poems the tribunal received, which were preserved among trial documents. The more liberal Cardinal Consalvi, who had unsuccessfully tried to battle the reactionary *zelanti* and their anti-Jewish edicts, had an unusual role in the history of the Ferrarese Jewish community. He tried to limit the restrictions Pius VII imposed upon Jews of the Papal States, viewing the renewal of these restrictions as disastrous examples of how the conservative cardinals in Rome wanted simply to return to the past. To this end, he wrote the papal representative in Ferrara in 1814, where this story was to unfold, with regard to the city's Jewish population. Making the Jews return to the humiliations of the past, particularly after they have enjoyed freedom and emancipation, would bring further problems to the Papal States, he wrote; it would cause the Jews to leave the Papal States altogether, which would have severe economic consequences for the state.[46]

It is no coincidence that Consalvi addressed these worries to the papal delegate of Ferrara, the same city whose Jews so vociferously opposed the removal of Cavalieri's wife and children. While the Jews of Rome and cities near Rome had enjoyed the freedoms that the French instated for a short period, the Jews of more northern cities such as Ferrara, Bologna, and Cento had enjoyed similar freedoms for almost twenty years. When Napoleon's troops were forced to withdraw, the Jews of this area found themselves under the control of the Austrians, who spoke out against returning them to the ghetto. Thus the Jewish communities in these cities hoped that their emancipated status would endure—a belief that surely enflamed tempers more when Piccoli and Tabacchi came to remove Cavalieri's family. As noted earlier, Consalvi's attempts to ensure these freedoms were overruled by the pope himself. Consalvi's failure to mitigate the anti-Jewish desires of some of his colleagues is also demonstrated by correspondence surrounding the Cavalieri affair. I refer in particular to a letter that the Cardinal of Ferrara, Lorenzoni, wrote the Father Inquisitor at the Sant'Uffizio in Rome about the trouble that had arisen with the attempted "extraction" of Cavalieri's family. The letter speaks only briefly of the violence surrounding the Cavalieri affair. But in an unequivocal rejection of the fears Consalvi expressed several years earlier, Lorenzoni uses the rebellion of the Cavalieri affair to propose that Ferrara completely separate its Jews from general society, arguing that the city would be better off without a Jewish presence—even the contribution of Jewish economic successes—in its midst.[47] Indeed, Lorenzoni's letter argues that Jews of the Papal States, like those in other European states, competed against and threatened their non-Jewish counterparts in the economic life of the city. The cardinal's letter taps into traditional stereotypes of usurious Jews, providing further evidence that the Jews represented a foreign culture in the midst of the Papal States—much like Marchiò viewed the Jewish policeman Marace in the Labani Affair.

The Vatican solution that Lorenzoni endorsed was to remove Jews from society by more restrictive laws or convert them to Christianity in an attempt to assimilate them both religiously and culturally. This turn away from the conciliatory politics that Consalvi had endorsed reflected the reactionary and intransigent attitudes the Vatican was adopting as its response to the ideology of the French Revolution. In addition, Lorenzoni's desire to separate Ferrara's Jews both socially and economically reflects a more general phenomenon that Mosse notes: "The accusation that Jews were a state within a state dates back to the very beginning of emancipation and led, almost inevitably, to the belief that Jews must once again be excluded from European life. Jews were thought to desire domination over Europe through their economic skills supposedly based upon their ingrained materialism."[48] While Mosse refers to Jews' exclusion from life in the twentieth century, efforts to this end began as soon as the

Napoleon's emancipatory laws could be undone. In other nations, where Jews often had civil rights, the hope was that they would assimilate into the society at large. Thus emancipation was driven by the assumption that it would enable Jews to assimilate into the general populace, allowing them to shed the negative qualities that were tied to their Jewishness. The Vatican hierarchy, as Lorenzoni reveals, never viewed assimilation without conversion as a viable option. Rather, conversion was presented as the means to creating a unified community, and if conversion was not possible, Vatican officials sought to isolate Jews from the general society.

As far as the Cavalieri case was concerned, the Archbishop of Ferrara sought very specific punishments against the "perpetrators." In his desire to punish the Jewish community for its flagrant disrespect for authority, he recommended that economic sanctions be imposed on the leaders of the community until they, or the community they represented, provided information on the Cavalieri children and their mother: "Since all other attempts at persuasion that I have tried have been in vain," wrote the archbishop, "the Edict of this Holy Congregation compel[s] us to take compendiary and economic measures for the continual violation of *Jewish Leaders* or *Heads*."[49] He went further, stating that, as a result of not having produced the mother and children within forty-eight hours of the order, certain members of Ferrara's Jewish community were fined three hundred *scudi* "for every day until the moment that they obey." In spite of great pressure from the Vatican, however, and despite the hefty fine imposed upon the Jewish community, none of Ferrara's Jews revealed the whereabouts of the family when questioned. Indeed, the community both refused to give information and refused to pay the fine. As a result, tribunal records document that papal police raided various shops in the ghetto, gathering objects equal in value to the sum owed. To this end, a papal representative entered the ghetto shop of one man, Rubino Pesaro, on May 10, 1821, "accompanied as always by armed forces." The shop contained wax products, and the papal representative instructed his men to gather up the merchandise to cover the fine incurred.[50] Almost daily the same papal representative and his armed force entered the shops of various Jewish merchants to confiscate goods. Each time, the shop owner protested the papal actions, explaining that he, along with the other shopkeepers, was appealing the case and awaiting the final verdict before paying the fine. The papal representative and his men were in no mood to wait, however, and, saying that they had received instructions from the Inquisition tribunal, they removed candles, clothing, thread, and other goods to cover the fine imposed upon the community.[51]

Given that the Tivoli and Astrologo families did not live on papal soil and claimed to be Tuscan citizens, Inquisition forces could not act as quickly or as forcefully. First, Vatican officials had to prove their claims that the Tivoli and Astrologo families were papal subjects. To this end, the office of the Holy Inquisition carried out a trial in which witnesses attested that both Ricca Astrologo and Salvatore Tivoli and their families were originally from Rome. In the trial testimony, dated July 18, 1814, two Christian shopkeepers—both of whom had shops near Tivoli's—testified that Tivoli had resided in Livorno for about eight years, that he was born a Jew, converted to Christianity, and then returned to the practice of Judaism. Neither seemed to know if Ricca knew of her husband's baptism or if the Tivoli-Astrologo relatives had helped the couple escape. Oddly enough, the only Jewish witness the Vatican called upon was the Livornese Jew Abramo Jacob Marace, the same police officer who had been suspended from his job at the request of Consul Marchiò.[52]

Marace testified that it was common knowledge among the Jewish community that the young man had been baptized in Rome. In Livorno, however, Tivoli was an active member of the Jewish community, and Marace described the apostate's involvement in the Jewish community and its practices: he went to synagogue on the Sabbath and Jewish holy days, fasted on Yom Kippur, and bought unleavened bread for Passover. When Tivoli decided to marry Ricca Astrologo, testified Marace, the couple was married civilly and according to Jewish law. Marace hesitated in his testimony for the first time when the interrogator asked Marace if Ricca knew that the man she married had converted to Christianity: "I do not know," responded Marace, "but it appears that she had to know, since this was public knowledge, and available to everyone." Did Ricca's family know about Tivoli's baptism, the interrogators asked? Marace responded that the parents had to have known, especially because they were Roman and had left Rome only after Tivoli had been baptized. Though he might not have realized it, Marace's assertion that Salvatore's apostasy was common knowledge was, from the Vatican's perspective, substantial proof of the complicity of the Astrologo family and Ricca herself in Salvatore's crime. When asked if any family member helped the couple escape Livorno six weeks earlier, Marace carefully avoided implicating anyone, saying he did not believe they had any part in the affair. Finally, in response to questions regarding Tivoli's present hiding place, Marace testified that he had heard that the young man had gone south of Livorno, to the coastal Tuscan town of Portoferraio.[53]

While the Tuscan government welcomed the proceedings of the trial, they ultimately claimed that the Vatican had failed to prove adequately that the Tivoli-Astrologo family members were still papal subjects. Having lived in Tuscany for over ten years, argued Tuscan officials, the arrested family members, including Ricca, were considered Tuscan citizens. In addition, despite Marace's testimony, the Tuscan court found no decisive proof that Ricca or her family were complicit in Salvatore's act of apostasy: "It appears moreover proven that Ricca's complicity, and that of the relatives with regard to the apostasy is nonexistent, and that the former married Tivoli believing him positively a Jew, as results from the civil act of their marriage."[54] This ruling regarded only one aspect of the case, however. The other issues, namely the arrest of Salvatore Tivoli and custody of the couple's unborn child, were much stickier questions, and much more important to all the players involved. These issues became even more pressing in mid-June, 1814, when, Vatican documents record, Tuscan police discovered Ricca hiding in the city of Pisa—Salvatore was still at large. In Consul Marchiò's letter to his superior, Cardinal Pacca, he reassures the secretary of state that he did everything possible to make Ricca comfortable and not upset her; and seeing that the young woman was due to give birth any day, he convinced her to get into a carriage and had her brought to a women's hospital in Livorno.

Even before Ricca gave birth, the Jewish community of Livorno was aware that her child might very well be turned over to Church officials: according to Inquisition law it was not only illegal for a convert like Salvatore to marry a Jew, it was illegal for the child of a Catholic father to be raised in a Jewish home. In contrast, in Tuscany, the question of paternal authority and parental rights were legal areas that changed after the French invasion of Tuscany. In a letter that Jewish community members wrote on Ricca's behalf, and in an interesting assertion of a mother's rights, they argued from a legal standpoint that, with Salvatore's absence, paternal authority passed to the mother, and Ricca should thus decide the destiny and religion of her child. With this argument, they were clearly reminding the Tuscan authorities of their obligation to the French law that was practiced in the duchy, and the vast legal differences that existed between Tuscan and Inquisition law.[55]

The same day that leaders of the Jewish community sent off this letter, Ricca, who remained in police custody at a nearby hospital, gave birth to a baby girl. Anticipating the Vatican's desires to take the baby, Jewish community members again wrote the governor, asking that the security of the newborn be guaranteed until the Florentine courts had ruled on her future. At the same time, Consul Marchiò did everything he could to isolate the mother and child from such support within the Jewish community, hoping that such actions would bring him one step closer to removing the child from her mother. Suggesting that the kosher food Jewish visitors brought might be used to poison the mother and child, or that these community members would sneak the child out of the hospital, he placed mother and child under constant police supervision and tried to prohibit Jewish visitors.[56] In a second letter, he similarly complained that government officials allowed Ricca to communicate freely "with her fellow Jewish nationals," which he considered unwise because of the subversive intentions the Jewish community harbored with regard to mother and child.[57] And not only did Marchiò accuse the Jewish community of such malevolent intentions, but in a letter addressed to Secretary of State Pacca he warned that Ricca, rather than permitting her child to be baptized, "could in the excess of passion commit the terrible infanticide of the child."[58]

Vatican fears were great enough that Cardinal Secretary of State Pacca himself wrote to the Tuscan government to request the removal of the newborn from her mother's care. Once again a Church representative depicted the Jewish mother as a threat to the child's survival: "This [baby] cannot be left for even a moment near her Jewish mother, who, because of the perfidy of that nation in many cases already seen, could mistreat her, and even obfuscate her in hatred of the [Catholic] faith; much less then can it be permitted that she be educated growing up with Jews, in evident disfigurement of that indelible character that the sacrament of the holy baptism imprinted upon her soul."[59] The sharp vocabulary of Pacca's words is noteworthy: the "perfidious" Jewish mother will abuse her child, and, even worse, turn her against Catholicism. Particularly striking is the contrast between the baptism that will be "imprinted" on the baby's soul and the "disfigurement" that Judaism will effect on her. The indelible imprint of baptism completes the soul and leaves the body whole; Judaism mutilates the soul, reducing the body to something incomplete as well. Once again the Vatican uses a vocabulary of conquest: conversion to Catholicism erases the alterity of foreign corruption that Jewishness imposes on its members; baptism masters the soul in the same way that colonial powers sought mastery over the nations they conquered.[60]

In this context, the language of conversion and conquest takes on a narrative of gender as well: the preparation of food, a domestic activity associated with women, is brought into question as Vatican representatives question the purity of kosher food, suggesting that it is contaminated to a dangerous degree. And finally, mothering and nurturing itself are questioned, as the Church suggests that the newborn is at risk of being murdered by her Jewish mother. Such an accusation is hardly new: in the Church's eyes, because of Tivoli's conversion, the baby is a Catholic. The accusation on the part of Vatican leaders and adherents that Jewish parents kill Christian children can be traced back to the Middle Ages. Generally, however, these accusations are made of men, and Jewish women are largely exempt from any role in ritual murder because of their exemption from the bulk of Jewish ritual that the Vatican also finds dangerous.[61] The suggestion that a Jewish woman could also perpetrate such a crime, to her own child no less, increases the anti-Jewish narrative of this official writing: the accusation against Ricca provides a link to the historical crime associated with Jews from the Middle Ages, namely the murder of Christian children, and expands upon this history to include Jewish women.

Such a suggestion reflected papal fears that the Jews had gained Tuscan support. The Livornese governor, for example, expressed great sympathy for Ricca. Reversing Marchiò's orders, he permitted the woman to receive food from home, enabling her to eat food in accordance with Jewish dietary laws and to see any visitors she desired. Sympathy such as this made papal authorities fear that the Tuscan government was responding to Jewish protests over the affair and would ultimately allow both the mother and child to return to the ghetto: "Judging from the excessive uproar that the Jewish Nation makes, we have strong reason to believe that Ricca Astrologo and her child will be returned freely to her home if Signor Valentini [a Vatican representative] does not convince that government at least to concede to their division, with the longed for baptism of the latter carried out without the knowledge of the government itself."[62] That Vatican officials linked the Jewish community's loud protests to its ability to manipulate Tuscan officials to decide in their favor perpetuated the belief of the threat that Jews presented to papal law and order and the unfortunate powers that emancipation had granted them. Furthermore, the aforecited note suggests that faced with Tuscan inaction over the case, the Vatican was preparing to take matters into its own hands, baptizing the newborn with or without Tuscan consent.

In his discussion of medieval anti-Semitism, James Shapiro writes of different forms of criminality attributed to Jews in medieval times, ranging from a desire to abduct and kill Christian children to a wish to destroy all Christians. Accusations of the former generally included the claim that Jews used the blood of Christian children in their rituals; accusations of the latter often included a claim that Jews had tried to murder Christians by poisoning their food. More than one of these accusations was made of Ricca and the Livornese Jewish community while Ricca's child remained with her in the hospital. Marchiò's fear that Ricca would flee with her child was a twisted version of this old medieval tale: in essence he was suggesting that she would kidnap an allegedly Catholic child. The claim that Jewish visitors would try to poison the mother and her child or that Ricca would murder her own baby rather than allow her to become Christian repeated these old stereotypes of blood libels, endorsing the view that the baby was Catholic and as such was at risk in the arms of her Jewish mother and the Jewish community. In addition, the Jewish mother who denies the Catholic identity of her children is represented as a foil to the mothering Church: whereas the Church nurtures and nourishes, the Jewess will brutally kill her children rather than see them adopt the ways of Christians. The brutality of the imagery of the Jewish mother as kidnapper or murderer is further endorsed by the legal vocabulary Vatican leaders employ, since their use of words such as "perfidy" and "obstinacy" resonate both morally and religiously with readers. Thus this language of the Inquisition contributed to a legal system that endorsed official stories in which the stories' narrators have the ability to reinterpret the facts surrounding these conversion stories to their advantage.[63]

An image perpetuated in the Cavalieri story as well is the contrast between the upstanding, loving Catholic community and a Jewish community that did not value its children and had no qualms about treating them violently. The accusation of the "kidnap" of the Cavalieri children, predicated by the rebellion at their school, fed into these views of Jewish criminality. In contrast, the clergymen of Ferrara depict the institution they represent as emotionally aware of the preciousness of these children; their desire to keep them safe suggests necessarily removing them from the arms of the Jewish community. The repeated imagery of the "dear," innocent Cavalieri children, violently and abusively taken by rapacious Jews, set up a moral contrast between the good Catholic community who rightfully sought its latest acquisitions and the evil Jewish community who held them captive. With this perspective, the Cavalieri children are portrayed as innocent Catholic victims of a corrupt Jewish community.

Not only did the archbishop define the Jewish community's actions as kidnap, but his description of the "notorious kidnapping" bespoke the amount of attention the case attracted, which must have been substantial. In a letter that the Cardinal wrote the city's Father Inquisitor, he expressed openly the interest the case had generated and the urgency with which Church leaders wished the affair to be resolved. Lorenzoni reiterated the anti-Semitic stereotypes the city's archbishop had voiced: the city's Jews had too much liberty and too much wealth; they lacked respect for the law of the land, and in the recent political turmoil following the French Revolution, they had sown the seeds of rebellion and revolution among the general populace. These accusations appeared fairly generic, but the way in which the cardinal tied them into the Cavalieri case is significant. In his letter, which was really a request that the tribunal support the trial against the accused in the Cavalieri affair, Lorenzoni tried to convince his superiors to hold the trial and of the legitimacy and justness of his position in the affair: "I write to Your Most Revered Eminence only in order to implore your most efficacious protection for a trial whose good outcome abound[s] in glory and benefit[s] of our religion and the Church, not to mention [that it is] to the advantage and health of innocent souls. These two indisputable truths speak sufficiently to the virtuous heart of Your Most Revered Eminence, and they affect the justice, religion, and honor of the most respected Congregation of the Holy, Supreme Inquisition of the Sant'Uffizio."[64] A favorable outcome of the trial, he argues, would provide the Catholic religion with the advantage of victory. Second, it would provide for the salvation of the innocent souls who are converted. Thus Lorenzoni presents both political and religious reasons as significant considerations for the tribunal. He suggests that both issues would surely interest the Inquisitors and the population at large. In addition, he argues that the religious and political achievement produced by a verdict against the Jews would heighten the religious and political consciousness of the populace. Such an outcome, he reasoned, would make the papal government more popular and hence more powerful.

In his letter, the Cardinal made no bones about the fact that he did not believe that the papal police would ever find the children. Nonetheless, he argued that an Inquisition trial was an important show of force. His reasoning reflected another ingredient in the growing politicization of the Catholic movement: public opinion. Even if the police returned empty-handed, he reasoned, the trial, sure to be well-publicized, would produce great admiration for the Holy See among Catholic inhabitants of the Papal States, who would surely be scandalized by the affair:

> In conformity with the determinations of the holy supreme inquisition of the Sant'Uffizio the case was remitted of the formerly Jewish Cavalieri, who demanded and demands the rescue of his dear children kidnapped from him by the Jews of this ghetto. The case was, as I say, remitted to this

> most distinguished legate cardinal in order that a criminal trial be constructed. It would never be that I wish to censure such a determination, but I believe, as all believe, that by this means those innocent souls that were stolen will never be rescued, despite being legally offered to the church by their father. [That there is no other means to rescue the two kidnapped little children] literally scandalizes citizens.
>
> In such circumstances I sought to produce in public a defense in the name of the father, which I pass on to Your Most Revered Eminence as well so that you make of it that use that in God will judge more favorable for the reason of the lord. I heartily recommend this to your illustrious piety and religion. Forgive this part of my words that is perhaps premature; but I say it also with a view towards satisfying the vows of the city and citizens who ardently desire that a new enemy arise to make a show of zeal in honor of the church and its sanctuary.[65]

The Cardinal refers to the Cavalieri children as "kidnapped" or "stolen" three times in the first paragraph alone. Again, he creates a contrast between these "dear children," who are "innocent souls," legally offered to the Church by their father, and the Jewish kidnappers of the ghetto, the perpetrators of an illegal and immoral act that challenges the pontifical constitution. Why would the Inquisition tribunal want to carry out a trial that had little hope of procuring the children, he asks? He answers his own question, assuring the tribunal that the papal government will gain "great admiration." Even more important, perhaps, the case will scandalize the country's citizens, making them support the Vatican even more ardently. Thus the cardinal recommends continuing with the trial to demonstrate solidarity and support of the newly converted father and as a sign of the Inquisitor's "illustrious piety and religion." Such reasoning reflects the twofold motivation for the trial: to punish the Jews responsible for hiding the children and to rally support among the people for the Church. The former rationale reflects the uncompromising stance of anti-Jewish papal policy in this period; the latter speaks of a calculated political move that responded to changes wrought by the new order.

Despite the different circumstances of these two cases, the Vatican ultimately came out victorious. Not only did Tuscan Governor Spannocchi allow Ricca and Salvatore's child to be baptized, but, worried about how Ricca would respond to this development, he demanded that no one tell her about it until six weeks after the fact.

Her anger and dismay prompted the papal representative Valentini to again request the separation of the mother from her child.[66] While the Vatican pressed for custody of the child based on her religious identity and the threat to her life if she were left with her mother, for the Tuscan government the fact that the child had been baptized had no bearing on paternal definition. Baptism was a religious matter; to remove the child from Tuscan territory was a question of citizenship, and the Tuscan government was prepared to defend the baby's rights to stay in Tuscany until the Vatican proved that her parents were papal subjects. Nothing Marchiò could say would convince the government to allow the Church to take the child away from her mother before this ruling occurred: "In spite of all this, the aforementioned government does not believe it to be sufficiently authorized to remove the child from the mother without receiving from the government of Florence special authority."[67] While the governor of Livorno felt free to rule in the Church's favor on a matter of religious identity, custody of the child was a different matter, and the Church was not allowed to take the child from its mother because of both mother and child's potential rights as Tuscan subjects.

On August 30, the head of the Tuscan government finally ruled on the case. While Ricca and the couple's relatives were found innocent because they had lived in Livorno before 1808, Salvatore Tivoli, who had come to Livorno after that date, when the French-controlled the city, was not a beneficiary of the same privileges. Thus Tuscan officials condoned his arrest and his extradition to the Papal States, were he ever found. Resulting from this decision, the government declared that Ricca's child needed to be handed over to the Church as well: "She should be removed from her mother and her Jewish relatives, and she will be received at the House of the Catechumens in Livorno, where she will remain at the disposition of the government of Rome."[68] With this deceivingly neutral vocabulary, the Florentine government allowed Vatican desires to be fulfilled. A wet nurse brought baby Fortunata to Rome's Catechumens, where, upon entrance, she was declared an illegitimate child: in the eyes of the Church her father was considered a Christian, and no valid marriage existed between a Catholic and a Jew.

In 1823, two years after the Vatican attempted to remove Cavalieri's children from the Ferrara ghetto, papal police discovered that Cavalieri's wife and children were residing with relatives in Mantua. The network of Italian Jewish communities had proven itself fundamental to the family's escape from Ferrara, but fleeing the Papal States did not provide absolute refuge. On May 16, 1823, the Vatican spokesman in Ferrara wrote the city's Father Inquisitor: "With regard to the Jewish affair I can finally give you the most cheering news. Magnanetti's wife and children have not only been found; they were arrested in Mantova following our searches and demands."[69] A month later, the spokesman again wrote, this time to announce triumphantly, "The Jews are in my hands." The success of the arrest was due to providence and the persistence of the Vatican's procurator, who had achieved what even the cardinal of Ferrara deemed impossible, namely custody over the Cavalieri children. The Ferrarese spokesman wrote glowingly of his colleague, stating that the procurator "had the courage to cross the Po, go to Mantua, search for them, find them, and press a petition for their recovery, which was obtained."[70] If the ghetto provided a geography of difference internal to the Papal States, the Po represented the geography of difference between the Papal States and its neighbor, between Inquisition law and secular rule. The implication of the spokesman's words was that travel north of the Po—similar to crossing the border into the ghetto—was dangerous to the ideals, society, and culture maintained by Vatican ideology. In this sense, the language with which the Vatican spokesman depicted the procurator's travels reflected the ideological tension that existed between the Papal States and her neighbors. Finally, the procurator's success in furthering the Vatican's objectives across this frontier suggested a conquest similar to that of Consul Marchiò in Tuscany: both men negotiated around the politics of their secular neighbors to further the conversionary goals of the Vatican, victoriously emphasizing the importance of Catholicism even beyond the borders of the Papal States.

Despite the apparent dangers of traveling outside the Papal States, the fact that the Cavalieri family was in another state appeared not to have caused the problems for the Vatican that had occurred with the Tivoli-Astrologo clan in Livorno. Following the procurator's request, the Mantuan government allowed the Vatican custody over the Cavalieri children and their mother. They permitted the Jews to be arrested and brought first to Ferrara's and later to Rome's House of the Catechumens—on one condition, however: the procurator had to guarantee that the Vatican would not force Cavalieri's wife to convert through violent means. Upon hearing of this condition, the Vatican spokesman's response reflected his impatience with this demand: "But when is this violence ever practiced? She must be in our custody for forty days, and she will be."[71] The Mantuan government's implication that the Vatican resorted to force or violence to procure conversion, and its desire, however feeble, to avoid contributing to that process, clearly troubled Cardinal Lorenzoni. The cardinal wrote a letter to the Inquisition tribunal, repeating the papal spokesman's assurances that no violence would be used against Cavalieri's wife. Nonviolence would not be a problem, he wrote defensively, since "making Christians by force has never been practiced."[72] Similar to the cases described in chapter one, the Vatican sought to define its tribunal as just and impartial, despite the religious and political allegiances of its judges and despite the violence and bias of its language. Similarly, Vatican leaders had to ensure that the "making of Christians" was genuine and desired by the convert. Only through authentic, valid conversions could the political and spiritual unity of the Catholic community be ensured; indeed, anything but a sincere adaptation of Christian beliefs would threaten the very foundations of the society the Vatican was trying to strengthen and expand.

Despite his defensive tone, however, the cardinal appeared determined to find out who helped Cavalieri's wife and children escape. To aid in this search, when the family arrived at Ferrara's local House of Catechumens, the mother was immediately separated from her children. She underwent hours of questioning in an attempt to ascertain who among the Ferrarese Jewish community had helped her. Isolation, combined with these examinations, reflected the great psychological pressure to which Signora Manganetti was submitted, though clergymen never referred to these measures as a means of forcing conversion, or confession for that matter. In this case, reported the papal spokesman, Signora Manganetti was greatly pained when her children were separated from her, "but," he continued, she remained calm, "without conceding one point of her ideas."[73] Thus, while separation and isolation did not constitute violence, the councilor's phrasing here, his use of the word "but" suggested that he recognized the Vatican's procedures as measures meant to pressure the woman to reveal her accomplices and sacrifice her beliefs. Finally, his description and his earlier response to the Mantuan government reflect an official perception of Jews that lacked any identification with their plight.

While these interrogation methods met with no success with the mother, the future of the Cavalieri children, like the Tivoli-Astrologo baby, seemed assured. The Vatican representative's commentary on their welfare is noted with a sense of satisfaction that appears all the more noticeable after his frustrations with Cavalieri's wife: "They no longer know anything about Judaism, they are always with their father, they already pray, they can already understand that which everyone else their age understands."[74]

Tuscan officials' sympathy toward Ricca and the family members suggested that they did not take the portrayals of the new mother's possibly murderous tendencies or the conspiratorial capacities of her relatives too seriously, although their reluctance to tell Ricca of her child's baptism may in some way have reflected a fear that, as Vatican sources argued, she would harm her own child. Similarly, despite concern over the Vatican's treatment of converts, the Mantuan government acquiesced to Vatican demands, most likely in the interest of diplomacy. Whether or not Tuscan and Mantuan officials believed Vatican stereotypes, however, the division between Jewish outsider and Christian insider was one with which they grappled. Thus the portrayal of Jews as separate from the general population, together with the Vatican's pointed reminders of government officials' own personal identity as Catholics, translated into official acquiescence to Vatican wishes when it came to deciding the fate of Ricca and Salvatore's daughter and the remainder of the Cavalieri family. The Tuscan government and its Mantuan counterpart, torn between serving its citizens and maintaining good relations with its political and geographical neighbor, overlooked issues of sovereignty and voted with their religious allegiance instead.

As for the Vatican, archival documents do not mention whether Tivoli was found and arrested or if he managed to find safe haven in another territory. Similarly, records at the Sant'Uffizio do not indicate if Cavalieri's wife acquiesced to the demands of her interrogators and agreed to convert or if she continued to refuse to cooperate with Vatican officials. One thing is clear, however: in both cases, the double sword of conversion of the children and isolation of the mother once again lent power to the laws and practices of Inquisition Rome. Indeed, while the diplomatic initiative that produced the Labani affair began with an attempt to punish an apostate Jew, interest in the case increased significantly with the news that Tivoli was soon to be a father. Likewise, while the Vatican continued to seek out and punish the "pernicious" Jews who thwarted the early arrest of the Cavalieri children and their mother, the main thrust of their diplomacy was to gain custody of the children. Winning custody meant bringing an apostate to justice through his progeny, just as it served as a powerful reminder to the entire Jewish community of Ferrara of their precarious standing as a minority religion in the Papal States. In addition, it symbolized a victory—albeit a small one—against the spread of secularization. Indeed, as young people especially became increasingly enchanted with revolutionary ideals—as seen in the next part of this project–the Vatican felt increasing pressure to reverse this trend and counter the conquests of secular leaders with their own ideological triumphs. By pursuing a culture of conversion, particularly regarding children, the Vatican sought to effectuate a new identity for and among young people that firmly established Catholic beliefs and ideals in a new generation.

The trials discussed within these first two chapters have focused on the issue of early nineteenth-century Catholic culture and the legal institutions that represented it in the Papal States. By narrating two trials at length, I have sought to explore how the Church defined its cultural, religious, and political identity toward its supporters and toward those opposed to it. One of the reasons the Church went to such great lengths to initiate such trials was the idea that the Church was located at the heart of civilized society, a society over which morality and justice reigned.[75] Indeed, as Giovanni Miccoli notes, a primary aim of nineteenth-century Catholic culture was to present the Church as the model of civil society.[76] To this end, however, Church supporters argued that the only guarantee of a civil society was to entrust the state to Catholic hands and imbue it with Catholic principles. Indeed, many ecclesiastical leaders argued that the new values of liberty and equality were antithetical to Catholic doctrine. Their arguments were based upon the belief that the elimination of the judicial value of religion, the secularization of the state, and the granting of political and civil rights to non-Catholics threatened the power and values that the Vatican represented. Thus the Vatican's belief that it was at the center of Western civilization provided the basis for its assertion that Catholic identity should be an attribute of all subjects of the Papal States, if not of Europe more generally.

This desire led to an inevitable conflict: while not wishing to be accused of coercion, the Vatican sought to ensure that any Jew who wished to identify as a free, upstanding inhabitant of the Papal States divorce himself completely from his local community. To reinforce this view of conversion, the Vatican understood Tivoli's act of apostasy as the ultimate heresy: the man infiltrated Christian society without perpetuating its values. Similarly, the Vatican's particular interest in Cavalieri's children resulted from its conviction that the father's conversion also resulted in the "making of Christians" of his offspring, who could easily be inducted into the Catholic community. Conversion thus became a metaphor for the necessity of identifying the government and its inhabitants with Catholic ideology.

A second result of the association between Catholicism and European civilization was a reinforcement of the view of the Jew as outsider. As Sander Gilman notes, the relationship between Christianity and anti-Semitism resulted from the "Europeanization of Christianity," or the association of western civilization with Christianity—an association the Vatican sought to enforce.[77] When conversion was not possible, the push toward a separation and exclusion of Jews from the general community appealed to many clergymen as the only viable policy for maintaining a Catholic identity within the community at large. The anti-Jewish edicts that sent Jews back to the ghetto reflected this mentality, as did laws prohibiting the interaction between Jews and Catholics. Indeed, the Church had been trying to keep the Jewish and Catholic communities separate for many years, and records at the Sant'Uffizio demonstrate that these efforts went on well into the 1850s, when Vatican officials were again considering closing the ghettos of the Papal States.[78] In the early nineteenth century however, when Napoleon's military failures enabled the Holy See to return to Rome, Pius VII's reactionary legislation reconfirmed the traditional connection between Church and power. These two trials show how, through the texts provided by legal narratives and official correspondence, the Vatican elaborated a cultural initiative that corresponded with Pius's reactionary beliefs and those of his many supporters.

The separation that Vatican Consul Marchiò sought for Ricca when she was in the hospital and the isolation Cavalieri's wife suffered when she was arrested all point to a division the Vatican encouraged in its efforts to emphasize that acceptance into the larger community depended on one's Catholic identity. Such marginalization became a means that the legal system perpetuated in its desire to control a perceived social threat. That is, the Vatican's desire to enclose and restrict Jews appears ultimately to be a response to the fear of Jewish expansion into the fabric of society. Portrayed as Other, Jews represented a people, as Susan Zickmund's writes, "whose very presence within the nation is sufficient to destroy the social stability and the special values which made the nation strong at its founding."[79] The use of imagery and language to create an official perception of the dangers Jewishness posed to the larger Catholic community thus encouraged a policy of isolation that in turn, many Vatican officials believed, would ensure the continuance of Catholic identity on the peninsula. Indeed, the Catholic identity the Vatican desired for its society was in some sense better defined by projecting the Jew as embodying all that should *not* be included; by disparaging so-called Jewish attributes, papal representatives thus sought to enhance Catholic identity and authority. The Vatican in this sense was similar to a colonizer whose identity, as Michael Pickering writes, "depended upon this projected Otherness of difference in every confirmation of itself."[80] In other words, the identification of "Italian" with "Catholic" was rendered more explicit by the exclusion of other religions from the citizenry and by creating an image of the Jew as the opposite of the ideal human being and citizen.

In the era of the Tivoli and Cavalieri trials, the gradual strengthening of the reactionary *zelanti* within the Church further enabled this policy of separation and prejudice.[81] Religious diversity was viewed as a guarantee for fracture and a risk to the Catholic fabric that defined the general community. To this end, Vatican officials perpetuated images of Jews who threatened the lives and livelihoods of those around them. Viewing Jews as outcasts and foreigners was not new; indeed, even the stereotypes contained in these trials often duplicated those of earlier eras, particularly medieval portrayals of Jews.[82] Vatican supporters in Restoration Italy often resuscitated these stereotypes, I would submit, from a desire to return to the culture and society of the Middle Ages more generally. As a result, the connection between medieval and modern times that Giovanni Miccoli so persuasively develops with regard to Catholic society more generally can be seen in a return to medieval attitudes toward Jews as well.[83] With the onset of the nineteenth century, however, supporters adjusted medieval stereotypes to fit the context of the times. Thus the medieval depiction of the wayward Jew, still considered a threat to the Christian forces of morality, gave rise to the belief of a quality innate to Jews that led them to have central roles in the rise of modern economic systems and associations with secular, revolutionary groups—both viewed as detrimental threats to Christian authority and rule. Clergymen thus reinvented medieval stereotypes to make them resonate with the new circumstances that the French Revolution produced in the Papal States and across Europe.

As expressed here, these stereotypes, like papal anti-Jewish laws of the nineteenth century, present evidence that church-instigated anti-Judaism contained both religious and cultural aspects. For example, accusations on the part of Ferrarese clergymen that that city's Jews sought to disempower the entire Inquisition tribunal with their money reinforced medieval stereotypes of usury, combining this financial immorality with the modern accusation of Jewish support for political revolution and mayhem. The language that accompanied these accusations, with its regular use of terms such as "obstinacy" and "perfidy," connected Jewish criminality to accusations of deicide and a rejection of Catholic theology.

Indeed, Jews who rejected the Catholic faith were regularly portrayed as criminals, a threat to Christian society and to individual Christians, particularly children, as well. Salvatore Tivoli's apostasy was portrayed not simply as heretical but as a dangerous and divisive brand of criminality that needed to be punished. In a revised version of the medieval blood libel, his wife Ricca was depicted as a potentially murderous mother, the exact opposite of the "true" nurturer and mother of her child, the Catholic Church. And, like the rebellion of the Cavalieri affair, the arguments regarding Tuscan citizenship that the Jewish community used on behalf of Ricca and her child brought new "evidence" that Jews were active participants in revolutionary efforts to de-Christianize society and limit Catholic authority. Similarly, papal insistence that Marace was an infiltrator in the Livornese police force hinged upon the fact that his Jewish allegiances meant that he could not be trusted as an enforcer of state law. While this type of accusation was not new, the Vatican official's disparaging depiction of Marace as a member of the Jewish nation struck a particular chord in the nineteenth century, when questions of nationhood were so pressing. Thus the accusations leveled at the Cavalieri family, at Tivoli, and at their respective "accomplices" reflected the tension that existed over the issue of nationality and citizenship in the Papal States more generally. By belonging to the local Jewish community—or the "Jewish Nation," as it was called—these Jews were unable to belong to the larger Catholic community that, for the Vatican at least, defined the desired Italian community.

Finally, the stories that the Inquisition Tribunal reported, the language and imagery employed, lent these official narratives to that which Peter Brooks terms "the modalities of narrative presentation."[84] That is, the ideas and ideologies expressed in the Vatican's legal storytelling fostered a tacit agreement between narrator and reader, in which the former expected the latter to adopt its ideology in return for the story it told.[85] Thus the trials served more than a legal system that simply sought to deter or punish threatening conduct: first, these trials reinforced Catholic organization, mentality, and culture with their authority; second, they cultivated a shared reference for moral and political beliefs between narrator and reader. As a result, the stories narrated here shed light on the political importance papal supporters placed on Catholic identity, just as they explain why the Vatican devoted so much energy to these cases. In sum, Vatican officials' use of threatening stereotypes, clergymen's expressed fear of Jewish perfidy, and the general consensus of the harm Jews brought Catholics exposed further the absolute impossibility of the motto Cardinal Pacca quoted in his memoirs. The saying *If this is true, let us go immediately to the Ghetto and make ourselves Jews* can only be understood by its inverted form, in which the very plausible—indeed, desired—story of Jews converting and leaving the ghetto is narrated. In Restoration Italy, Jews, problematic because of their religious beliefs and threatening because of their supposed support for revolution, could only be accepted fully if they bowed to the conversionary pressures surrounding them. For this reason, the figure of the convert and the rhetoric of conversion that the Inquisition Tribunal expounded were reimagined as a response to Napoleon's invasion and the threat this presented to the future of the Papal States. By rewriting the Jew in the context of legal documents and the "law's stories,"[86] Vatican officials strove to define their community into a political and geographical referent that coincided with a citizenry that was wholly Catholic.

Part II

Novels

Chapter 3

Proselytization as a Nationalist Project*

Alessandro Manzoni the Convert(er)

The most popular story told of Alessandro Manzoni's conversion links him to Napoleon, contrasting the religious conservatism of one of Italy's leading intellectuals with the leader of revolution and secular modernity. On April 2, 1810, the story goes, Alessandro Manzoni was in Paris with his wife Henriette. The City of Lights was celebrating the wedding of Napoleon and Marie Louise, and some of the fires that the crowds lit grew out of control, causing a great deal of confusion and panic. The Manzonis found themselves caught up in the crowds, and to escape the throngs of people Manzoni sought refuge in a nearby church. Accounts of the story diverge at this point: Some versions suggest that Manzoni went in to escape the crowds and that he had a sudden revelation as he sat in the Church of St. Roch.[1] According to other narrators, Manzoni's conversion was precipitated by his separation from his wife in the Parisian crowds. Desperate to find her, Manzoni entered the nearby Church of St. Roch and exclaimed: "God, if you exist, reveal yourself to me, let me find Henriette."[2] Upon successfully finding Henriette in the church, amid the chaos of the celebration, Manzoni declared his renewed faith in God and the Catholic Church. In both versions, the backdrop of Napoleon's wedding and the references to the Parisian crowds appear to be a narratological attempt to explain Manzoni's agoraphobia and his deep-seated misgivings about the unruly nature of the populace, a volatile element of the French Revolution that he wished to avoid during the process of Italian unification.[3] In a similar vein, the Church of St. Roch may have been named as much for the identity of Roch, the patron saint who protects individuals from the plague, as for its location in Paris.[4]

In other, modified versions of this story, Napoleon's wedding does not play a role, although the events surrounding Manzoni's conversion are remarkably similar. One version claims that Manzoni, inspired by religious anxiety (according to some) or by ill health (according to others), entered a church that he was passing. Once inside, he experienced an epiphany that resulted in his conversion to Catholicism.[5] Similarly, Davide Norsa, a young Jewish man whom Manzoni converted to Catholicism, claimed that Manzoni described entering the Parisian Church of St. Roch and exclaiming immediately: "Oh God, if you are there, make yourself known to me."[6] From that day forward, Manzoni "believed, and found peace in the true Faith."[7] Manzoni's daughter, Vittoria, used similar language to describe her father's conversion. While Vittoria did not detail where her father's conversion took place, she reported that Manzoni's conversion came about by a revelation, recalling that her father compared his conversion to the moment when God revealed himself to Saint Paul on the road to Damascus: "Daughter of mine," she reported her father to have said, "thank God who had pity on me. . . . That [same] God who revealed himself to Saint Paul on the road to Damascus."[8]

One final version of Manzoni's conversion story rejects the setting of Paris and the Church of St. Roch altogether. The Englishman J. H. Wynne, whom Manzoni also inspired to convert to Catholicism, claims that Manzoni's conversion did not occur in Paris but at an unspecified church in Lyons, where Manzoni and his wife stopped en route from Paris to Milan. Manzoni decided to attend mass one day, during which the priest delivered a sermon; Manzoni felt that the priest was speaking directly to him: "He said it seemed to him that Almighty God was talking to him by the mouth of the priest, filled his soul with the light of faith, and his heart with horror and compunction at his apostasy." [9] After the mass, Manzoni reportedly asked to see the preacher and upon meeting him declared his newfound faith and was reconciled with the Church.

Whether Manzoni's conversion took place in Paris or en route to Milan, and whether or not it was connected to the events of Napoleon's wedding, one element of these stories remains constant: the moment of conversion. That is, the revelation that resulted in the apostle Paul's conversion appears to be the model that Manzoni drew on to describe his own conversion to Catholicism. The mirroring of Paul's conversion is significant for several reasons: Paul, influenced by his Jewish roots, used Judaism as a model for his vision of Christianity. Indeed, many scholars argue that Pauline Christianity is a "transvalued" Judaism: the law of the New Testament and Jesus replace the law of the Hebrew Bible and Mt. Sinai, and a new covenant and a new people replace the old. In Romans, Paul even assures his readers that the Jews' future lay in the Christian faith. In Paul's times, replacing the law of the Hebrew Bible with that of the New Testament had political implications. As Kenneth Stowe notes, the Hebrew Bible was essentially a civil constitution for Diaspora Jewry; replacing it with the law of Jesus and the New Testament meant changing society's laws as well as the beliefs of the individual convert.[10]

With his emphasis on the role of religion for the individual and the society, Manzoni coheres, albeit in a modern context, to the model Paul provided as a convert and promoter of Christianity. Like Paul, Manzoni's conversion to Catholicism was the result of an epiphany, a Pauline moment of revelation. In addition, Manzoni envisioned a model, Christian society based on the politically and religiously engaged community of the ancient Israelites, with Italy rather than biblical Israel at its center. And finally, Manzoni advocated the morality of the Church and its laws as being of primary importance for society as well as for the individual. That is, while Manzoni did not envision a politically engaged papacy, he viewed Catholic identity and belief on the peninsula as a key unifying factor among Italians, who, ideally, would live under the moral guidance of the pope. Like Paul, Manzoni's conversion embodied a religious ideology that defined the development of his political vision for Italy as well.

Thus it should come as no surprise that the Pauline model that inspires stories of Manzoni's conversion can be seen in many of Manzoni's literary projects. Indeed, an examination of Manzoni and his works within the context of conversion suggests a writer who is far more conservative than scholars have generally argued. Manzoni regularly addresses the theme of conversion in an attempt to underline a vision of Italy in which lapsed Catholics and non-Catholics turned—or returned, as Manzoni himself did—to the Church. The theme of conversion that permeated Manzoni's work was influenced by the tumultuous events that he witnessed: the overthrow of absolutism, the French Revolution, the counterrevolution, and the Restoration were all events that resonated deeply with the Italian author. Manzoni, like other Vatican supporters of his day, opposed the antireligious sentiment that generally accompanied revolution and the so-called nationalization of the masses. As a practicing Catholic, he suggested that the group was always counterbalanced by the importance and value of the individual and his destiny.[11] The conversion story that places Manzoni in the crowds of Paris in large part reinforces these sentiments, with its portrayal of the rowdy masses that appeared as perilous as they were celebratory.

Manzoni's poem *Il Nome di Maria*, part of his *Inni Sacri*, exemplifies the Pauline influences on Manzoni's work in its advocacy of the conversion of Jews to Catholicism. In the poem, to which I will return in a later section, Manzoni urges Jews to follow the example of Mary and convert to Christianity. For Manzoni, such conversion was proof of the biblical unity between the people of the Hebrew Bible and the people of the New Testament. Furthermore, Manzoni's celebration of Christian triumph over Judaism echoes the Pauline relationship between Christianity and its Jewish roots. That Paul converted from Judaism to Christianity suggests the model Manzoni drew on for his *Il Nome di Maria*. Most significantly, however, Paul's conversion led him to advocate a society guided by the laws and morality of the New Testament. Thus Paul's conversion involved elements both religious and political, providing the model for Manzoni's personal conversion to Catholicism and for his political goal of unifying Italy.

This chapter explores the theme of conversion that is so fundamental to Manzoni's view of the individual, both as human being and as citizen, and that individual's role in a moral society. I examine aspects of Manzoni's own conversion to Catholicism and the conversions he encouraged of those around him, such as his wife and several literary admirers. In particular, I examine the stories of the Jewish Marco Coen and Davide Norsa and the Anglican J. H. Wynne, young men who sought out Manzoni while they were exploring their religious identity.[12] All three men attribute their conversions to their discussions with Manzoni, and their stories are significant both because of the spiritual quest that they describe, which culminated in their conversions to Catholicism, and because they in turn become narrators of Manzoni's conversion. Furthermore, the men Manzoni converted to Catholicism share Manzoni's vision of an empowered papacy and the need for continued Catholic hegemony on the peninsula, with the result that each of these individuals becomes himself a part of the trope of conversion in Risorgimento Italy. Finally, I explore the clerical correspondence of the clergymen who converted Manzoni, and who were also responsible for converting Manzoni's wife Henriette; their correspondence presents a rare window on how representatives of the Church interpret and understand religious identity in the case of an *un*forced conversion, and particularly in the case of one of Italy's great writers. The two priests who administered pastoral care to the Manzoni family in Paris and Milan viewed the author's new religious beliefs as a triumph of religion over liberalism and the freethinking intellectual, their letters providing further evidence of the culture of conversion that papal representatives advocated in Italy before unification.

That conversion marked a turning point in Manzoni's own life is reflected in his writing, where he again explores the relationship between his religious and political beliefs, portraying the Church and Catholic identity as a necessary component of an independent Italy. In particular, the Pauline elements of Manzoni's conversion are echoed in his writing, further displaying the parallel he sees between the Church father's religious and political vision and his own. After returning to *Il Nome di Maria*, I examine the role of conversion in his novel *I Promessi Sposi* (henceforth *PS*), a historical novel that depicts numerous religious conversions that restore morality and hope to an Italy torn apart by the plague. I will discuss how Manzoni, adhering to his identification with Paul, sought to portray Italy as the reestablishment of the political and religious society of the biblical Israelites in a modern, Catholic context. As my discussion of these works will show, conversion appears to be a significant topos in the author's perception of *italianità* (Italian-ness) and as a means of promoting a Catholic identity for Italian society. In sum, in the stories surrounding Manzoni's conversion, and in the conversions that he advocates in his writing, Manzoni maintains a singular role that one critic aptly defines as that of an "ideological operator."[13] That is, Manzoni hopes to instill an Italian identity that is inherently Catholic in his young, fictional heroes and in his impressionable, real followers. This desire defined Manzoni as a Pauline proselytizer in two senses: he converted individuals from other faiths, and he proselytized on behalf of his beliefs in the need for unification. In so doing, Manzoni lent a political dimension to religious conversion that was crucial to his view of nation building.

When, in the fall of 1807, Manzoni met Henriette Blondel, the daughter of a Swiss Protestant banking family, he was living in Paris with his mother and her companion, Carlo Imbonati.[14] During this period, the young Manzoni cultivated ties with a group of intellectuals known as *les idéologues*, whose ideology was based upon its opposition to the political conservatism and societal hierarchy Napoleon advocated following the French Revolution. Rather, its members, who included Count Antoine Louis Claude Destutt de Tracy, Charles-Claude Fauriel, and Pierre Jean George Cabanis, advocated the antiestablishment, antireligious ideals associated with the Enlightenment. Thus the fact that Henriette Blondel had been raised in a strictly Calvinist family posed no difficulty for the liberal Manzoni. Indeed Manzoni's letters suggested that her Protestant roots made her more desirable. In a letter to his Parisian friend Fauriel, Manzoni wrote of Henriette and her admirable qualities, including her religious affiliation: "I find that she has a good heart; she thinks only of her household, and of the happiness of her parents, who adore her. . . . Furthermore, she is Protestant; indeed, she is a treasure."[15] The couple was married on February 6, 1808. Because receiving a dispensation from the Catholic Church to marry a Protestant would have been a long and arduous task, Manzoni, reflecting his secularism, chose to be married by a Calvinist pastor.[16]

After the birth and baptism of their first child, Manzoni decided that he and Henriette should remarry in the Catholic tradition. In the name of family unity, Henriette chose to convert. Her abjuration provided the first correspondence among the family's priests regarding Manzoni's conversion and, while Henriette's conversion is not the subject of this study, her Catholic baptism is noteworthy because of the responses it evoked in the clergymen converting her. Abbot Eustachio Degola and his Milanese delegate Monsignor Luigi Tosi expressed concern that Henriette's closeness to her parents would impede her conversion.[17] This concern in part resulted from a letter Degola received from a Manzoni family friend who was involved with Henriette's conversion. He wrote asking Degola to help Henriette fight her filial sense of duty through prayer: "Our virtuous Catholic suffers unspeakable torment in the conflict between her pious, irrevocable resolutions, and the filial sentiments inspired by nature. Help her with fervent prayer and sage advice. I think that as soon as she is able to receive the holy sacraments, including that of confirmation, she will feel better."[18] When Tosi wrote Degola sometime later, he too admitted that Henriette's closeness with her parents made him fear that she would change her mind about converting: "Signora Henriette cannot behave better; she acquired a greater openness with her mother, for whom her affection and pusillanimity initially gave me worry"[19] Both letters display a paternal attitude toward Henriette, which was repeated constantly by those involved in her conversion. In addition, the suggestion that Manzoni's wife go through the steps of conversion as quickly as possible in order to root her to Catholicism and distance her from her parents were methods that the Church employed in the forced conversions described in earlier chapters. In other words, because of Henriette's fragility and her concern for her parents, the Church appears to have treated her as the equivalent of an unwilling convert.[20]

The fairly aggressive measures that these Church officials employed not only resulted in trying to push Henriette's Catholic education ahead at a fast pace, but they had a proselytizing aim as well. Those converting the young woman openly stated their hopes that Henriette's conversion would bring about that of her "heretical" parents: "I will learn with great joy of the perseverance of your courageous neophyte, with more joy still that her good and wise and Christian firmness is for her blind parents a means of the mercy of God for them to open their eyes. . . . The grace that overcame the young heretic can triumph equally over more ingrained, more obstinate errors that plague the new proselytizer."[21] This desire to convert as many non-Catholics as possible also contains echoes from the earlier stories of forced conversion, just as the description of her parents as "obstinate" parallels Catholic portrayals of Jews who refused baptism. And in this case, like converted Jews who wished to "offer" their families to the Church, upon converting Henriette appeared to be a willing partner in further efforts at proselytization by the Church.[22] To this end, she expressed the hope that her conversion would convince her parents to convert in a letter that she wrote Degola.[23] Indeed, her efforts to convince others to convert to Catholicism went beyond the members of her family; in a letter Henriette wrote Degola in March of 1813, she described her efforts to convert a Swiss Protestant family to Catholicism. Two years later, Henriette reported that the family had decided to convert to Catholicism, suggesting that members of the family had turned to her for guidance in their decision to convert and that she was thus in some way responsible for this "conquest." [24] Such proselytization efforts are often attributed to converts in an effort to make their conversions all the more complete, since the conversion of a nonbeliever "is the surest sign of the conversion of the self."[25]

Manzoni seemed far removed from the proselytizing efforts of his wife. Indeed, in the same letter in which Tosi expressed optimism about Henriette's progress, he hinted that Manzoni did not exude the same enthusiasm for religion. And in his letters to Degola around the time of Henriette's conversion, Manzoni himself avoided any discussion of religion insofar as it pertained to himself, speaking only about the conversion of his wife.[26] His reserve and general attitude toward the priest made the priest assume that he was not interested in returning to the Catholic Church.[27] However, when the Manzonis arrived in Milan after an exhausting long journey from Paris, Manzoni asked Tosi to minister to him and his mother as well as his wife. The Milanese Tosi wrote to Degola and recounted the strange transformation that had taken place in Manzoni: "Oh what a miracle is that of Divine Mercy! Not only Henriette, who is an angel of naïveté and simplicity, but Madame, and even the by now so proud Alessandro are little lambs, who receive the most simple instruction with extreme eagerness. . . . Alessandro embarked on this undertaking with extreme docility and submission; tomorrow we will again have a long lecture and if the Lord preserves and augments His blessings in him [that is, Alessandro], he too will soon make great progress."[28] Degola reacted to Tosi's news with happy surprise: "I did not foresee that Alessandro would make rapid progress such as that in which you must have found him to grant him such a good time in the participation of the Sacred Mysteries. God bless a work begun so happily."[29] With these words, Degola surmises that Manzoni's change in heart is due to a miracle. Tosi, too, did not appear to have any explanation for Manzoni's sudden about-face other than divine intervention. These men's view that the changes in Manzoni were miraculous suggests the Pauline epiphany that so many stories of Manzoni's conversion relate. The bookish intellectual, whom Tosi seemed to indicate was overly proud, turned subdued and submissive in the face of simple Catholic instruction. In Tosi's description, Manzoni's conversion was preceded—and therefore aided—by his being stripped of the attributes of an intellectual: he received simple instruction despite his intellectual stature, he was docile rather than argumentative, and thus he was included in God's presence rather than excluded. Manzoni's humility was further emphasized by Tosi's use of conventional vocabulary; that is, in joining Jesus' flock, the Italian author achieved a kind of anonymity by joining the ranks of the pious. Equated to an angel, the quiet, willing, relatively anonymous Henriette rose above her famous husband.

While the liberal politics Manzoni had been exposed to in his early years were ideals that he would always advocate, he saw great flaws in the aftermath of the French Revolution. Above all, Manzoni viewed the bond between Church and state as necessary to fight the secularization that occurred with the French Revolution. Manzoni expressed these views in his *Adelchi*, written in 1822, in which he expounded the important societal role of Catholicism and the role of the Church in Italian history. In this work he depicted Charlemagne as conquering the Lombard kingdom in the name of the pope. His message was clear: on a peninsula that had been conquered countless times by foreign invaders, the Church was Italy's only legitimate representative since the fall of the Roman Empire, and as such it should have a role in the modern state as well. His convictions regarding the necessity of Italian unity and independence were tied to his understanding of Christian morality such that the unification of Italy was desired by God, in the name of justice; and it was an event that could only occur with the support of the Catholic Church. Ultimately, Manzoni's Catholicism led him to advocate an Italian identity that balanced unchanging Catholic values and the changing society of the modern world, effectuating, as Spinazzola writes, "a return to politics under the rule of morals."[30]

A decade after writing his *Adelchi*, Manzoni began to correspond with Marco Coen, providing the earliest account known of an individual who was inspired to convert because of the Italian author. The correspondence culminated in 1842, when Manzoni urged his young follower to convert to Catholicism. His meeting and correspondence with two other eventual converts, Davide Norsa and J. H. Wynne, began shortly thereafter, in 1847. The time period that these conversion stories encompassed is significant. The first version of *PS* was published shortly before Manzoni's correspondence with Coen began, in 1827; the final version was published more than a decade later, between 1840 and 1842, not long before Manzoni began writing to Norsa and Wynne. However, the synthesis of nationhood and Catholic morality that Manzoni put forth in his novel, a topic to which we will turn shortly, had yet to come to fruition in reality. As Dionisotti writes, "The Catholic revival, as conceived by him [Manzoni], should have been conducive to peace and freedom in Europe. In fact peace had been precariously enforced through an intolerable loss of freedom. Inevitably the alternative of an un-Christian revolution was looming ahead once again."[31] The prospect of not realizing his vision, of facing the secularization and loss of Christian values that a repeat of the French Revolution would inevitably bring to the peninsula, was undoubtedly one of the great incentives that led Manzoni to pursue the conversion of the non-Catholic individuals with whom he interacted.

Marco Coen, the son of a Jewish Venetian banker, was being sent into the family business, despite the fact that he wished to become a writer.[32] He wrote Manzoni for advice on how to continue his literary ambitions, and in June 1832, Manzoni responded. Manzoni's letter is relevant not only because it regards the subject of conversion—Coen eventually converted and attributed his conversion to Manzoni—but also because it highlighted the literary reforms that Manzoni undertook upon his own return to the Church. In his letter, Manzoni immediately established a connection with Coen, writing that Coen reminded him of himself as a young man before his conversion.[33] In 1842, many years after the two initially made contact, Manzoni again wrote Coen, this time openly encouraging the young man to convert:

> The God of your fathers granted you the indescribable gift of knowing the sense and the fulfillment of the promise made to them: you feel the duty to correspond to such a gift; you see very well that the difficulties, which could in any case be predominant, in this are nothing: all that you are lacking is the resolution. This only one [being] can give you; and he gives it infallibly to he who desires and prays and together does, for his part, that which he can.
>
> . . . Who knows, perhaps you are the first in a family upon whom God wants to extend his mercy? In the meantime, the duty to obey Him imposes upon you another dear and easy duty: to be . . . the most loving, most respectful, most submissive son ever, and to show that you place nothing before paternal authority except that which lies at the origins of it and consecration. But above all ask from Him the powerful intercession of that saintly, blessed, glorious, merciful daughter of David, who recently gave such a plain and comforting sign.[34]

Manzoni's reference in the first line to "the God of your fathers" is a phrase regularly used in Hebrew liturgy; that Manzoni uses it to promote conversion again displays his Pauline belief that Catholicism is the fulfillment of the covenant promised to the Hebrew fathers. Using language that echoed that of the correspondence surrounding Henriette's conversion, Manzoni urged Coen to become Catholic, suggesting that his conversion might convince his entire family to do the same. In addition, Manzoni appeared to reiterate the concept of paternal authority that the Inquisition authorities advocated so vociferously in the cases we examined in previous chapters. That is, while he encouraged young Coen to act respectfully toward his Jewish parents, his first obligation was to his religious father, Jesus, and to the mother of all Christians, the Church. Finally, Manzoni's oblique reference to the divine intervention of the Virgin in the last line recalls the reference to Mary in *Il Nome di Maria*, in which Manzoni asks his readers *"Non è Davide il ceppo suo?"* ("Is not David her root?"). In so doing, he again recalls the relationship between the Hebrew Bible and its fulfillment, the laws and beliefs of the New Testament. Not only is the reference is typological, however;[35] the "recent sign" Manzoni mentions in the final line cited above refers to the most famed conversion of his day, that of Alphonse Ratisbonne.[36]

A Jew from Strasbourg, Ratisbonne converted to Catholicism after purportedly seeing a vision of the Virgin Mary in the Roman church of Sant'Andrea delle Frate. The event, which occurred on January 20, 1842, garnered much attention in Catholic communities throughout Europe and was publicized in a series of propaganda pamphlets distributed by the Restoration press.[37] Ratisbonne's story is remarkably similar to that of Manzoni: touring Rome with a Catholic friend, the Frenchman went to the Church of St. Andrea delle Fratte so that his friend could pay his respects at a funeral there. As he waited inside the church, he experienced a vision of the Virgin Mary. The power of what he saw, he later recounted, knocked him to the ground and blinded him with its light. Like St. Paul, who was knocked off his horse, Ratisbonne's conversion was the result of an epiphany and thus similar to Manzoni's own conversion story.

The recall of this event placed Manzoni squarely within the movement of a larger Catholic project of exalting the role of the papacy in modern Italy and of a Christian "conquest" in which the social and political order would be reconstituted. Manzoni surely did not advocate the intransigent Catholic ideology that many Church supporters desired and to which Antonio Bresciani, as we see in the next chapter, fully adhered. Nonetheless, his attempts to convert others, and the political tone these conversions often took, reflect the extent to which he strove to identify a modern Italy with Catholic leadership and a faithful populace. He confirmed this ideology with his reference and clear support for the warmly welcomed and widely publicized conversion of Ratisbonne.[38]

That Manzoni sought to unify Italy—and even Europe—under the moral guidance of the pope was further reflected in a visit he had in 1847 with three visitors from Britain, J. H. Wynne and two companions, J. H. Pollen and T. W. Allies. All three men were practicing Anglicans, and their trip appeared to be inspired by their desire to reconcile the Roman Catholic Church with the Anglican Church.[39] The visit came nine years after the well-known Englishman William Gladstone met with Manzoni. Gladstone, who had just completed his work *The State in its Relations with the Church*, also met Manzoni to speak about the possibility of creating a unified church. Manzoni insisted on the supremacy of the pope as essential to Christian identity, and thus the meeting, while amicable, ended inconclusively. While Manzoni and Gladstone could not agree on the issue of unifying the two churches, Manzoni's reaction to Gladstone showed that the issue of a pan-European Catholic identity, and the desire to foment a Catholic revival across Europe, was on Manzoni's mind.[40] In 1847, when Manzoni met with the three aforementioned visitors from Britain, circumstances had changed substantially since Gladstone's visit. Pope Pius IX was still considered somewhat liberal, his antiliberal stance hardening only after the revolutions of 1848; and in England the growing urgency of the Irish question, as well as the conversion to Catholicism of a number of English clergymen, reflected a growing religious crisis and the beginning of a Catholic revival. (I return to this issue in the final chapter, in my discussion of the Catholic press.)

Any hope of garnering support for reconciliation between the two churches by meeting Manzoni, of succeeding where Gladstone had failed nine years earlier, failed once again. As a Catholic convert and strong papal supporter, Manzoni was adamant regarding the supremacy of the Catholic Church. His strong support for the papacy is well documented, and thus the vehemence of his beliefs comes as no surprise. But his meeting with the three Englishmen is striking because in their conversations Manzoni told his visitors about his own conversion to Catholicism—his motivation being, it appeared, to encourage them to convert as well. The meeting struck a chord with the Englishmen; two years after these discussions, Allies and Wynne converted to Catholicism, attributing their change in faith to their conversations with Manzoni. Pollen followed suit several years later. Wynne resided in Italy after his conversion, studying in Rome from 1852–1857 and becoming a Jesuit priest. Many years later, in December 1882, he wrote of his visits and conversations with the Italian author and recounted one of the stories of Manzoni's conversion with which I began this chapter. However, while Manzoni may have inspired Wynne to convert, the latter was vehemently opposed to Manzoni's political vision. As a Jesuit clergyman, he did not simply view Italian unification as problematic; he saw Italian independence as the downfall of religion. Indeed, he harshly criticized Manzoni's support of the Risorgimento, remembering that Manzoni "tried to draw me into seditious conversations on the politics of Italy. . . . At the slightest allusion to Italian politics, Manzoni ceased to be himself; he became fierce, morose, passionate, an evil spirit seemed to possess him, and he talked like a Communist, a Carbonaro, a Conspirator."[41] In sum, Wynne suggested that the author's desire for Italian independence was anomalous to his religious ideals, and he viewed Manzoni's advocacy of a modern Italian state as heretical and antithetical to Catholic interests.

Wynne's criticism of Manzoni reflected the reactionary Jesuit attitudes that Bresciani displays in his novel as well. In contrast, Wynne's companion Allies recounted Manzoni's passion for political discussion in a different light: "He spoke with compassion of the miserably infidel state of France and quite admitted my remark that a great change seemed to be passing over the mind of men everywhere and that they were in the process of being won back to the faith, as in the last century they were falling from it. The Church was the best friend of all governments, for they must be bad indeed for the clergy not to support them."[42] That Manzoni viewed the outcome of the French Revolution with compassion rather than condemnation reflected his continued support for many of the ideals associated with the modern nation-state. In other words, while Manzoni's conversion led him to anchor his ethical and religious beliefs in a faith shared by the vast majority of Italians, it did not lead to a renunciation of the Enlightenment ideals instilled in him as a young man in Paris.[43] In his desire to moderate the ambitious revolutionary aspirations that accompanied these ideals, however, he turned to the papacy as an institution that would temper the "pagan charm of war" with its moral leadership and message of peace and charity.[44] Allies' words, accurately reflecting Manzoni's advocacy of Christian values, are also notable because of the theme of conversion that once again permeates such a vision. As we will see in the following chapter, the Catholic press actively perpetuated the perception that conversions to Catholicism were increasing as proof of Catholic victory in Italy and greater Europe.

The same year Manzoni met Wynne and his companions, he began corresponding with the Jewish Davide Norsa, who also sought to speak to Manzoni about religion. His epistolary conversation with Manzoni, a turning point in his search for religious fulfillment, preceded a journey that the young Norsa took to Egypt. The story he tells of his return to Italy seems heavily influenced by Manzoni's Catholic ideology. On board a ship, Norsa meets a monk with whom he feels compelled to speak. The monk appears to be the last reassurance Norsa needs—after his conversation with Manzoni, that is—that conversion to Catholicism is the right path to pursue. The geography of these details is significant; just as Manzoni uses biblical stories to depict the Italian struggle for independence in his *Inni Sacri*, the voyage out of Egypt evokes the larger, biblically referenced exodus. The only difference in Norsa's account is, of course, that Italy becomes the Promised Land, and the Moses-like monk leads Davide across the sea, from Egypt to Italy, convincing him of the truth of the Catholic faith. The religious implication of the journey is clear: Italy is home to the center of Catholicism, just as the Promised Land was home to the Israelites and their faith. Thus Norsa's conversion story contains the same transfer of values that Manzoni advocated in his Pauline vision of Catholicism as the replacement for and perfection of Judaism. The connection between Norsa's conversion and allusions to the Hebrew Bible is further strengthened by the fact that Norsa appears to accede to the exhortations Manzoni expresses in his *Il Nome di Maria*: while he does not deny his heritage, he happily accepts conversion and Catholicism as the true religion.

Only two weeks after Norsa began the process of converting, in a turn of events oddly reminiscent of the French gendarme Jochanan (in the Labani Affair), revolution broke out in Lombardy. The upheaval prolonged the conversion process by a year. As Norsa writes, "the revolution of February [1848] and the others that followed, . . . made the ancient struggle that still has not come to its end begin again. Having won with arms is nothing if souls are not won, if the spirits are not calmed with a reasonable reorganization."[45] Revolution without the guidance of a moral force will never end the "ancient struggle" of Italians to establish an independent state. With words that come remarkably close to mirroring Manzoni's views, Norsa goes on to explain the necessity of religion in the modern state, writing that the absence of religion in a Christian civilization will lead to paganism, and that this lack of faith is one of the greatest problems with the French Revolution.[46] Indeed, Italian supporters of revolution, he writes, had essentially advocated war against Catholicism, and such a war was "no longer about independence, but about religion; no longer national, but between brothers."[47] Revolution was not about ousting a foreign power; it was a war against Catholicism, and hence a war among Italians. Like Manzoni, the converted Norsa thus suggests that war against Catholicism is akin to civil war; the unity of religion, and the role that Catholicism had on the peninsula, defined an integral aspect of Italian identity.[48]

As in his correspondence, Manzoni addressed both issues of religious and political identity on the peninsula in his literary texts, tying together his profound support for Italian independence and unification with his support for the moral leadership that only the Vatican could provide. In so doing, Manzoni sought to ensure a cultural and political role for the Catholic Church on the peninsula, while simultaneously making room for a modern, independent Italy. Indeed, Manzoni's religious conversion coincided with a rupture in his poetic writing: despite his ideological opposition to neoclassical values, he began his literary career by writing in precisely this style of poetry, expressing his opposition to Restoration ideology by replacing traditional content, with its respect for authority and the Church, with revolutionary ideas associated with Jacobinism and anticlericalism.[49] Ultimately, however, the limitations imposed by this style of writing proved too restrictive: stylistic regulations severely constricted the content of his writing; he could not condone the conservatism that neoclassical poetry championed; and finally, Manzoni had to reject the mythological writing that was a fundamental aspect of neoclassical style because of his newfound religious beliefs.[50] While one might consider mythology a literary tool used to reflect and express a classical culture, other aspects associated with mythology, such as paganism and sensuality, repelled Manzoni.[51] In 1809, Manzoni decided once and for all to stop writing neoclassical poetry, moving instead toward more popular poetry that concentrated on political and religious subjects that a wider audience could relate to and understand. To this end, he wrote his close friend Fauriel, "I may write worse poems, but I will never write anything like that anymore."[52] The date of this letter is noteworthy, as it was written just after Manzoni rediscovered his belief in Catholicism.

Manzoni's new writing sought to establish a strong tie between the public audience, the political mood of the times, and literature.[53] And yet, while Manzoni's literary transition supported to a certain degree a revolutionary ideology, the author's conversion to Catholicism tempered this change with his desire for the papal authority to play a central, unifying role in any newly independent Italian nation.[54] As Spinazzola so aptly put it, Manzoni sought "certainly to reform the old idea of literature, but in order to reorganize it immediately; to change the modalities of production and the perception of aesthetic values, but without iconoclastic breaks from tradition."[55] Manzoni's belief that life and faith provided the best subject for art can be seen in his further advice to Marco Coen, who lamented the fact that his father was forcing him away from writing to enter the business world. Manzoni admonished the young man not to think badly of the business world, reminding him that business was a profession that "not only does not put an end to all means of progressing in letters, but is itself a means."[56] The Italian author's words to his protégé reflect his own abandonment of the composition of classical poetry and mythology, and his interest in writing that incorporated modern political values and traditional religious belief.

Manzoni's *Inni Sacri* provides one response to his rejection of neoclassical poetry. He envisioned the work to be a series of twelve poems dedicated to Christian holidays that reflected the narration of history as Christian time and which mended the fractures of society. *La Resurrezione* (*The Resurrection*), *Il Nome di Maria* (*The Name of Maria*), *Il Natale* (*Christmas*), and *La Passione* (*The Passion*), the only poems realized of the *Inni Sacri*, laud the value of collective ritual by using sacred events to bind together a Christian populace; they reflect Manzoni's desire to understand and represent Christianity as an integral part of life, rather than as an esoteric theological meditation.[57] With this aim, the works emphasize Manzoni's newfound faith and advocate a return to the Church, just as they mark the author's turn toward a subject matter,

Catholic practice, to which a wide audience from a variety of social and economic backgrounds could relate. Indeed, Salvatore Nigro describes the collection as Manzoni's "first station 'on the road to Damscus,'" referring to the author's conversion and its effect on his writing.[58] As mentioned briefly earlier, *Il Nome di Maria* in particular contains the topos of conversion that Manzoni often reflected upon in his work:

> So much it pleased the Lord on top to see
> this simple Hebrew lass!
> O Israel's descendants, O so low
> once fallen and oppressed by such long wrath,
> is it not the Lady that we honor so
> sprung from your very faith?
> Is David not her root? Your prophets' old
> vision began her triumph to foretell
> when they announced the Virgin's trophies bold
> over defeated hell.
> Oh, raise your every prayer to her at last—
> that she may save you, too, who saves her own;
> and may all tribes and countries, as they must,
> this song with us intone:
> Hail, You, made worthy of the second name,
> O Rose, O Star that saves all men astray,
> as dazzling as the sun, fierce as an army
> in battle array.[59]

With these verses, Manzoni attempts to share the salvation he experiences with other nonbelievers, in this case the Jews. By tracing Mary's heritage back to the Hebrew Bible figure of David, Manzoni reminds his readers that the Virgin Mother, and Jesus himself, were Jews. Thus Jesus' ancestry is one that Jews can share. However, while Jews are historically connected to Jesus, without accepting Christianity they will never gain salvation. Thus the poem contains a break between those who belong and those who do not. Jews belong in the history of Christianity, but whether they belong to its present condition depends on their conversion. Their dubious future is reflected by the fact that the two specific times Jews are mentioned—*prole d'Israele* ("descendants of Israel") and *Davidde* ("David")—they are referred to in the context of questions. That is, their place in history is assured, but their fate and their acceptance into the populace, are placed in doubt. The final verse of the stanza, *"e non sia gente né tribù che neghi / lieta cantar con noi"* ("and may all tribes and countries, as they must, / this song with us intone") attempts to erase differences between Christians and Jews by erasing the status of Jews as a different people or tribe. This change will only occur when the Jews sing the praises of the Virgin, that is, when and if they convert. Thus Manzoni suggests a historical role for the Jews, but not one that carries into present times. Instead he encourages conversion as a means of saving Jews, encouraging a Catholic identity, and contributing toward the second coming of Jesus. And finally, just as Manzoni's conversion story embraces the Pauline model of epiphany, here Manzoni's writing supports Paul's view of Christianity as the fulfillment and completion of a religion that the chosen people of the Hebrew Bible, the Jews, initiated.

The theme of redemption that is played out in *Il Nome di Maria* is striking because of its use of a Catholic figurehead in its attempt to unite readers and draw them toward a shared icon. That the icon is Mary, the mother of Christianity, and that this poem was written with a large audience in mind, reflects Manzoni's efforts to establish and define an Italian identity that has an inherently Catholic element to it. That is, the poem reflects the author's attempt to reconcile poetically his aspirations for a united, independent Italy with the continued role and presence of the Catholic Church on the peninsula. With this project, the dialogical relationship between art and history in Manzoni's work is illuminated; Manzoni's personal devoutness provides the driving force behind his literary projects. Religious conversion, adherence to Catholic belief, and national independence are brought together, and proselytization is articulated as a nationalist project that unifies religious belief with modern, independent statehood.

Manzoni's effort to advocate a strong religious presence on the peninsula and the theme of conversion itself are also key ingredients of *PS*. More specifically, the relationship between converter and converted in Manzoni's life is replicated literarily in *PS*, in which many of Manzoni's characters undergo conversions and live out Manzoni's belief in participation in the modern state together with practice of traditional religious ways. Manzoni scholars often note that Manzoni's conversion led to a great religious presence in *PS*. Prieto, for example, explains the religious content of the novel as follows: "It does not obey a propagandistic plan, but rather the characteristic of Manzoni as the convert."[60] Indeed, I will argue that Manzoni's novel is really a story of numerous conversions; its synthesis of nationalism and religion, of conservative *classicismo* (classicism) and revolutionary ideology reflects the author's story of a man who both found God and enthusiastically supported the modern ideals of Italian unification. Once again, fiction and reality overlap: just as Manzoni's conversion inspired the narrative of *PS*, it also inspired fictionalized narratives about the author that were as politically and ideologically motivated as Manzoni's own writing.

Like many historical novels, *PS* tells the story of a new generation who rejects the ideals of the old regime and struggles to establish itself within a changing society. To combat the atheistic tendencies often associated with the French Revolution, Manzoni depicts the heroes of *PS* as ethical subjects whose religious rebirth absorbs and directs their "revolutionary" tendencies toward the civic good. His ideological project is, therefore, "to bring the revolutionary stimulus within the moderate limits of Christian reason."[61] Thus, in Manzoni's novel, the attainment of a new identity takes a different twist from the traditional historical novel: rather than moving away from tradition to live the liberal ideals of a new individualism, the male heroes of the novel experience a religious conversion that marks a return to tradition and belief. These conversions mirror Manzoni's personal history, reflecting the author's desire to firmly establish Catholic ideals in a new generation and to anchor unified Italy within this shared system of beliefs. In this sense, Manzoni's novel depicts the return to faith of his characters as a fundamental ingredient that would make Italian unification more successful, in both a moral and a social sense, than the French model. Indeed, by making Catholic identity and conversion such a key element of the novel, Manzoni carefully walks his readers down a different path from that established by the French model. The French Revolution, too violent to imitate, is also dangerous because of the atheistic tendencies that accompanied it. Thus, aside from his desire to portray a nation free from foreign domination, Manzoni's novel seeks to show that an ideal modern society is based upon a synthesis of liberal ideals and Christian values.

To combat his fear that Italy would follow too closely the model of the French Revolution, Manzoni depicts every character in his novel as, first and foremost, an ethical subject. And, similar to the many conversion stories that exist about him, he creates different conversion experiences for his characters.[62] Indeed, it appears that the author experiments with as many combinations as possible of sinning and repentance, good and evil, and nonbeliever and believer to display the link between individual existence and social order.[63] Manzoni scholars generally focus on two conversion figures in particular: Father Cristoforo and the *Innominato*, or Unnamed. The former—as his name, meaning "bearing Christ" suggests—converts to strict religious practice, becoming a Capuchin monk and abandoning the life of luxury he lived until then. His conversion occurs after he murders a young man in a fit of rage at the age of thirty. These events occur many years before the main events of the novel, however, and while Father Cristoforo always has to battle the impulses that were so uncontrollable in his youth, his faith is never seriously threatened or challenged in the novel.

In contrast, the dark character known only as the *Innominato*, the Unnamed, converts to a moral and religious way of life within the time frame of the novel. His spiritual biography is introduced against the backdrop of a long history of wrongdoing that falls outside of the main time frame of the novel: "These [crimes], accumulating in his memory if not in his conscience, rose up before him again."[64] Thus the beginning of the *Innominato*'s life of immorality occurs before the novel's beginning. Several scholars compare Manzoni's conversion to that of the *Innominato*, since the latter's conversion occurs at the moment when he accepts "that his existential crisis itself proves the existence of a God who has wrought in him 'the miracle of mercy.'"[65] Indeed, striking similarities exist between this character and some of the portrayals of the author's conversion. The story Davide Norsa tells, for example, in which Manzoni enters a church after experiencing a crisis, parallels the *Innominato* conversion story, once again blurring the lines between fiction and "truth" such that the conversion appears relevant and possible in both spheres. Similarly, in his novel Manzoni describes the regret and anxiety the *Innominato* experiences as he remembers the vengeful nature he displayed as a young man: "In the early days, the frequent examples, the almost continual sight, of violence, revenge, and murder had inspired him with a fierce competitiveness, and had also served him as a kind of authority against the voice of conscience. Now the confused but terrible idea of an individual responsibility, of a reason independent of example, would rise before his mind."[66] The description not only is reminiscent of the anxiety Norsa claimed Manzoni suffered before his conversion but also reflects Manzoni's belief in the need for individual responsibility and in the idea that the un-Christian acts of violence and revenge are enhanced when this form of responsibility is lacking.

Also similar to stories of Manzoni's conversion is a local man's description of the *Innominato*'s conversion: "He described the solemn ceremonies, then digressed to talk about the miraculous conversion. But the thing which had made most impression on him, and to which he returned most often, was the cardinal's sermon."[67] The similarity to accounts of Manzoni's conversion, in which the author felt that the priest's sermon was directed specifically at him, is striking. In addition, the Unnamed's miraculous conversion results from an epiphanic moment of religious lucidity, a conversion clearly modeled on the story of Paul and one that resonates with many of the accounts of Manzoni's own conversion.

The importance of this mirroring of Paul's story becomes clearer upon discussing one of the few conversions that takes place entirely within the novel, and one that differs quite dramatically from the others: the story of the male protagonist of the novel, Renzo. Renzo's conversion—or "moral purification,"[68] as Riccardo Verzini calls it—is not epiphanic or revelationary in the traditional Pauline sense, and yet, as we will see, this character embodies many of the characteristics associated with Pauline Christianity. His conversion enables him to acquire an identity that is simultaneously Catholic and Italian, a synthesis that Manzoni envisions as the Italian identity of the newly forming nation. In addition, his turn to religion marks a transition from old societal values to new, much like the Pauline transvaluation from the morals and law of the Hebrew Bible to that of the New Testament. As the protagonist, Renzo exhibits many of the characteristics of a young man with local roots ready to be made into a national figure. Indeed, the narrator of the novel recognizes this fact when he writes that Renzo is "a bit too high-spirited, to tell the truth, but shows every sign of growing up into a decent citizen one day."[69] First, he comes from a small village in the area of Lecco, with little to no knowledge of Italian lands outside of his own. Thus, for example, when he learns that Father Cristoforo has been sent to the city of Rimini, he is forced to ask the friar who supplies him with this information: "To . . . ? . . . Where's that?" [70] Not knowing the geography of the peninsula, Renzo has a world view constricted to the tiny area of Brianza, the territory of Lecco.

Second, Renzo is an orphan, with no roots in the *ancien régime*. Indeed, the hierarchical society of the old regime is the source of his troubles, and thus young Renzo is eager—at times even too eager—to act against it. When the novel opens, Renzo is preparing to marry Lucia. Their wedding plans go awry, however, when a young nobleman, Don Rodrigo, takes an interest in Lucia and demands that the parish priest not marry the couple. After being discovered trying to trick the local priest into marrying them nonetheless, Renzo is forced to run away until things settle down. This departure marks the break from the past that enables Renzo to become an Italian of the new generation. He leaves behind the parochial identity and hierarchical relations that are part of the social landscape of his hometown, and his travels force him to become gradually more acquainted with a larger part of the national landscape. Thus movement between the private world of Brianza and the public space of greater Italy serves to unite the elements of Renzo's personal life with those of Italian history. As Angelo Marchese notes, this movement is represented geographically by the River Adda, which represents the border that Renzo must cross upon leaving his hometown.[71] Marchese suggests that the Adda is spiritually symbolic of the Red Sea, which the Jews crossed as they left Egypt for the land of Israel. As such, the Adda is not simply a frontier; by crossing it Renzo defines his role as a citizen of the new promised land, Italy.

Just as the Israelites' journey to their own lands was both a religious and political passage, so too Renzo's travels are united to his religious development. While he often forgets the behavior befitting a good Christian, he never strays too far from it:

> His home abandoned, his work gone, separated from Lucia—which was worse than anything—and now finding himself on the road without even knowing where to lay his head! And all because of that villain! When he allowed his thoughts to dwell on any of these things he felt himself overcome with rage and the longing for revenge; but then he would remember that prayer he had offered up with the good friar in the church at Pescarenico, and he would control himself. Just as his rage was welling up again he would see some shrine in a wall, doff his hat to it, and pause a moment to say another prayer: so that he must have killed Don Rodrigo in his heart and brought him to life again at least twenty times during that journey.[72]

Turning to God neutralizes Renzo's violent intentions, and Manzoni intends Renzo to be the example of how the new generation of Italians needs to act in the face of upheaval and imminent independence.

Indeed, final proof that Renzo becomes a modern son of the new Italy occurs when the young man learns to temper his indignation at the injustices he has suffered with a belief in God. In other words, the secular Renzo experiences a de facto conversion and a new belief in the power of Christian charity and prayer. For, unlike the pious Lucia, Renzo fails to display a strong belief in God in the early parts of the novel. Indeed, his inability to entrust his future to Providence is one of the great obstacles he must overcome on his journey. Renzo's non-religious identity throughout the first half of the novel is displayed through his expressions of frustration at the unjust situation in which he finds himself. When Don Abbondio, the local parish priest, tells him that his wedding must be postponed, Renzo's immediate response is to demand to know who is responsible for the delay and to reach for his dagger.[73] When he tells Lucia and her mother Agnese of Don Rodrigo's machinations, he lashes out even more energetically: "'Ah, the scoundrel! The damned swine!' Renzo began shouting, striding up and down the room, and clutching now and then at the hilt of his dagger."[74] Several chapters later, in another conversation with Agnese and Lucia, Renzo is unashamed of his desire to kill Don Rodrigo: "I'll finish him off. Even if he's [Don Rodrigo] got a hundred or a thousand devils in him, he's still made of flesh and blood. . . . I'll do justice myself, I will; I'll rid the village of him, I will. How many people will bless me!'"[75] His reaction to his oppressor reflects his tendency toward violent impulses, and throughout the novel he continually envisions killing the powerful nobleman. Unlike the *Innominato* or Father Cristoforo, however, Renzo never actually carries out a crime of passion. Nonetheless, he is portrayed as a potential killer, and he must overcome this identity before being reunited with Lucia and successfully participating in the new state.

At a societal level, Renzo also displays his weak character on numerous occasions. Rather than go to a specific church, as directed by Father Cristoforo, the impressionable Renzo becomes caught up in the Milanese crowds that are rioting over the price of bread. His attendance at a rally ends disastrously: he is arrested and only barely escapes the clutches of the Milan police force, clearly representatives of an old social order, who view him as a villainous revolutionary. These scenes of the novel appear uncannily similar to several of the conversion stories told about Manzoni himself. The similarities between Renzo getting caught up in the whirl of activity at the scene of the Milan riots and the wild festivities surrounding Napoleon's wedding in one version of Manzoni's conversion in Paris are striking. Particularly significant is the relationship between the fictional and historical events: the fictional stories of *PS* are comparable to the story of Manzoni's own conversion. Renzo's conversion enables him to become the ideal citizen of the new Italy, providing a literary embodiment of Manzoni's vision for Italian statehood. There is no way of knowing how much Manzoni actually told those who became the narrators of his conversion story and how much is their own embellishment. Nonetheless, the conversion stories about Manzoni apply the conventions of his own fiction to himself. In an ironic conflation of history and fiction, Manzoni becomes both author and character in his own national story. That is, his own conversion story parallels the text he authors. In addition, as a protagonist of a conversion story, he becomes the hero of a text scripted by fellow converts who share similar visions for modern Italy. The result of this intertextuality reflects the extent to which conversion is relevant and encouraged in both nonfictional and fictional narratives.

The narratives that embellish Manzoni's conversion story with images of the tumultuous Parisian crowd are efforts to explain the origins of Manzoni's fear of crowds, which is clearly evident from their portrayal in *PS*. His desire to escape the crowd was what moved Manzoni to enter the church. In contrast, the crowd arouses Renzo's curiosity, drawing him in rather than making him try to escape. And yet, while Manzoni-the-novelist expresses his critical view of the masses, Renzo, unlike the author, is not overcome by the crowds. Indeed, the opposite is true: "In all popular tumults there are always a certain number of men who, either from excited passions, or fanatical conviction, or evil intentions, or just from a cursed taste for disorder, do all they can to push things as far as possible. . . . But, to balance these, there are always a certain number of others who are working with equal ardour and persistence to produce the opposite results. . . . May Heaven bless them!"[76] Renzo is one of the latter individuals who balance out the passions of the group mentality. He even goes so far as to control the crowd, holding them back with his broad shoulders: "Renzo . . . was now able to join one of the two front rows of well-wishers, who were acting . . . as a breakwater against the two surging waves of people."[77] Thus, while Renzo joins the crowds, he is not seduced by their power to join in.

Indeed, Renzo does more than hold back the crowd. Earlier on that same day, when one inhabitant diabolically brandishes a hammer, rope, and nails in the air with the intention of crucifying the Commissioner held responsible for the price of bread, Renzo is the only individual to react: "'Hey! Shame on you!' burst out Renzo, horrified at . . . the looks of approval he saw on many faces around, as well as encouraged at seeing others showing the same horror that he felt himself, silent though they were. 'Shame! Do we want to do the executioner's job? Commit murder? How d'you expect God to give us bread if we go and do atrocities like that? He'll send thunderbolts down on us, not bread!'"[78]

The idea of crucifying a leader to procure bread is the ultimate perversion of the story of Christ, and when the possibility of murder goes from imagined to real, Renzo has no desire to perpetrate the deed. That Renzo expresses horror at the violence and injustice of these actions, that he resists the violence that escalates from the crowd, reflects his Christian heart and the good intentions it inspires. Indeed, for Manzoni, Renzo's misadventures are put forth as a means of correcting the young man's world view. Before the protagonist can settle down, he must understand that his social transformation is the result of divine providence, and his transition is complete only when his social status and his Christian points of view are reconciled. Only then can the protagonist overcome adversity and establish himself as a productive member of society. Thus his conversion is a story of Christian redemption that involves both a religious and sociopolitical element.

Renzo's journey ends in the *lazzaretto*, which houses those who are dying from the plague. The plague has led to a social breakdown, where human reason is almost nonexistent and where death triumphs. The *lazzaretto* symbolizes this breakdown both as a last stop before death and as a place that breeds and sustains the *monatti*, those survivors of the plague whose task it is to cart away the dead and their belongings. The *monatti*, with their disrespect for both the living and the dead and their greed to acquire the wealth and property of plague victims, profit from the death around them. They instate a grotesque system of justice all their own that is void of morality or charity; rather it represents a perversion of the modern, capitalist system as it would be without the guidance of a moral authority.

It is here, in the *lazzaretto*, that Renzo meets again with Father Cristoforo and explains his plans to find his betrothed. The thought of losing her to the plague and the possibility of finding Don Rodrigo fills the young man with a familiar rage: "If I find him . . . if the plague hasn't already done its justice . . . I'll do my own justice, I will!" [79] These words are the last expression of anger and revenge that Renzo utters, and once again the converted, this time Father Cristoforo, proves his piety by converting the vengeful Renzo. Father Cristoforo's identity as a man of the Church underscores Manzoni's message that the Church will lead Italy from this destruction.

To enable Renzo's conversion, the monk scolds the young man harshly, telling him that charity should replace his anger and vengefulness. Surveying the horrific scene around him, Cristoforo shakes Renzo: "'Look and see who is the One who punishes. The One who judges, and is not Himself judged. The One who chastises and who pardons. But you, you worm of the earth, you want to do justice. D'you know, you, what justice is?"[80] His harsh words convince Renzo to forgive his former oppressor. Father Cristoforo brings Renzo to the dying man, the symbol of societal corruption who has earlier caused Renzo such hardship:

> Bless him, and you will be blessed yourself. He's been here four days in the state you see, without giving any sign of life. Perhaps the Lord is ready to grant him an hour of consciousness; but He wanted to be asked for it by you; perhaps He wants you and that innocent girl to pray to Him. Perhaps He is reserving His grace for your prayer alone—the prayer of a heart that is afflicted and resigned. Perhaps the salvation of this man and your

> own now depends on you, on your feelings of forgiveness, of pity . . . of love.[81]

While the repeated use of the word "perhaps" makes it impossible to know if the text is suggesting that Don Rodrigo repents, there is no doubt that Renzo forgives him and that, as a result, he is blessed. Indeed, with his act of contrition, Renzo redefines himself: "Only the words of forgiveness of Father Cristoforo in the *lazaretto* unite us to Renzo in a confused prayer for his soul, about which, glowing with health and wealth he had had no thought."[82] No longer is Renzo a potential killer controlled by emotion; he is a figure whose Christian charity renews society in a period when death has almost completely trumped life.

Manzoni provides his readers with clues to Renzo's upcoming conversion and renewed faith in Christ throughout his journey. The most prominent clue resonates with a theme from Manzoni's earlier poem, *Marzo 1821* (*March 1821*). In this poem, written eight years after *Il nome di Maria*, Manzoni again uses biblical imagery to articulate the Italian struggle for independence. By drawing a parallel between the experience of the Israelites and that of the Italians, by making an analogy between the national identity and alien population of both nations, Manzoni reiterates a main theme of Pauline Christianity. In the poem, Manzoni uses the power struggle of the Jews against their oppressors to depict the Italian struggle for independence:

> Yes, that God who in the vermilion wave
> closed in on the wicked who pursued Israel,
> He who in the fist of the brave Yael
> placed the hammer and guided the blow.[83]

In the first two lines, Manzoni refers to the splitting of the Red Sea, which occurred as Moses led the Israelites in their flight from slavery in Egypt. The second two lines refer to the biblical story of Yael, who lured a Canaanite general—the Israelites were living under the oppressive rule of the Canaanites at the time—into her tent, killing him while he slept by driving a tent peg through his temple. This patriotic reading of biblical stories, the analogy between the enslaved Israelites of yore and the oppressed Italians of his day, reflects Manzoni's ardent support for Italian unification and independence. Indeed, with its biblical archetypes, the Hebrew Bible appears the ideal history with which to synthesize modern religious and national aspirations; the story of the Jews becomes the patriotic story of an oppressed people that could be transferred to other national stories in the nineteenth century.[84]

First, Manzoni picks up on the biblical analogies of *Marzo 1821* with his portrayal of the figure of Father Cristoforo and the monk's relationship to Renzo. Similar to the biblical Moses, Father Cristoforo leads Renzo, at times charitably and at times almost brutally, to his new identity as a practicing Christian and to the threshold of a new society. Like Moses, who killed a man in a fit of rage, Father Cristoforo also committed a murderous act in his youth. And just as Moses was denied entrance to the Promised Land as a result of his uncontrollable anger, so too, Father Cristoforo's actions as a young man prevent him from physically leading Renzo into the new Italy.[85] He dies in the *lazzaretto*, unable to enjoy the rebirth of Christianity in an independent Italy, even though he has contributed to its outcome. Reading Father Cristoforo as a "Christ bearing" reembodiment of Moses, Manzoni creates another modern, Catholic parallel to a biblical story. In so doing he recalls once again his similarities to Pauline Christianity. In addition, the analogy between homeland and holy land that the conversionary act of both Father Cristoforo and of Renzo makes possible emphasizes the role of conversion and proselytization in the nationalist project that circumscribes Manzoni's vision of modern Italy.

Manzoni picks up on this Hebrew Bible theme yet again with his reference to two different gates to the city of Milan in *PS*, the *Porta Orientale* ("Eastern Gate") and the *Porta Nuova* ("New Gate"). When Renzo arrives in Milan, and in the misadventures that follow him throughout the novel, he is constantly asking for directions to, and subsequently being diverted from, the Porta Orientale. The church that Father Cristoforo initially directs the boy to as a sanctuary lies near this gate. Later, when Renzo is forced to flee the police and take refuge in Bergamo, the gate that leads to Bergamo is again the Porta Orientale. Jerusalem and the Promised Land of the Hebrew Bible are also east, projecting images of the biblical Holy Land to readers. [86]

Not coincidentally, the same Porta Orientale is the district of the city first struck by the plague,[87] and once the disease spread, the *lazzaretto*, the ultimate symbol of death and destruction, is located just outside this gate. When Renzo arrives in Milan for the second time, the reader is alerted to a change immediately. Renzo arrives at the walls of the city, somewhere between the well-known Porta Orientale and the next gate, the Porta Nuova. Not knowing which way to turn, the protagonist "stood there for some time, then turned right at a venture, going, without knowing it, towards the Porta Nuova."[88] The protagonist's return to Milan fails to repeat the mishaps of the first journey. Like Davide Norsa, who began his spiritual quest heading East but who found his faith returning West, Renzo's return to Milan through the Porta Nuova foretells his future as one of new beginnings and directed by the teachings of the New Testament. Entering Milan through the Porta Nuova, Renzo slowly makes his way through the city until he finds himself back at the Porta Orientale, a gate surrounded by the dead and dying who are headed for the *lazzaretto*. As he walks through this gate for the last time, Renzo stops and surveys the degradation of the society around him. The *lazzaretto*, connected to the Eastern Gate, is a tribute to the old society that he leaves behind following his Pauline confirmation of faith.

The ultimate sign of Renzo's conversion occurs shortly after the encounter with Don Rodrigo: he finds Lucia alive and well. As they are reunified, a baptismal rain begins to fall, washing away the death and destruction of the *ancien régime* and introducing a modern, unified society bound to a Christian ethical system as Renzo finally leaves the *lazzaretto*:

> Hardly had Renzo crossed the threshold of the lazaretto . . . than a few big scattered drops began coming down . . . a moment later they were falling thick and fast, and before he had reached the lane they were coming down in torrents. Renzo, instead of being put out, wallowed in it, rejoicing in the freshness of the air, in that murmur and stir among the grass and leaves, all quivering, dripping, reviving, and glistening; he drew long, deep breaths; and this sudden change of Nature's made him realize more freely and vividly the one that had taken place in his own destiny.[89]

The rain washes away the vestiges of disease that wracked Milan and marks the end to the plague altogether. As Renzo and Lucia prepare to set out on their new life together, marking a final departure from the old society destroyed by the plague, they leave the area of the Porta Orientale, connected to the Hebrew Bible and to their former life; similar to the new start reflected by Renzo's arrival at the Porta Nuova, the new couple's departure marks the rebirth of society, renewed and guarded by the New Testament and the Catholic Church. This new society depicts the triumph of Christianity even as it spells out a vision of society that is not a return to the world of prebourgeois Christianity but the advocacy of a modern society that does not forget its Catholic roots. Renzo, the formerly secular-minded young man, returns to religion, and with this conclusion, Manzoni advocates a return to religion for the secular-minded bourgeoisie.[90] Thus Renzo's conversion and his reunification with Lucia mark the conversion of Italian society itself from the lawlessness and death that the plague produced to the charity and regeneration that come with the recognition of the value of religion. In sum, it is a Pauline vision of the triumph of Christian law and society in a modern, Catholic context.[91]

In his discussion of Manzoni, Dombroski writes, "Manzoni's great work no doubt centers on the populace, but it does so not with the purpose of knowing and representing it objectively, rather with that of reforming it and, thereby, determining its ideological physiognomy."[92] This act of re-formation that Dombroski describes, the moment in which Manzoni determines the ideological thrust of his work and defines the future of his characters, hinges upon these characters' conversions. Manzoni formulates the issue of conversion to Catholicism in terms that define national identity. Because of his fear of revolution and his appreciation for history, Manzoni seeks to establish a relationship between morality and politics, between a changing society and unchanging Christian values. In other words, while Manzoni shares the political goals of liberal and moderate-liberal thinkers of his time, his religious faith leads him to reject ideas of social progressivism as he tries to place liberal doctrine within a Catholic framework.[93] Manzoni's synthesis of conservative religious morality and liberal Enlightenment ideals leads him to envision the conversion of modern society such that it defines itself by the ethical code of Catholicism. *PS* reflects this synthesis by rehabilitating and converting even the most evil character, the *Innominato* (Unnamed). Those who refuse to convert have no place in the rejuvenated society described at the novel's end. With this conclusion, Manzoni's message to his readers is clear: Italy can begin building a modern identity as long as it adheres to a model of Christian belief as it modernizes and unifies. This message, and its inherently conservative nature, displays the defining nature of Manzoni's conversion and the strength of his subsequent religious identity: in an attempt to ensure a sense of morality in a time of change, he advocates a return to Catholicism for the inhabitants of the peninsula.

Similarly, in the narratives of Manzoni's conversion, and in the tales of those Manzoni converted, the authors insist upon their relevance, as authors and as protagonists, in the dialogue regarding the unification of Italy. The stories of Manzoni's conversion draw upon references from the Bible and from contemporary culture. These Pauline influences reflect the belief of both narrator and subject that Catholic-ness is a critical element of a new Italian homeland. By means of the stories of his own conversion and the fictional conversions of *PS*, Manzoni and his supporters suggest that Catholic identity has to precede any unification movement and that the new nation-state has to adhere to a model of Christian belief if it is to be successful. By writing an ideology of conversion that Manzoni practices in real life, by arguing that Catholic belief and national independence are the two components that define Italian statehood, the author establishes conversion as an essential experience in the making of a "new" Italy.

Chapter 4

Conversion and National Identity

A Reading of Bresciani's *L'Ebreo di Verona*

In the last chapter, I argued that Manzoni's novel advocated conversion to Catholicism as a means of establishing a modern Italian nation-state that retained its Catholic identity. It may seem surprising to suggest that a liberal Catholic like Manzoni would vigorously pursue conversion. And yet this was not unusual among neo-Guelph and liberal Catholic thinkers. Vincenzo Gioberti advocated conversion with his vision of an Italian nation-state based on Christian principles. Carlo Maria Curci, a Jesuit opponent of Gioberti, criticized the Giobertian conflation of Catholicism and nationhood, stating that Giobertian ideology was one in which "in the name of the Gospel, Parliament is proclaimed, in the name of the Pope, the Italian confederation, and in the name of Christian morals, the expulsion of the Germans from Lombard-Veneto."[1] While Gioberti condemned the persecution of religious minorities, his argument for open-mindedness was itself aimed at conversion. That is, rather than be persecuted, he argued that Jews be treated with Christian charity, since such kindness would lead them to convert of their own accord. Similarly, the liberal Catholic Giovanni Vicini criticized the Church for its excessive force in dealing with the Jewish community. And yet his seemingly liberal views, like Gioberti's, were ultimately directed at dismantling the Jewish community: if the Church treated the Jews with tolerance and friendship, Jews would convert voluntarily.[2]

Reactionary Catholics, opposed to unification and to the emancipation of religious minorities, a movement associated with modern nationhood, viewed conversion as a way to anchor and stabilize Vatican power after the disastrous blow dealt by the French Revolution. For Antonio Bresciani, the Jesuit priest and novelist whose work is the subject of this chapter, conversion was not simply about spiritual hegemony; it lent power to the political policies that these conservatives supported. In this sense, papal intransigence, which the reactionary Bresciani fully endorsed, was more than a return to the Old Regime; non-Catholics became useful scapegoats, and gaining their conversion to Christianity demonstrated to all of Europe how the Church and Rome were able to overcome the crisis of revolution.

Reflecting the differences between liberal and reactionary Catholicism, Manzoni and Bresciani differ dramatically: Manzoni championed the views of a liberal Catholic ideology; he proposed a vision of a modern Italy that gave the pope moral and religious authority, but he advocated the bestowal of temporal power on a secular governing power. Bresciani could never accept such a possibility, advocating instead that the Vatican should maintain both temporal and religious control of its lands; he was deeply suspicious of anything associated with liberalism and was, for example, a vociferous critic of Italian and European Romanticism, a subject to which I will return. As opposed to Manzoni, who avoided any mention of Rome in his novel because of the difficulty he had in balancing his desires for nationhood with his papal allegiance, the more reactionary Bresciani makes the city the central locus of his work. Perhaps the most telling differences between the two are encapsulated by Manzoni's own words. When asked for his opinion of Bresciani's recently published novel, *L'Ebreo di Verona* (henceforth *EV*),[3] Manzoni responded: "I have read the first two sentences; they are like two sentries who say, 'Go no further.'"[4]

Despite their obvious differences, however, Manzoni and Bresciani have some critical similarities that tie them together—commonalities that are integral to understanding the Church's position within the modernizing Italian state. Both men envision a modern Italy that is inherently Catholic, and so both authors advocate conversion to Catholicism as a prerequisite to becoming a productive member of society. Thus, ironically enough, despite representing different ends of the Catholic spectrum—liberal on the one hand and reactionary on the other—both thinkers believe conversion necessary to maintain the Catholic-ness of Italy. For Manzoni, conversion is a topic that reinforces the spiritual power of the papacy, and the conversion of key figures such as Father Cristoforo, Renzo, and the *Innominato* in *PS* confirms and celebrates Catholic spiritual hegemony over modern Italy. While the title of Bresciani's epic novel specifies the religious identity of one young man—notably the only Jew in the story—the novel narrates the lives and conversions of numerous other characters who initially proclaim themselves to be atheist, lapsed Catholic, or Protestant.[5] The events of the early years of Pope Pius IX's papacy are the subject matter of the novel, and the resultant vicissitudes of the political fortunes of the Papal States become a moral and political lesson that Bresciani hopes to impart to his readers. The religious and political drama of the novel is created by, as Gunzberg notes, "the general scheme of oppositions—evil versus good, sectarian violence versus ecclesiastical repression, Romanticism/Risorgimento versus Jesuitism."[6]

That the heroic converted characters reject the French Revolution, dealing a blow to the revolutionaries and the secret societies, reflects Bresciani's conflation of political involvement and religious belief. In other words, conversion to Catholicism defines both a political and religious allegiance to the pope, and the novel's conversions depict a Vatican victorious in its battle against liberalism and unification. Furthermore, by viewing the French Revolution and the subsequent revolutions of 1848 as actions of godless extremists, Bresciani exonerates Church supporters from taking any responsibility for the fall of the Old Order. At the same time, he portrays a conspiracy against the Church on the part of Jews and other revolutionaries that negates any possibility for real dialogue with the Church's enemies. Indeed, the Roman Curia that Bresciani exemplifies does not aspire to a compromise in the Church-state relationship; it seeks Catholic absolutism as the answer.

Simply put, Bresciani uses the novel to reveal his conviction that liberty can only be achieved through a return to religion and that only the Church can be the agent for the reorganization and rediscipline of society.[7] As a result, only one positive outcome for Bresciani's characters exists: conversion to Catholicism. The conversion of many of the characters—and the subsequent death of the most important of these converts—reflects, I will argue, Bresciani's response to the societal changes occurring in the mid-1800s. Through the conversion and subsequent deaths of the eponymous Aser and a heretical woman revolutionary, Polissena, Bresciani posits a victory for papal authority and Christendom. The return to Catholicism of Lando and Mimo, two young aristocrats caught up in the headiness of the Mazzinian call to battle, allows Bresciani to display the return of youth to the Church, indicating that the revolution and the ideals of the new era cannot "kidnap" the children of Italy. Finally, the capture and death of an unapologetic revolutionary, Ciceruacchio, a historical figure who never returns to the Church, enables Bresciani to suggest that the future of Italy lies with Catholic and papal supporters; fomenters of revolution and unification will end in ignominious disgrace, and the very symbols of revolution and unification die with them.

Despite his tedious and predictably reactionary rhetoric, Bresciani's portrayal of the victory for papal temporal and religious authority is quite singular. In his essay entitled "Father Bresciani's Progeny," Antonio Gramsci compares the antisocialist reaction in Italy after the Red Years of 1919 to 1920 to the reactionary attitudes that Bresciani advocated after the revolution of 1848. In particular, Gramsci condemns Bresciani for fighting against the democratization and unification of Italy. To this end, in his essay entitled "Reaction and Revolution," Gramsci cites the nineteenth-century literary critic Francesco De Sanctis, who, in a harshly critical review of Bresciani's novel, wrote that Bresciani expropriated revolutionary language for the cause of reaction, presenting Catholicism as the "true liberty" and calling the liberals "libertines."[8] The very fact that Gramsci turned to Bresciani's work a century later reflects how substantial the latter's efforts had been to reinvigorate the position of the Holy See and papal supporters in Rome. As Gramsci recognized, Bresciani defined the issue of Catholic identity in terms that appealed to a wide populace, thus making the question of national identity one that could be answered with a Catholic cultural and religious ideology.

Indeed, Bresciani, all too aware of the power of the written word and the revolutionaries' skill at using it, responds in kind: within the novel, papal authority is regained through the pious letters, sacred books, and Catholic newspapers that gradually replace those of the revolutionaries. Thus Bresciani popularizes ideas regarding revolution, religion, and the significance of the Holy See that were already present among reactionary thinkers of the religious right, using the tools of the modernizing nation to reassert Catholic cultural, political, and religious ideals. A key aspect of *EV*, then, is how Bresciani addresses issues that accompanied the modernization of the nation-state, particularly those regarding a wider readership and the need to appeal to this diverse audience. Thus far, this system of interaction and publication had empowered revolutionary fervor to the detriment of Vatican supporters. By recognizing the significance of a wider reading public, Bresciani helps the Vatican grapple with issues surrounding the circulation of information and ideas. As I argue, Bresciani's awareness of the power of circulation can be found both in the serial form in which the novel was published (discussed in the following section) and within the drama of the novel itself, in which Bresciani suggests that the circulation of ideas and information can work together to strengthen a shared, Catholic culture and, more precisely, a national, Italian Catholic culture. For papal supporters, the connection between circulation and the imagination was just beginning to be realized. Bresciani's novel thus helped make explicit what was until then only implicit: the Vatican could use the press and the free circulation of ideas in its ongoing battle against the secularization and modernization that many associated with the Risorgimento.

Before we turn to the novel itself, a word needs to be said about its publication. *EV* first appeared as a serial novel in the newly established and immensely popular *Civiltà Cattolica*, a Catholic journal meant to counter the onslaught of liberal papers. The Catholic press in Italy already had a presence in the early nineteenth century, but these journals had a limited circulation, and the contents were often dry and theoretical—long theological discourses that held little appeal for the general reader.[9] (I return to the subject of these newspapers in the next chapter.) In 1848, Carlo Curci, a Jesuit priest, proposed that the Society of Jesus publish a bimonthly journal geared toward the lay community that contained articles of general interest that expressed Catholic values on the subject of familial, political, and social pursuits.[10] His idea was to create a publication that presented the Church as a model of civil society.

At this same time, Pope Pius IX made an about-face in his policies toward supporters of unification. Initially, when Pius IX succeeded the reactionary Gregory XVI as pope in 1846, the more liberal faction in the Vatican hoped that Pius would be a more modern leader—one who could successfully unite Italy into a confederation and even act as its leader.[11] During the first two years of his papacy, Pius did indeed appear to be a political and spiritual leader ready to confront the challenges of the Risorgimento and perhaps even to fulfill the Giobertian vision of being the new leader of unified Italy.[12] Departing from the policies of his predecessors, for example, Pius decided to appoint laymen to the newly created Council of Ministers. Reporting to this council, he established another legislative body known as the Consultative Assembly at Rome. When news of the constitution of the Second Republic in France arrived at the Vatican on March 5, 1848, news also came that the liberals who drafted this constitution wanted states on the peninsula to follow their example. On March 14, 1848, Pope Pius IX granted Rome its statute, constrained to do so after the precedent set by the kings of Sardinia and the Two Sicilies. For the first time, laymen had positions of authority within Vatican politics. This act, as well as other reforms that Pius instituted upon acceding to the papacy initiated what many believed to be a new relationship between the Church and modern society. His election had, among other things, even raised hopes of emancipation for the Jewish communities in the Papal States.[13]

Despite his willingness to reform the traditional, absolutist governments of the peninsula, however, Pius could never support the expulsion of the troops of his Catholic ally Austria from the peninsula, a primary demand of unification supporters. In this regard, Bresciani, who initially appears far more reactionary than Pius IX, stands ideologically hand-in-hand with the Pontiff. That is, Bresciani's novel is filled with glowing references to the Austrians, and he is openly deferential to the political power that enabled the Vatican to maintain its lands.[14] Likewise, despite his various reforms, Pius IX had no interest in doing away completely with the old system of government; indeed, he feared that modernization would weaken the Church hierarchy and its traditional authority, threatening the very foundations of Christian civilization with the corrupting influences of secularization and democracy.

When revolution erupted in Vienna in March 1848, revolutionaries in Italy saw it as the perfect moment to drive the Austrians out and declare Italian independence. For liberal Catholics, it was the moment to convince the pope to serve in some leadership role over unified Italy. Crushing any such hopes, the pope withdrew his support for a national war at the end of April, 1848. He explained that the Vatican could not be tied to the interests of any specific nation, and he publicly condemned Italian nationalists, rejecting any thought of threatening Austrian soldiers, and speaking strongly against the unification movement on the peninsula. To protest Pius's condemnation of the independence movement, the ministers of the newly established Roman government resigned. The statement created an immediate fracture in the Catholic public as well: on the one hand, there were those papal supporters who continued to support the papacy in terms of both its religious and temporal power. On the other hand, there were those Catholics who remained faithful on a spiritual level but who supported national ideals regarding the unification of Italy.[15] Pius's stance disempowered liberal Catholic supporters, who advocated a role for the pope in the new nation-state and led to the rise of a more staunch republicanism that sought to strip the papacy completely of its temporal power. Inhabitants of Rome and the Papal States were up in arms, demanding democratic reforms and the expulsion of Austria, and religious and secular factions respectively became more polarized as a result. The protests grew louder and more violent, and Pius's appointee as Prime Minister, Pellegrino Rossi, was assassinated in the unrest that followed.[16] In November 1848, fearing for his life, Pius fled the Vatican dressed as a simple priest and made his way south to Gaeta. One month later, Garibaldi marched into Rome with his volunteer army and, in February 1849, Rome was declared a republic, and the era of papal temporal rule was declared over.

Upon being forced into exile, Pius no longer maintained any sympathy toward those who sought to reform his government; he saw his job as that of reasserting papal temporal power and of regaining the power that had vanished in the past two years. To this end, he abolished the constitutional government that he had been pressured into establishing two years prior. In his desire to return to the hierarchical authority of earlier days, he also did away with the reforms of 1848. The humiliating exile of the pope during the crisis of 1848 thus ended the possibility of a more moderate Vatican voice. Gradually, a monolithic unity was built up within the Church, and any diversity or divergence was viewed as disobedience. In his battle against modernity and the movement toward secular, democratic statehood, Pius supported the establishment of a Catholic newspaper whose express goal would be to combat the secular press and spread the word and ideology of the Vatican. And, while the head of the Society of Jesus had misgivings about Curci's idea for a journal, Pius recognized the need for a publication that would counter the claims that liberal presses expressed. Indeed, having endorsed the venture immediately, Pius even financed the first issue of the journal, *Civiltà Cattolica*, which started on April 6, 1850.[17] Ironically enough, the Holy See's attempts to defend its actions and justify and reinforce its ideology led Catholic leaders to use tools that had until this point been viewed as signs of the secular, revolutionary, and antipapal camp.

When the journal began, it was based in the Kingdom of Naples, where Pius had fled in 1848. And, when Pius returned to Rome, the journal soon moved as well, indicating its close association with the Holy See. Bresciani was called to Naples to work on *Civiltà Cattolica*, and Pius IX supposedly asked that he be given the job of contributing novelist.[18] When Bresciani hesitated, saying that he had no idea what he should write about, the pope responded, "Write about things of Rome that you see with your own eyes and hear with your own ears. It is a fresh, well-known, universal topic: develop it as you like, it will always arouse the curiosity of Italians, and you can clarify for them the fallacies and lies that shamefully pass from the pages of the conspirators to those ill-fated days."[19] *EV*—the first novel to be serialized within its pages—was the result, and it provided the editors with the answer to the difficult issue of how to define a role for Catholicism in a political environment that was changing dramatically.[20]

The irony of Bresciani's appointment as novelist is particularly striking when one considers Bresciani's hatred of Romanticism—both its Italian and foreign varieties—as an outgrowth of liberal, revolutionary ideology. Thus, while Manzoni appeared to connect himself more and more to the Romantic Movement, distancing himself from the defenders of *classicismo* (classicism), Bresciani in a sense became a Romantic despite himself, adopting the genre of the romantic novel despite his dislike of the movement. His letter to his superior, Father Roothaan, written on December 29, 1831, expressed his unqualified disapproval of Romanticism, which he viewed as anti-Catholic and overly liberal: "Romanticism is an irreligious and antimonarchical literary sect. It always has in its mouth Christian topics, but only in order to bite easily into the saintliest institutions of the Catholic Church. . . . All of their writings tend to ask for Italian liberty: and they all yell: *Oh slave Italy, Oh refuge of pain!* Their novels, their tragedies, their songs are always about that. *The great priest has been trapped. Law and not King, Italy is existing.*"[21]

Driven by his desire to reach the greatest number of readers possible, however, he recognized the value and empowerment of elements of romanticism. Thus, much like Curci, who recognized that the Vatican had to adopt the press as a tool in its fight against liberalism, Bresciani became a novelist in his desire to add political momentum and strength to the Vatican's battle against liberalism and revolution. As a result, despite his hatred for the literary movement, Bresciani invented an exotic, Jewish protagonist for his novel. Aser's conversion is the act that justified Bresciani's placement of a Jew as the protagonist, since through conversion he could demonstrate that Catholicism and the Church are the ultimate victors.

Bresciani's technique of contrasting the extremely pious, moral Catholic character with the evil atheist revolutionary rendered a powerful tool that was immensely successful with his readers, who were generally practicing Catholics with little understanding of lay government. That the denouement of Aser's personal story—and that of numerous other characters—evolves around his subsequent conversion to Catholicism, demonstrates the intensely political role that religion played for Bresciani. In other words, by connecting the redemption of his characters with writing in general and letter-writing in particular, Bresciani found a way to explain why he was writing a novel and why it deserved to be read. Ironically, Bresciani accused the new order of having inverted the hierarchy and authority that he believed fundamental for the future of Italy; and yet he seeks to set straight this inversion by employing tools and communications of the press that had been the very weapons of his adversaries.

Bresciani's reactionary sentiments and the proselytization that is at the center of his novel were very much a result of the period in which he developed as a clergyman. In particular, his entrance into the priesthood in 1821 and his subsequent entrance into the Society of Jesus in 1826 coincided with a period marked by a rising fear among Vatican supporters regarding the growing modernization and secularization of the general populace. This fear led to a rise in reactionary thinking among some papal supporters that clearly resonated with Bresciani. Indeed, he was undoubtedly influenced by the significant number of reactionary *zelanti* who held powerful positions in the Vatican hierarchy. As historian Owen Chadwick notes, while extreme reactionaries may not have been especially numerous in the Papal States in this period, "the mood of the age brought some of them [reactionaries] into posts of authority. There they believed that religion supported authority, authority's interest lay in using religion."[22] The relationship between religion and authority that Chadwick describes appears particularly relevant to Bresciani's personal history; as a young man Bresciani rejected his father's authority and turned to that found in the Church instead. Indeed, in a somewhat dramatic tale, he ignored his father's wishes that he become a lawyer and ran away to Rome in 1815, at the age of seventeen, where he turned to local Jesuits for help in realizing his dream to become a priest.[23] In so doing, Bresciani set an ideological tone that he maintained for the rest of his life, namely that the authority of the Church and the power of religion must remain the ruling forces of the Papal States and the Italian peninsula. In other words, just as Bresciani subscribed to the authority of the Church in his own life, he invoked it in his writings and teachings as well. Furthermore, Bresciani's great wish upon entering the Jesuit order was to be sent to Paraguay to proselytize among the native population. Thus the issue of conversion, of spreading the message and authority of the Catholic Church, appealed to Bresciani long before his literary career began.[24]

The mood of the times, and the emphasis on conversion, was perhaps best reflected by two well-received and highly vaunted essays that appeared in Rome at the time. The first, which appeared two years after Bresciani joined the priesthood, was entitled *L'ebraismo senza replica e sconfitto colle sue stesse armi* (*Judaism without Objection and Defeated with its Own Arms*). Written by the Dominican theologian Filippo Aminta, the work was dedicated to Pope Leo XII, then Cardinal Della Genga, who had been instrumental in appointing Aminta *predicatore* (preacher) of the Jews. Aminta described this job as consisting of convincing Jews to convert to Catholicism,[25] and the aim of his text was also conversionary: in traditionally anti-Semitic language, Aminta proposed that Jews embrace the Catholic tradition and repent for their past iniquities. Furthermore, Aminta dedicates his work to his mentor, Cardinal Della Genga—the future Pope Leo XII—explaining that Della Genga acted as a mentor who aimed to fulfill the same conversionary goals. A second well-known reactionary voice was that of Father Ferdinando Jabalot, whose 1825 essay, *Degli ebrei nel loro rapporto colle nazioni cristiane* (*On the Jews and Their Relationship with Christian Nations*), questioned Jewish allegiance to the papal government and suggested that the Jewish communities in the Papal States were complicit with, if not overwhelmingly in favor of, the upheaval brought about by the New Order. The Vatican promoted the work upon its publication in the *Giornale ecclesiastico di Roma*, and both pieces reflect the reactionary and intolerant views to which many in the Vatican hierarchy subscribed.

When Cardinal della Genga became pope in 1824 (taking the name Leo XII), he added his voice to the reactionary, antimodern view of many of his clergymen. He strictly censured the press, forbidding newspapers from discussing any political topic; he reinstated the restrictions on Jews in the Roman ghetto; and he encouraged severity in the rulings of the papal court system. In 1825, in an attempt to promote a general return to Catholicism, he reinstated the celebration of the Jubilee, which had not been observed since 1775. In his encyclical to mark this event, the pope repeated his goal of a return to Christianity, warning his listeners that "the iniquitous convention between Catholics and heretics has grown. . . . Strive with all your ability to saturate youth with Catholic customs and rules of life, demanding this of them, of their parents, and of their teachers. Especially however, see that they are on their guard against seduction, so that they may shudder at the evil opinions propagated by these miserable times and at the books inimical to religion, morals, and public peace, from which this foul crop of wickedness has grown."[26]

Similarly, on Ascension Day, when he delivered the Bull that announced the holy year, Cardinal Wiseman recorded how Pope Leo first addressed his followers and then spoke to opponents of the Vatican, stating "in words of burning charity and affectionate forgiveness he invites them to approach him and accept him as *their* father too."[27] Wiseman's words clearly referred to heretics and nonbelievers, just as they appeared to refer subtly to secret societies, and the pope's desire that all such individuals become part of the fabric of a Catholic culture and society.

While the turmoil in the Papal States culminated in 1848, signs of unrest, and of the Holy See's gradual loss of control, were evident decades earlier. In 1831, two days after the reactionary *zelanti* managed to elect their candidate, Gregory XVI, to the papacy, a revolt broke out in Bologna, and the townspeople expelled the papal legate and flew the tri-colored flag of the Italian republic. It was only with the help of Austrian forces that the revolt was crushed and papal control reinstated. Later that year, new revolts broke out in the Romagna region, and once again the pope was forced to call upon Austrian troops to quell the violence. The Papal States' complete dependence on foreign power induced Gregory XVI to uphold ever more reactionary rulings. In the words of the aristocratic landholder Bartolo, father of the heroine in Bresciani's novel, Pope Gregory XVI had been "too much opposed to the progress of European civilization at the present time . . . an enemy to enlightenment and useful inventions [who] seems even to take delight in stifling the aspirations of Italian genius."[28] Gregory died in 1846, and historian Adolfo Omodeo succinctly summarizes the situation that Bartolo referenced in his description of Rome at the time of the pope's death. The deceased Pope, he writes, was "reactionary, stubborn, and inert, opposed to every sort of innovation, even to the building of railroads, Gregory XVI died after sixteen years of bad government, leaving a difficult heritage to his successor."[29]

As a historical novel, *EV* is unusual insofar as it concerns a period of recent history, namely the reaction of a papal supporter to the political upheavals of 1848. The novel opens with a reminder of the exile of Pope Pius IX, who, in 1849, moved from his refuge in Gaeta to the Villa Reale di Portici, in the Kingdom of Naples, where he stayed until his return to Rome in 1850.[30] In fact, the notion of movement, encapsulated by the pope's flight south, serves as a central component for the novel. The sign of modern nationhood is movement: the building of roads and a public transportation system enables people to travel, commercial exchanges between increasingly remote places, and, perhaps most significant, the transmission of written documents to many more places, near and far. People, coaches, letters, and newspapers all circulate across revolutionary Europe and the Italian peninsula, tying Bresciani's numerous subplots together. (Indeed, the novel's own success on the literary market is a part of this financial and written exchange.) These indications of progress stand in sharp contrast to the stasis invoked by Pope Gregory XVI, who resisted all forms of progress and modernization.

Thus, for example, he opposed the building of railroads in the Papal States, and his encyclical *Mirari Vos* emphatically denounced any separation between Church and State. More specifically, the work condemned the freedom of the press and called for a return to an earlier era, when the Church's control was not questioned.[31] In Bresciani's novel, movement has similarly negative associations: revolutionaries leave home to go to battle, with the young men of Italy naively following their example; the secret societies successfully send letters and newspapers up and down the peninsula and across Europe, transmitting information and plotting their battles; the pope and clergymen are forced to flee Rome, leaving the city and lands they believe are theirs.

But finally, Bresciani channels movement, essentially recognizing its manipulability. In this way, the phenomenon of movement and the theme of circulation are inherently intertwined with the numerous conversions that Bresciani narrates. That is, while movement is generally associated with nationhood and the New Order, Bresciani uses it to redefine the order and permanence of the Vatican and its rule, and the return of many to the Catholic Church. Thus the revolutionaries are killed in the very battles that they had promoted, with several of them converting on their deathbeds and rejecting the ideology they had advocated so energetically; the young men who followed these revolutionaries remorsefully return to their homes and to the values associated with the old order; the letters that circulate contain expressions of remorse, repentance, and piety, rather than the words of battle-hardened soldiers; finally, and most importantly, the pope and his followers return and reclaim Rome.

The development of the modern nation-state, with the forward motion suggested in the word "development," is associated with movement, activity, and exchange. Industrialization leads to a diminishing of the particularisms that define local identity. Thus, for example, paved roads and faster travel enabled commerce over a far wider domain. As arteries that aid all bodies in their circulation, roads become a means to recognizing that there is a greater Italy outside of any one particular village or town, thus stimulating an interest in national events that accompany a greater awareness of the larger nation. Making use of the newly built roads, military groups, revolutionaries, and the Civic Guard all have a further homogenizing affect, contributing to a new national awareness.[32] In sum, movement is a means by which different parts of a country and its citizens are connected to one another to create what has often been referred to as the imagined community of modern nationhood.[33] In his novel, Bresciani employs the elements most closely associated with modernization and nationhood, namely movement and exchange, and essentially turns them on their heads, illustrating how these forces are responsible for the Church's downfall. He then uses the tools of the revolutionaries to promote piety and Catholicism among his characters. Thus circulation, rather than promoting nationhood, becomes a means for spreading Catholic dogma and the Vatican's political ideology.

The plot of the novel evolves around the trickery and evil of the neo-Guelphs, who, according to the author, fool the masses into believing in their cause and into questioning the role of religious leaders and monarchical rulers. Many of the characters play a role in the revolution sweeping Europe: Aser, the hero of the novel; Polissena, a woman warrior, whose lies and disguises enable Bresciani to emphasize the duplicitous nature of revolutionaries, and women revolutionaries in particular; Lando and Mimo, young aristocrat cousins of the heroine Alisa who join the revolutionary movement; and Ciceruacchio, a popular historical figure. Throughout the novel, Bresciani strives to contrast Catholicism and morality on the one hand and revolution and atheism on the other; and the suspense of the novel derives from the necessity of reforming the book's evil characters. The conversion and repentance of these characters—all but Ciceruacchio, that is—enable Bresciani to claim a temporal and religious victory for the Church against the battle for Italian independence. The struggle between good and evil, between Church and revolution, between the old order and the new, is reflected in a conversation between Bartolo, a Roman aristocrat who is father to the heroine of the novel, and his friend Cardinal Mezzofanti, who visits him. Upon discussing the secret societies, and the anti-Catholics who belong to them, the Cardinal reminds Bartolo that "they pray for us as we pray for their conversion."[34] Thus the vocabulary of conversion is inherent to the battle that Bresciani envisions between the papal forces and the revolutionaries; the cardinal's words reflect not only a religious understanding of the secret societies but also the politicization of the Church's conversionary efforts.

Despite being the titular referent of the novel, Aser is not a central protagonist. Indeed, some critics suggest that the city of Rome during the period 1848–1849 is the true protagonist of the novel, and still others view the secret societies as the true protagonist.[35] These suppositions do not necessarily contradict one another; Bresciani clearly associates the secret societies with the Jews, since these societies are the modern manifestation of Christ's murder, an act perpetrated by the Jews. Furthermore, he views the secret societies as largely responsible for the papal exile from Rome. Underlying Aser's political and ideological commitment to the secret societies are numerous stereotypes that Bresciani employs to denigrate both the Jews and the revolutionary movement that they support: the young Jew is rich, of unknown origins, and speaks many languages.[36] Aser's association with money is also reflected in his name, a version of the Biblical name Asher, meaning wealth in Hebrew. In the Hebrew Scriptures, Asher was a brother to Joseph and was involved in the events that led to Joseph's being sold into slavery. The story of Asher has significant overtones for the role of Aser. In typological readings of the story of Joseph, Joseph is identified with Jesus, while his brothers, who sell him into slavery, are equated to Judas. By recalling the Joseph story and its relation as a precursor to the New Testament, Bresciani stresses the anti-Semitic stereotypes of his Jewish protagonist. As a revolutionary, Aser represents a people who are sustaining the crucifixion of Christ that the Jews initiated. In other words, by bringing down the Church, the revolutionaries—led by the Jews—are crucifying Christ a second time.

The words of Sterbini, a revolutionary and consort of Aser, underscore the wealth and power Bresciani attributes to the Jews and their separateness from the rest of the population. The Jews, he states, "crowd the universities; they move in the highest circles; they have merchant vessels in every port; they are mixed up in the affairs of every government; in short, they are excluded only from the most influential places in the palaces of kings."[37] With his constant use of the word "they," Sterbini emphasizes the differences between the Jews and Bresciani's Catholic readers and thus the nonbelonging status of the Jews in the larger Italian community. The Jew, according to Sterbini, is always an outsider, not completely understood or known even by his closest friends. For Bresciani to perpetuate this stereotype is particularly ironic, since the Italian for "Jesuit" or "Jesuitical" denotes in figurative terms "underhanded" or "two-faced,"[38] precisely the images he ties to Jews and revolutionaries. Aser's Jewishness defines him both as a latter-day Judas and an enemy to Catholicism: "It is neither magnanimity, nor generosity, nor courtesy, which binds them to us: it is the rage of Judas. The resurrection of Europe would crucify and bury again the Nazarene, and for this they would give the last drop of blood."[39] Thus Bresciani suggests that Aser's religious identity ignites his revolutionary passion. As a Jew, Aser embodies the perfidy of political as well as religious opposition; as a practicing Catholic, he becomes a respectable and virtuous citizen who has cut all of his ties to the secret societies. Thus his conversion is as political as it is religious; his newfound religious piety is matched by a political credo that endorses papal temporal hegemony.

Aser falls in love with Alisa, Bartolo's virtuous daughter, after seeing her from afar one morning. The young woman is seated outside with her governess, Polissena, reading a novel. The power of reading, and its ability to manipulate the reader and observer are striking in the description of Aser's vision of Alisa. He is "struck with the animated features of Alisa, who was at that moment stirred to the most lively pity for the sufferings of some heroine in the story. She was motionless, and seemed not even to breathe. Her color, heightened by excitement, came and went alternately, and her whole countenance denoted the rapid emotions which succeeded each other in her mind."[40] Bresciani, consumed by the belief that the revolutionaries use letters, newspapers, novels to manipulate public opinion, presents this scene as a demonstration of how powerful reading, and seeing, can be. Significantly, the discourse on motion enters even this descriptive passage. While Alisa's features are animated, the young woman's body remains motionless. Her stillness is a reflection of her purity, just as the emotions that are so easily readable in her face make *her* easily read. Her readability lies in sharp contrast to the duplicity and trickery of the revolutionaries—and the mystery surrounding Aser's identity, and her motionlessness stands out against their constant motion. Aser, struck by the vision of Alisa, makes a painting of the young woman, portraying her as a country girl with a lamb on her knees. By portraying Aser as an artist, Bresciani draws a parallel between his character and that of Mazzini's hero-poet-patriot.[41] Of course, Bresciani's decision to represent Mazzini's vision of a "son of the people" with a Jew allows him to mock an icon of Risorgimento ideology. That is, to posit this outsider as the Mazzinian native son was to ridicule the entire ideology of the Risorgimento, since the international nature of the Jewish community means that the Jews could have no allegiances other than to their secret societies and fellow Jews. Finally, the religious undertones to the painting, in which I would submit that Alisa appears as a Mary figure with the lamb, a symbol of Jesus, looking up at her, prefigure Aser's future conversion to Catholicism.

The two young Italians are thrown together by fate several days later. Both have joined the crowds that have gathered to witness the installation of Pius IX as pope, and the chivalric Aser risks his life to save Alisa from being crushed by a horse. The two are not united forever, however, since Aser must leave Rome to fight in the revolutions that are washing across Europe. Thus traveling and the theme of movement are inherent to Aser's character. Revolutionary fervor, amplified by the itinerant lifestyle often associated with Jews, leads Bresciani to create a protagonist that is regularly on the road, zigzagging across the continent. For

Aser, as for most supporters of the Risorgimento, travel helped define the borders of the new nation-state of Italy: traveling the country was a means of imagining it, knowing it, and hence possessing it. Indeed, the development of roads and the rise in travel is generally associated with nation building. Bresciani depicts these travels in the negative light of anti-Semitic stereotypes, however, suggesting that Aser's mobility serves the interests of a subversive group of people who are not anchored to Italy any more than to any other country.

Aside from travel, nothing symbolizes the boundaries of the new nation more than the control of information flowing into and out of it. Like traveling revolutionaries, the dispersal of information by means of journals and letters becomes yet another means of defining the imagined community of the larger nation. In other words, the postal system, and the power that controlled it, becomes a fundamental symbol of authority in the development of a new nation-state. When Austria occupied the Italian peninsula, one of the ways in which Metternich maintained control was by regulating the post. By the 1820s, he had established a network of *logge* (postal collection points) throughout the Austrian empire, with the center in Vienna. The Italian border had *logge* in Venice, Padua, Vicenza, Verona, and Mantua, and all the mail for central and southern Italy passed through these checkpoints. Post that traveled by sea was intercepted in Trieste, Venice, and Zara.[42] Papal reliance on Austrian military might further demonstrates the complete control Austrians had over the Papal States, and while Vatican officials did not like the idea of Austria possibly having access to their mail,[43] they viewed governance of the post as an imperative necessity to controlling the circulation of ideas more generally. The revolutionaries sought to undo precisely this censorship with innovative means of communication that circumvented Vatican and Austrian controls.

Bresciani's fear of the power of the revolutionary skills of communication is reflected in a letter that the revolutionary character Sterbini writes: "The Jews of Italy, Germany, Poland, Bohemia, and Hungary, will lend their aid in various ways. They are our treasurers and our printers; they supply us with books and every kind of prints; and what is infinitely more important, they have men of every condition, old and young, traveling apparently for purposes of trade, who render us, with perfect safety, the most faithful services. They pry into every corner, and through every keyhole; they thrust themselves everywhere: in a word, they are our electric telegraph."[44]

Sterbini thus suggests that Jews have an ulterior motive for traveling. That Jews and revolutionaries "pry" into private affairs again reflects

Bresciani's suspicion of the subversive intentions of the Jews. Finally, with his claim that the Jews represent the electric telegraph, Sterbini creates a direct connection between the circulation of people and the circulation of words—and the danger attached to each. Like the errant Jew, who is unsettled and unsettling, the circulation of information is a danger to be reckoned with and conquered. That he connects the Jews with a modern invention further associates Jews with the technology of modernization, of which many in the papal hierarchy were suspicious. Indeed, when Tomas Sömmerring introduced the first electric telegraph to the Munich Academy of Sciences in 1809, his words bespoke a new discursive means that Vatican officials, interested in controlling discourse, feared most: "It has been recently invented in order to expedite communications from the four corners of the globe, an electrical telegraph; a telegraph that . . . can transmit messages with the speed of thought."[45] Speed and distance are overcome with the telegraph, which presents yet another challenge to the Vatican and its desire to filter and control the information that reaches the citizenry of the Papal States.

Aser triumphantly describes the postal system that the revolutionaries have set up across Europe to his fellow revolutionary Sterbini. Not coincidentally, it is the first of his letters that appears in the novel:

> You will henceforth receive my letters and those of the brethren, from the couriers of Leghorn, where we have instituted a living telegraph, on the plan of those of the Chinese. Leghorn is the central point, and thence diverge rays which will extend over all Italy like the web of a spider. Every ten miles in every direction there is a secret post. A courier leaves Leghorn, and at the distance of ten miles he finds others; one for Rome, a second for Florence, a third for Turin, a fourth for Milan, one for Venice, another for Naples, and to these he consigns his message, which, if very important and short, he gives by word of mouth, and so it proceeds until it reaches its destination. In this manner, in a few hours we have a post communication, safe, active, and most rapid, and the police may in vain seek to penetrate or discover our secret devices.[46]

Improvements to the postal system changed the perception of distance on the peninsula by bringing distant cities within communicative reach, precipitating a chain reaction. The increase in communication, which Aser boasts about in the letter cited above, gave greater power and authority to the revolutionaries. The presence of these informal post offices, their ability to serve in the transfer of information, represents a national geography, one that, in its very breadth, denotes the creation of a national community.[47] Most significantly, however, Aser's description of the Italian postal system that the revolutionaries had put in place is at odds with the system that the Austrians had organized on the peninsula. When the Papal States were more securely under Austrian control, Austria and the Vatican had almost a monopoly on the power of discourse. In this hierarchy, every letter writer "was a subject of posting." The state's monopoly on the postal system "turned the state into the reason and guarantor that bodies and symbols could be reciprocally translated and sent."[48] Geography was the surface upon which mail linked people and letters. The spider web that Aser describes, with its center in Leghorn rather than Vienna, supplants the postal network, and thus the authority, of the papal government and its Austrian allies. With Aser's letter, which itself has traveled great distances and proved the capability of the revolutionaries' postal system, readers read evidence of the successful communication network within the secret societies.

Bresciani's fear of the revolutionaries' communication skills and their attempts to distribute information without the knowledge of the papal authority is portrayed by the presence in his novel of one historical figure in particular, that of Ciceruacchio. Ciceruacchio is a popular historical figure whom Bresciani depicts as a revolutionary cohort of Aser. He is, in Bresciani's words, "a gambling, quarrelsome character, tall and muscular, ready for every kind of disorder."[49] Both in fiction and in reality, Ciceruacchio is the epitome of all that Bresciani detests: he is a vulgar, popular figure who urges the populace to revolution. Ciceruacchio, who works delivering wine to local Roman taverns, has two connections to the theme of communication and exchange. First, he founded a periodical by the name of *Circolo popolare romano*, which flourished largely because he regularly supplied it with circulars and publications.[50] Second, Ciceruacchio headed continual demonstrations against Pius IX in Rome, expressing his desire to distance the clergy from the government, to arm the people, and to battle against Austria. Bresciani portrays him, for example, as a key figure in the taking of Castel Sant'Angelo and the Quirinale, suggesting that the Roman revolutionary instigated an audacious attempt to take the pope himself prisoner as he roused the masses to revolution. The narrator of *EV* bitterly complains that, despite his frequent violations of the law, "his deep cunning, concealed under an open and frank demeanor, had generally shielded him from punishment."[51]

For the last protest that he instigates, however, he pays with his life. Two months after the uprisings in Vienna and Lombardy, Ciceruacchio confirmed the growing strength of the revolutionaries by forcibly invading a Roman post office. Supported by locals and members of the Civic Guard, he invaded the post office of Piazza Colonna in the hopes of stealing the papal correspondence—specifically that written by a group of cardinals—that lay inside. He believed that the letters contained proof that the Curia was planning to carry out strong punitive measures against the masses for any support they voiced in favor of revolution. The bag of letters was brought by carriage to the Campidoglio, accompanied by Ciceruacchio and other revolutionaries, who shouted to the populace, inviting them to gather at the Palazzo dei Conservatori to help read the Cardinals' letters.[52] The Austrian representative in Rome attempted to regain possession of the letters, but failed; the envelopes had already reached the hands of the masses. In describing the events at the post office, Bresciani describes how Ciceruacchio and his henchmen led the populace in the theft of letters:

> In the midst of this Pandemonium, one honest voice was heard. "Infamy! Abomination! Letters are sacred and inviolable: the rights of mankind are entrenched beneath every seal; he who breaks it is a traitor, a felon to security, and civil liberty!"
>
> "What liberty? What security? Tyrants are deserving of neither! To the Post, brethren!"
>
> "To the Post! To the Post!" shouted those madmen. A crowd of villainous wretches rushed to the Post-office: "Deliver up the letters or die, all of you!"
>
> . . . Never, from the foundation of Rome to the present time, did the Capitol behold so criminal a breach of trust, nor a transaction so foul as this.[53]

For Bresciani, Ciceruacchio's actions, like Aser's first letter, encapsulate the threat facing the Papal States. Indeed, in a certain light, the attack on the postal system is a micro version of the attack on papal temporal authority. By its very nature, the postal system is a hierarchical system; things arrive at their destination, on time, by means of orders from a higher authority. Overpowering the authorities that control the postal system is a symbolic toppling of the temporal control of the papal government itself.[54]

Rather than trying to enforce stasis by banning travel and communication, like the reactionary Pope Gregory, who preceded Pius, Bresciani offers a different solution. He ensures that his main characters reject their revolutionary and religious past by means of conversion. For those figures such as Ciceruacchio, who will never repent, there is only one possible solution: punishment by death. Indeed, unlike the figure of Aser, who is offered the opportunity to repent, Ciceruacchio, true to his real-life story, never converts but dies because of his revolutionary actions. While the populace was never punished for their role in the affair, Ciceruacchio and his sons were later captured by the Austrians and shot to death.[55] And, while Bresciani does not mention Ciceruacchio's death, Ciceruacchio was a figure that most readers of the day would have heard about. Indeed, he mentions only the vaguest details of the post office heist, clearly assuming that his readers knew the story. While Ciceruacchio may have challenged Vatican order and authority with his actions, Bresciani restores it, and in so doing, reinstates the values of the Church without suggesting a complete return to earlier times, as other reactionaries were prone to do.

Reflecting the change taking place in those characters that choose to return to the Church, Bresciani reformulates the use and nature of letters. Aser's earliest letter exposes the power of the revolutionaries. With his conversion, however, Aser uses letters as a means to confess, and to relay his newfound Catholic beliefs. He writes to seek forgiveness rather than to further the aims of the revolution. Thus letter writing, letter reading, and even the circulation of letters take on a different meaning by the end of the novel: the letter represents not just a textual body but a spiritual one. Before his conversion, reading the text of Aser's letters consisted of reading a web of deception and divisiveness—a description of how to evade authorities and foment revolution. As Aser begins to rethink his position as a revolutionary, however, the text of his letters changes as well. Rather than containing boasts as to the communication prowess of the secret societies, the letters contain warnings of upcoming violence caused by revolution. And with his actual conversion, Aser's letters change further, becoming confessional and introspective. In other words, Bresciani renders a convert a character in which reading text is about reading self.

The confessional nature of Aser's last letters, like those of other converts, remains informed and directed by a sense of Bresciani's authorial power and influence, and hence of his desire to change the uses and conception of letter-writing and reading. In her work *Epistolarity*, Janet Gurkin Altman describes the letter as "a totally amorphous instrument in the hands of its creator."[56] By calling a letter an "instrument," Altman emphasizes the ease with which authors can manipulate it. For Bresciani, epistolarity is a means to manipulate a tool used by the revolutionaries for his own ends: to redefine who controls circulation by taking away the very actors who implemented this network and to place the new letter writers squarely under the aegis of the Church.

Several elements of the later letters of *EV* mark Bresciani's use of the letter as a means to send a different message. First, unlike most of the letters of the revolutionaries, which we, as readers, catch only an incomplete glimpse of, the letters of the convert are conveyed in their entirety, and the addressee reads these words in a moment of acquisition and appropriation. They are simultaneously read by a larger reading public as well. As readers we assume the same position that Alisa did when Aser first sighted her: animated, yet rendered motionless by the words in front of her. Just as Aser could read Alisa's interior by looking at her, the interior of the convert is made visible and readable by the act of converting. As opposed to the revolutionaries, who circulate their own physical bodies as instruments of change and inscribe the corrupt ideas associated with revolution in their letters, the convert declares his faith in a moment of stillness and naked vulnerability. The accessibility of the convert's[57] words is evidence of the accessibility of his soul, contributing a sense of purity, probity, and clarity to his newly formed character. In contrast to the letter writing of the secret societies, the circulation of expressions of belief demonstrates the unity, power, and authority of the pope over his lands.

The change in the content and circulation of Aser's letters is thus inextricably linked with his conversion. Like Renzo, Aser's conversion is a gradual awareness rather than an instantaneous realization. Indeed, the reader's first clue that Catholicism resounds in Aser's heart occurs through the use of the postal system as well; when Alisa hears that Aser is leaving Rome to fight, she sends him a pendant of the Virgin Mary. The gift does not arrive through the mail, however; rather than use the postal system, Alisa asks her English professor to deliver the gift, introducing the reader to exchange that emphasizes the local, real community rather than the imagined, larger one.

Aser's regret at being part of the revolutionary movement increases as the novel continues and is reflected in the young man's letter writing. His second letter contains none of the boasting of the first. It is addressed to Mimo, Alisa's young, impetuous cousin, and in it he begs his friend to leave Rome and to tell Bartolo to do the same. He warns Mimo that the Mazzinian faction of the revolutionaries has lost patience with diplomacy and is about to use force to conquer Rome: "It has been decided by the Mazzinians to dispose of the Pope, the Cardinals, the Prelates, and the entire clergy; they will either effect this, or they will resort to unheard of atrocities. You good people don't know these fiends; they are capable of blowing up St. Peter's, the Vatican, the Quirinal, and whatever else you have of beauty and excellence in Rome, and if they stop short of that, it will not be through good will"[58]

Aser's words warn of dire consequences when the revolutionaries arrive in Rome. He contrasts the "good people," namely the aristocratic, propapal Bartolo, with the Mazzinian "fiends." His prediction of the destruction of things "you have" refers to buildings and monuments owned and associated with papal Rome. The "beauty and excellence" of these landmarks differs starkly with the ruin and devastation the atheistic revolutionaries will perpetrate.

The events that Aser forewarns of relate to the rebellion that occurred in Rome. Instead of reflecting triumph and excitement at the impending victory of the Mazzinians, however, Aser's words describing the revolutionary violence in Rome are severely critical. Furthermore, in his desire to protect his friends, he suggests they move either to their country villas or to another country entirely, and names Vevey and Geneva, Switzerland, as tranquil destinations. While Aser makes no mention of the pope's departure, he too is forced to flee because of the impending violence. Thus the people who symbolize the permanence and immobility of the Papal States, its very leaders, are forced into motion by the revolution. The aristocrats own the land around Rome, making them a constant presence of the Papal States. The pope symbolizes Rome itself, as the narrator reveals: Rome is "the centre of Christianity, the sovereign seat of Faith, the august residence of the Head of the Church, and the queen city of the whole Christian family."[59] Making the pope and his followers flee reflects the lawlessness of the revolutionaries, and rather than demonstrating nationhood, the enforced movement produces something akin to anarchy. Indeed, in his description of these events, including the pope's flight to Gaeta, Bresciani notes that Catholics from all over the world sent their leader letters, conveying their allegiance to him and to the Catholic faith. Catholics "sent forth protestations, acknowledging and reverencing him, not only as the Head of the Church, but, also, as the Supreme Ruler."[60] Bresciani's conservatism and antirevolutionary stance is illuminated in this passage. While revolutionaries have forced the pope's removal from Rome, thus connecting his movement to theirs, Bresciani writes of the pope as a fixed point, "Head of Rome," "Supreme Ruler," and this stands true in Gaeta or in the Eternal City, Rome.

The savageries against which Aser warns Mimo, and those he continues to see as he travels through Hungary, lead him to regret his involvement in the secret societies, until ultimately Aser heeds the advice he gave Mimo. He leaves the war and decides to break off contact with the secret societies.[61] In other words, he determines to end communication with the network he earlier supported. His decision to defect produces drastic results. Rather than use the network of communications established by the revolutionaries, Aser is forced to write Mimo secretly of his future plans, and his letter only reaches Mimo after a circuitous route in which it passes through many hands. Nonetheless, the letter reaches its destination, and for the first time, the revolutionaries' communication network does not appear impenetrable.

The other body that comes to an abrupt halt is that of Aser himself: shortly after Aser leaves Hungary, seeking refuge in Switzerland, he is touched by the misfortune that he evaded so adeptly as a soldier. The young Jew falls down a steep precipice and is knocked unconscious—literally immobilized from further travels. Indeed, Aser barely escapes death and is saved by a priest who discovers him in the woods. Gradually, the stage is further set for Aser's conversion; he comes to terms with his revolutionary past, renouncing any sympathy for the secret societies and any affiliation with Judaism. His growing disgust with the religion of his fathers is further illustrated by the derogatory term that he uses, *giudeo*, rather than *ebreo*.[62] His conversion, as political as it is religious, is marked by cutting ties to both communities.[63]

The ultimate reward for converting is that Aser and Alisa can finally be reunited. Until now, not only have Aser's travels kept the two apart, but his Jewishness, kept a secret from Alisa, presents an insurmountable obstacle, and assimilation through intermarriage was not a solution that Bresciani condoned. Aser travels to Schwyz, Switzerland, where he receives a letter from Mimo, whom he immediately writes describing his fall and his rescue.[64] He includes a note to Alisa in which he finally reveals the mystery behind his former identity: "Will you forgive me, Alisa, if I confess that, besides being a Jew by birth, I was an impious enemy of God?"[65] The letter is the written equivalent to the confession he gave the priest who converted him, and his newly discovered faith prompts his newfound mobility. Alisa takes Aser's conversion as a sign of redemption, and this understanding is reinforced by the fact that Aser's name spelled backward creates the word "resa," or surrender. Attaching such meaning to Aser's name suggests that he has finally submitted to the will of God with his conversion and that he has been destined to do so. By intimating that Aser was destined to convert, Bresciani puts forth his belief that it is Italy's destiny to be a Catholic nation, under the leadership and guidance of the pope.[66] Before reuniting with Alisa, Aser visits the local *carbonari* to tell them of his decision to reject fighting and abandon the cause of the secret societies. The carbonari view Aser's change of heart as a political liability and a religious betrayal, and Aser's former comrades stab him to death. The military hero thus dies the most honorable of Christian deaths: that of a Christian martyr.

The other revolutionary significant to the theme of movement is Polissena, who at the beginning of Bresciani's novel poses as a governess and is hired to be Alisa's tutor. In actuality, however, she is an undercover revolutionary, completely dedicated to the revolution and to converting people to that cause. In an attempt to convince her ward to join the cause, she lectures Alisa on the need for unification and on the evils of the clergy. She even goes so far as to replace the girl's pious books with political novels that support the revolution. Indeed, if Aser represents the Mazzinian hero-poet with his military prowess and artistic ability, Polissena exhibits the romantic sentiments of Mazzinian ideology that Bresciani blamed for corrupting the Catholic youth of Italy.[67] Polissena's manipulative actions, even her use of dangerously persuasive literature, have no effect on the incorruptible Alisa. The young heroine escapes entrapment from liberal ideology by preserving "unbroken in her heart the good dispositions, which had been engraven there by the religious education of her childhood."[68]

As a revolutionary, Polissena is responsible for dispersing information. She acts as a messenger for revolutionary groups, passing messages and traveling the peninsula to deliver them. The messages are written on silk and carried in her corset so they make no noise and remain completely hidden. As a carrier of hidden messages, Polissena's own body becomes likened to the cash value generally associated with the postage of a letter. That is, the association of Polissena's body as a subversive means of circulating letters cheapens her identity with its suggestion that her body replaces the need for a postage stamp.[69] The correlation of Polissena's body with money and the suggestion that the female revolutionary sells herself by willingly transporting secret notes are not the only means by which Bresciani hints at Polissena's moral corruption. Her letters are hidden by her body, but in order to retrieve them, Polissena must somehow undress herself, thus rendering her exposed and indecent. With this imagery, Bresciani implies that the political woman resorts to the immodesty and lewdness of a kept woman, whose body, readily uncovered, also has a monetary value. Indeed, the contrast between the politically savvy Polissena and the naïve, apolitical Alisa is stressed again at the novel's end when Alisa receives a letter—her only letter in the novel—from Aser. Displaying proper manners for a woman of her position, and in harsh contrast to Polissena, Alisa asks her father's permission before she opens it. In contrast to this propriety is Polissena's indecent portrayal, directly linked to her role as messenger and spy for the secret societies. Polissena's dexterity at transporting messages again points to Bresciani's fear at the success of the revolutionaries' prowess in communication. In the nineteenth century, governments considered a unified postal system a sign of national control, authority and organization;[70] Polissena challenges this authority with her alternative methods and successes.

With the revolt in Austria, and the subsequent rebellion in Lombardy, Polissena drops her façade as a governess, puts on a soldier's uniform, and abandons her charge, leaving a note for Alisa in which she explains that she is leaving to fight for the unification of Italy: "My country calls me, and I respond to her call. . . . Whoever has the heart of an Italian can never remain in inactivity; and while the heroic sons of Italy face the perils of battle, it is an indelible disgrace to remain home in luxury." Polissena accuses Alisa of bigotry and a lack of patriotism: "I wished to make you valiant, classical, heroic—in a word, *Italian*—and you have issued from my hands an insipid and despicable votary of superstition."[71] Bresciani's use of italics to emphasize the word "Italian" mocks the nationalist impulses that drive Polissena to violence in the name of the *patria* and against the express wishes of the pope. In addition, the note exposes Polissena's identity for the first time, but her perfidy is only discovered when Bartolo searches her closet. He discovers a number of burnt letters, upon which is written "We will rid the world of monks, priests, and cardin." And on another piece were the words "Protestant . . . Rome, free and happy."[72] The burnt notes are not meant for Bartolo's eyes; indeed, it is the only one of Polissena's secret correspondences that we, as third-hand readers, catch a glimpse of either. Secrecy vies with the confessional as Polissena's sacrilegious letter remains partly accessible. Exposing the readable parts of the letter exposes Polissena for the revolutionary she is, empowering the reader and the Church.

The confessional nature of these notes is reiterated in a letter Polissena writes her sister, telling of her decision to join the fighting for Italy's war of independence. As one might expect, Ombellina, a nun, rebukes her sister for the violence of her desires and advises her to try to reform herself rather than others. Bresciani views Polissena's decision to write her sister as a sign of a hidden admiration for her sister's piety, particularly because she knows that she will meet with disapproval: "Polissena, always deaf to the invitations of Ombellina, yet opened her heart to her with sincerity and candor on many occasions, informing her faithfully even of those acts which would draw upon her the just reproof of her sister."[73] Bresciani himself thus understands Polissena's letter to be read confessionally. Thus, like those of Aser, Polissena's letters appear to graduate from seditious pieces of information to a more genuine confession, foreshadowing Polissena's conversion to Catholicism. After being mortally wounded in battle, the atheist begins to feel remorse for her actions. She passes on a letter of confession and apology to Mimo, Alisa's cousin, who discovers her shortly before she dies. As she dies, Polissena recites the Ave Maria, and with these words she returns to Catholicism. Her body serves no longer as a conduit of revolutionary activity but as a reservoir of faith. Thus, like Aser, Polissena's letters are a transmission of herself. Her early letters are angry, disrespectful, and rebellious, reflecting her inner impiety. Her last letter, in contrast, is confessional and remorseful. Thus, the letter itself has changed within Bresciani's novel, moving from being a tool of the revolutionary to being a tool of the believer.

Polissena is not the only one to be caught up in the revolutionary fervor; when accounts of the Lombardy rebellion reach the ears of the Roman populace, throngs of men and boys throw their support behind the revolutionaries and enlist. As a Vatican supporter, Bresciani viewed this latest development particularly harshly, interpreting it as the kidnapping of the youth of Italy. Thus he describes mothers abandoned by their sons because of the tempters—that is, revolutionaries—who persuade their sons to take up arms. As Bresciani's narrator pointedly exclaims, "The Sovereign Pontiff, with the eye of a watchful father, saw clearly that the impious were wounding the most sensitive point of the glory of Rome. The hearts of his beloved and ingenuous youth were robbed of the precious treasures of piety and virtue. He wept over the scene, and exclaimed: 'Ah! They are robbing me of my young children!'"[74] While Polissena does not succeed in her efforts to corrupt Alisa, Italy's other children, representatives of the next generation, succumb to the propaganda that the liberal press and the revolutionaries spread.

The family of Bartolo and Alisa does not go untouched by this wave of patriotism; Alisa's two cousins, Mimo and Lando, join the Civic Guard, leaving their mother fainting with grief. Their mother, Alisa's aunt, tells Alisa of their military training, how they socialize with rough-looking young men, and their disrespect toward their elders. These impetuous young men curse, read inappropriate journals, and worst of all are no longer interested in attending Church. In other words, the military does not simply take the country's children—it de-Catholicizes them. The tension between the old generation and the new is not an unusual topic in the nineteenth-century novel. Manzoni's Renzo's ties to his past, even if he does not completely reject the values of the elder generation, loosen when he is orphaned and are further cut when he is forced to leave Lecco for Milan. In the throes of their militaristic fervor, Lando and Mimo are no different: there is a pervasive tension between that which this new generation wishes to do and what the Risorgimento seeks from them, and that which the older generation and the Church wish for their future. The Civic Guard represents yet another manifestation of modern nationhood: Mimo and Lando unite with men and boys of other classes and areas of Italy; the army provides a shared experience and memory, and it provides a chance to travel the nation.

Readers are reminded of this national geography every time Bartolo receives a letter from Lando: his first action is to look at the postmark and see where the letter originates. In so doing, he inadvertently writes a map of a larger Italy. Bresciani, however, counters this map with one of his own: when he cites the numerous letters of support the pope has received in exile, he names specific places the world over from which they have come. Indeed, in his desire to prove the authenticity of these letters, Bresciani reminds readers in a footnote that the letters have all been published in *Civiltà Cattolica*, the same journal that publishes *EV*. In so doing, he writes a geography of Christendom whose heart is in Italy and that reimagines the boundaries of the modern world according to the Catholic vision.

Bresciani, who maintained great disdain for the lower classes and who advocated the hierarchical system associated with the Old Order, clearly found the Civic Guard, and the enthusiasm with which many joined it, to be a problematic and threatening manifestation of the Italian Risorgimento. He relays the tension between the revolutionaries and the young generation on the one hand, and the Church and the family elders on the other when the boys leave Rome for battle: "The two young men, whose hearts had been hardened by the crafty and seditious conspirators, replied harshly to their uncle [Bartolo]. They were determined to go; their country was more holy than the weaknesses of a mother."[75] Thus the sons break from their family and the values of an old era to join up with the new, sealing, at least for now, their change in faith from practicing Catholicism to secular patriotism.

Mimo and Lando's separation from the Church and the values of the old era is short-lived. Shortly after they leave to fight for the unification of Italy, Bartolo receives a letter from Lando in which the young man begs forgiveness from his elders for acting so disrespectfully: "Yes, my dear uncle, on my knees I beg that you will forgive me. Believe me, I had not even passed through the Porta del Popolo before remorse for the disrespect with which I had treated you tore my heart. . . . The image of my mother was ever before my eyes; I could see her falling insensible, I heard her sighs, and, oh! How I longed to press her to my heart, and wipe away the sweat of death."[76] Thus the youthful enthusiasm for revolution that led Mimo and Lando to join the Civic Guard is countered by the boys' later repentance for their brash acts and their decision to leave the army and return home. Such apologies could not be any further from the traditional *Bildungsroman*, in which the young man breaks with the older generation by leaving home and never turning back.[77] When Lando and Mimo return home to their mother, repentant of their former actions and filled with renewed piety and respect for their elders, Bresciani's fears that the military service of the Risorgimento will kidnap the youth of Catholic Italy are literally reversed.

On his travels with the Civic Guard, in a fantastical twist of fate, Mimo stumbles upon the dying Polissena. After asking for his forgiveness, Polissena makes Mimo swear that he too will renounce any allegiance to the secret societies. With her conversion of Mimo the newly reformed Polissena proves the sincerity of her own conversion. Mimo writes Bartolo, his uncle, to tell him of the dramatic change that Polissena underwent before dying and his own promise to leave the Civic Guard. The letter, however, is somehow misplaced, and thus the information Mimo relays does not reach its intended readers for quite some time.

Bartolo only hears the news secondhand, in a letter he receives from Mimo's brother Lando, who describes Polissena's death: "What a beautiful end!" writes Lando, "How God touched her heart! How passionately the poor creature longed to confess her sins! How fortunate to die, as she did, the death of a Christian and a heroine!"[78] Eager to read Mimo's description of the events he witnessed firsthand, Bartolo goes to the post office, where the clerk eventually discovers the misplaced letter. Reading as he leaves the post office, Bartolo is so moved at the story of Polissena's contrition and religious ardor that he bursts into tears. The story of Lando's letter is not simply a demonstration of the power of words and the need for information to flow; Bresciani goes to great lengths to describe the letter, and Bartolo's anxiety results from the possibility of having lost it.

Thus two different kinds of movement appear in Bresciani's novel. The revolutionaries, with their money and their internal communications, differ from the persons of the pope, his clergymen, and his followers, figures who are destined to be stationary and forever positioned in the Eternal City but are nonetheless forced to flee their geographic home. Rather than representing letters of intrigue and murder, the letters of this second group are letters of repentance, confessions. Bresciani thus uses his letters to challenge the generally accepted use of the post as a revolutionary tool of communication. In this sense, writing parallels life: Aser, Ciceruacchio, and Polissena all die, but Polissena and Aser die as repentance for their earlier sins. Their deaths depict a religious martyrdom, a conversion from the political crucifixion that Bresciani deemed appropriate for those who remained secular revolutionaries. Ciceruacchio, the nonconvert, is also killed; in effect, death ends the movement of his body, and with it destroys a symbol of the new nation. Indeed, his death is not mentioned in the novel precisely because doing so would be to remember him as a martyr, rather than those who died as faithful Catholics. By introducing the second kind of letters into circulation, Bresciani illuminates the need for an established social order; he redefines the sanctity of the letter such that it inspires piety and even martyrdom rather than revolution.

Bresciani attempts to show that the circulation of bodies, letters, and money is proof of the problems of modern statehood rather than an example of its benefits. Lando and Mimo enter into this world of circulation when they join the Civic Guard. Aser, Polissena, Ciceruacchio, and other revolutionaries are blamed for the destruction of the nation (not to mention Christian morality) with their alliance to the secret societies. Through their physical bodies, by means of subterfuge and disguises, with money and their own network of *logge*, the revolutionaries are able to convey their messages across Europe. While the populace might not have been aware of these intrigues, they are subject to yet a different kind of circulation: that of the secular press. Letter writing and the press are not unconnected. As Bernhard Siegert notes, the invention of the printing press "unfolded the paper again and relegated the future distinction between 'public' and 'private' to the realm of the text, which was no longer divided into parchment and paper, but instead into typography and chirography."[79] Siegert here refers to the impact of the Gutenberg press on writing. I would argue that the growing circulation of the printed word in journals bore similar effects. That is, with the spread of information, the distinction between public and private changed dramatically, as did the control of information that reached the public and what slant the stories took. The uncontrolled flow led to a democratization of discourse that Bresciani, a supporter of the hierarchical Old Order, sought to monitor and restrain.

The privacy of Polissena and Aser's communications, their success at passing on their messages and at overwhelming the post office, and the link between revolutionaries and the telegraph, all identified the power of control with the revolutionaries. Their control extended further when they won the populace to their cause by means of liberal newspapers that espoused their ideals. Bresciani changes the aim of the privacy that letters engender with the confessions that Aser and Polissena send to their loved ones; he then sends his own cross-border letters to demonstrate the power and possibility that the Vatican and propapal supporters have in using what had been a weapon of the revolutionaries. Similarly, he fights the democratization of discourse by concentrating for the first time on his own ability to produce compelling discourse for the populace, rather than focusing on limiting the spread of the news that others produced.

In Chapter 27, entitled "Gossip and Falsehood," the narrator addresses his readers directly and describes how liberty has "poured forth paper enough to cover the walls of the Vatican."[80] Those responsible for the torrent of gossip that advocates revolution are, above all, newspaper editors. As Bresciani writes, "Those who had obtained the royal patent for gossip and falsehood in the cause of the Italian war were the newspaper editors. Why, of course, the Press!"[81] Bresciani's invective does not end there; he goes on to suggest that the liberal newspapers are conspiring together against the Vatican, and he specifically names the *Contemporaneo, Bilancia, Epoca*, and *Speranza* as transmitting Mazzini's orders to the general public.[82] The problematic circulation and growing readership of liberal newspapers is countered by the establishment of the Vatican-approved *Civiltà Cattolica*, which gave Bresciani the possibility of countering the romantic, secular novels of the Risorgimento with his own Catholic novel of conversion, repentance, and faith as the bonding features of a modern Italian nation. In so doing, he suggests that the Vatican should impose a Christian history, culture, and even memory on the peninsula to enforce a unity wholly based on religion. These views are made explicit in the introductory note to the first issue of the *Civiltà Cattolica*, when editor-in-chief Carlo Curci writes: "It is by this time an irrefutable fact that other than European there is no civilization in the world, and in Europe, civilization has been a Christian, Catholic, Roman work; a glance at the planisphere can convince anyone who has doubts about this: where Roman influence stops, one finds an insurmountable barrier to civilization, to the point that in Europe itself we have maintained two regions, one with everything, the other half savage, even today."[83]

Curci's words are striking for their reaffirmation of the close connection between Christianity—Catholicism to be more precise—and civilization. Indeed, for Curci, as for Bresciani, there was a causal relationship between Christianity and the civilized world: without the former, the latter would not exist. The logic of Curci's argument points to a belief in the need for Catholic hegemony that Bresciani, too, clearly advocates in his novel. Judaism is the root of anarchic revolution; Protestantism is the source of secular nation-hood; only Catholicism maintains the proper balance between government and society, and only if Catholicism is secure can the cohesion and morality of the Italian nation be ensured.

Part III

The Catholic Press

Chapter 5

Private Letters, Public Stories

From the De Joux Conversion(s) to the Mortara Affair

In November 1847, the Archbishop of Ferrara wrote the Holy Office of the Supreme Inquisition regarding a request he received to reprint an article that had appeared in a Roman newspaper, *l'Artigianello.* That the article had been printed at all scandalized the Ferrarese clergyman, and its title, "Jews Must Be Respected," with its jab at the state's anti-Jewish edicts, suggests why. Indeed, despite its initial publication, the Ferrarese Archbishop wrote that the piece "contains doctrines that are not only extremely dangerous but completely erroneous," and he recommended that the Inquisition Tribunal censor the story.[1] The incendiary article hinges upon a (fictional) dialogue between three characters: Antonio, a shopkeeper; Andreuccio, a shoemaker; and a parish priest. The topic of discussion is Pius IX's recent decision to open the Roman ghetto and to allow its inhabitants greater civil rights, including the freedom to live and work outside of the ghetto. About two and a half months after his first letter, on February 10, 1848, Ferrara's archbishop addressed a second letter to the Inquisition Tribunal in which he revealed that Bresciani's fears about the spread of the liberal press were not completely unfounded. The clergyman wrote to express his dismay that, despite the archbishop having acted to censor the *L'Artigianello* story in Ferrara, the article had appeared in the Bolognese newspaper *Il Povero* and was being distributed throughout the Papal States. Reiterating the stereotypes that Bresciani so often expressed, and perhaps indirectly criticizing Pius IX's latest "liberal" acts, the Ferrarese archbishop expressed his view that *Il Povero* managed to print the censored article because the journal was run by Jews: "[The newspaper] is completely controlled," he wrote, "edited, I believe, by Jews, and without my being able to intercept it, it has been circulated even here in public shops and cafes, to the great scandal of the virtuous."[2] The Jews were responsible not only for publishing the article but also for publicizing its contents within the Papal States—a seditious act in the eyes of Inquisition officials and evidence of their anti-Catholic sentiments.

What were the subversive contents of the article, and why was its distribution attributed to Jews? In the story, shopkeeper Antonio expresses his concern to Andreuccio the shoemaker that, with the relaxation of the anti-Jewish laws that regulated Jewish commerce, Jewish merchants would be able to undersell their Christian counterparts. A merchant himself, Antonio clearly feels threatened by the prospect of such competition, and thus voices typically anti-Semitic views of Jews as usurers and Christ killers. His reaction reflects the sentiment of many citizens and clergymen throughout the Papal States, who received the news of Pius IX's opening of the ghetto with hostility. In Rome, news of this legislation led some citizens to attack the ghetto in October 1848, at about the same time that the Archbishop of Ferrara was corresponding with the Inquisition Tribunal regarding the problematic news story.[3] Such reactions were hardly surprising, since papal legislation before Pius IX's declaration had been driven by a desire to limit, rather than expand, the economic and social ties between Jews and Christians. Furthermore, it should be noted that as part of the fallout from the revolutions of 1848, Pius himself reversed his liberal decree.

Acting as a foil to the conservative Antonio, the more liberal Andreuccio hesitates to brand the opening of the ghetto a threat to Christian society and suggests stopping a passing priest to ask his opinion. The suggestion in and of itself demonstrates a level of deference for the priest and the church he represents; his views surely must reflect the political and social sentiments initiated by the leader of the Catholic Church. The priest's views, however, surpass even those of the shoemaker in their liberalism; he lauds Pius's decision to give the Jews' greater freedom, suggesting that this act moves the Papal States closer to the revolutionary ideology of liberty, equality, and fraternity. Antonio's continued reluctance to welcome the opening of the ghettos spurs the priest to recount a story to prove that Jews threaten neither Catholic identity nor its practitioners. He narrates a parable of a Jewish Livornese merchant who employs a female Christian servant. The woman, now old and in poor health, has worked in the household for many years and has always attended Church regularly. It is a cold winter, but despite the merchant's worries about the woman's health, he does not prevent the servant from going to Church, fearing that she will misinterpret his objections as anti-Catholic. The merchant's foreboding proves to be justified: the woman falls deathly ill. Rather than abandon her, however, the merchant cares for her and asks a priest to hear her last confession, displaying loyalty to his servant and respect for her religious practices. The priest concludes his story with a lesson for his listeners (and the author's readers): "May this example make you generous," he intones, "and always remember that God wishes that we love each other as brothers."[4]

While the story is not viciously anti-Catholic, the reason for its censorship is clear: Antonio, who represents the oft-expressed views of reactionary Vatican supporters, is depicted as misinformed and bigoted. Instead of condoning his repressive views and urging policies of conversion or subjugation for papal Jews, the priest provides readers with a story that celebrates religious difference and makes a Jew the hero of the celebration. In this sense, the newspaper article represents a *non*conversion narrative. Unlike the stereotypes and accusations expressed in the conversion narratives we have examined thus far, the Jew of this story does nothing to corrupt, kidnap, or convert his servant. Indeed, the commercial and social interaction between the Jew and his Catholic servant enable the servant to maintain her high level of piety, and harm befalls the servant only when the Jew, fearing that his words will be misconstrued, holds himself back and does not speak of his concern for her health. Finally, the priest who narrates this parable never expresses disapproval or disgust for Judaism, nor does he display any desire that the Jew become Christian; instead he seeks to repair the reactionary misinterpretations that many Catholics have had against Jews. To this end, he defends the Jews from accusations of deicide by explaining that Jesus' death was predestined. And in his advocacy of equal rights, he suggests that despite the power structure between employer and employee, the Jewish employer encourages, rather than threatens, the religious identity of his Catholic servant. Most significantly, by placing a Jew as the hero in his parable of ethical behavior, the priest suggests that the boundaries that have kept Jews separate from general society are unnecessary; brotherly love and mutual respect should define the relationship between the two communities. One has only to think of Aser's converter or the rector of the Catechumens in the Labani and Cavalieri affairs to realize the radical nature of these ideas of religious diversity and equality within the Papal States. Thus, not only does the story fail to advocate conversion, it promotes a society in which Catholicism does not occupy a hegemonic position as the religion that all citizens of the Papal States must practice.

The story is significant not only because of the absence of any reference to a conversion theme but also because the letters that passed between Vatican officials regarding the news article provide an important subtext to the narrative. The archbishop's frustration, his failed attempts at censorship, and his anti-Semitic views indicate that the communications revolution, even within the Papal States, was becoming difficult to control and that Jews were largely viewed as responsible for this development. In addition, the letters provide a view of how the Vatican reacted to a tool that Church critics used so handily. As we saw in the previous chapter, Pope Pius IX heralded the establishment of *Civiltà Cattolica* as a means of using the power of journalism to combat the secular, liberal forces that had previously employed it so effectively. While printed materials created a different language of power than that of the courtroom, the Vatican felt it had to counter the voices of the liberal press precisely because of the power these forces discovered with the growing circulation of printed materials. To this end, Catholic journals not only printed fictional conversion narratives such as Bresciani's *L'Ebreo di Verona*, they also reported "real" conversion stories that proved the victory of Catholicism and countered the liberal equality championed in nonconversion narratives such as the *Il Povero* story. In this sense, the Ferrarese archbishop's letters, which brought the Inquisition Tribunal's attention to this article, contributed to a more general Vatican belief that secular narratives had to be countered with stories that endorsed Catholic identity.

In this final chapter I examine conversion narratives published in the Catholic press from the 1820s through the 1850s. In particular, I explore how journalism became a venue that Vatican supporters and Catholic reactionaries used in their fight to maintain the Catholic identity of the modernizing Italian peninsula. The confidential letters that surround the publication of these stories, like those of the Ferrarese archbishop, provide an essential commentary on the news articles to which they refer. Often they provide the kernel for the Catholic version of a controversial conversion, or for a news article that counters anti-Catholic—and, often, anticonversion—stories of the secular press. Consequently, the influence of such letters in shaping newspaper stories is inestimable. In the first half of the nineteenth century, these letters and conversion stories pertained to conversionary experiences of both Jews and Protestants. As we will see, however, the parallel worlds of publication and private correspondence are employed very differently in Protestant and Jewish conversion stories. That is, while both types of stories rely on confidential letters as the base of their writing, as a genre, Protestant conversion stories are either reports on a conversion *en masse* of a large group, or, if they are the story of a single conversion, are generally short, factual, and based on "real" letters that the converts themselves write. Stories of the former echo the group conversions of pagans to Christianity in early Christian centuries, and suggest a conversionary experience as a "gradual collective transformation."[5] The latter letters are published as proof of the writer's newfound convictions and as a means to show the triumph of the Catholic Church over the divisiveness first initiated by the Protestant Reformation.

In contrast to these factual write-ups, Jewish conversion stories are more suspenseful dramas that become as much rooted in the imagination of the writer as in the history of the convert. Never do they entail a group conversion, as the narrative does not—nor does the writer wish it to—denote a gradual transformation. Rather, the individual Jew had to reject the Jewish community to enter the Christian community. This conversion was marked physically by a transferral outside the ghetto and psychologically by the fact that the Catholic communities of the Papal States largely defined themselves in contrast to the Jewish community in their midst. In so doing, not only did the Catholic Church's adherents suggest that Jewish converts were in some sense more prized than their Protestant counterparts; such stories also resonate with a distrust toward those who have suddenly switched sides, with the text acting as a means to make the conversion more concrete and more real, even if the text of the story is itself fabricated or inflated. Evidence of this suspicion can be seen by the very type of story that recounts a Jewish conversion in Catholic newspapers. That is, the story is not simply a letter the author addresses to his reader; it is an embellished, fictionalized story that Catholic journalists, editors, and Catholic officials work together to produce. Thus, as we see here, letters do not play a prominent role within the published article; instead, they are a fundamental component of the behind-the-scenes communications that help develop and shape the public conversion stories and articles of the Catholic press. By examining the private correspondence of papal leaders in conjunction with the news stories the Catholic press produced, we see first how private information translated into public articulation, and second how fundamental concerns over power and the struggle for public opinion defined the Catholic press's treatment of its subjects and its citizens.

As early as the 1820s, the Catholic press in Italy regularly published stories about individuals who converted from Protestantism or Judaism to Catholicism. Like Bresciani's and Manzoni's novels, these stories sought to depict Catholicism as a moral, unifying force. Catholic clergymen and journalists exploited the narrative form of the newspaper to aid in the Vatican's battle to promote an identity that is both culturally and religiously Catholic.[6] Robert Weisberg notes, "The desire to narrate is the desire to represent authority, whose legitimacy depends on establishing certain grounding facts."[7] The Vatican's desire to narrate—through trials, novels and, as we will see in this chapter, newspapers—was precisely this: an attempt to project an image of Catholicism as religiously and politically dominant in an era when its actual authority was severely weakened. To reflect this dominance, the conversion stories related in newspapers involved individuals from a variety of places, from nearby Italian towns to distant cities in North America, the wide geographical range revealing papal visions of worldwide (and peninsular) conquest. Stories of Protestant converts were meant to show Catholic supremacy over the discord originally sown by the Protestant Reformation, and they often included letters the converts had written on the subject. Stories detailing Jewish conversions were meant to reflect victory over the heretical revolutionaries of modern times, and they often included highly dramatized accounts of the conversionary moment. Internal letters regarding conversion stories from both religions regularly passed through Vatican hands as the Catholic press published its articles, providing a diplomatic and political subtext to conversion narratives that illuminates the Vatican's perception of its battle against heretics, revolution, and the secularization of the new era.

In 1826, for example, a journalist for the *Memorie di religione di morale e di letteratura* narrated the conversion of the well-known political minister Pietro De Joux, a story that was reprinted in the *Giornale degli apologisti della religione cattolica*. De Joux, an inhabitant of Geneva, and formally the president of the Concistory of Nantes, traveled extensively in Catholic Europe and finally converted on October 11, 1823 in Paris, where he wrote a letter explaining his conversion. This letter became a central component of numerous news stories that reported on his conversion. In the *Memorie*, De Joux described the political events that produced his change of beliefs: "I was convinced that the spirit of Protestantism, essentially a friend of new events, independence, and freedom of opinions with regard to faith and government, produced the French Revolution, the most vast system of destruction of the social order that ever occurred in the frightened world, from which an inaudible competition of circumstances, marked by the hand of God, was the only thing that could liberate us."[8]

De Joux's words perpetuated the newspaper's Catholic ideology by encouraging a view of Catholicism as a unifying, moral alternative to the fracture of revolution and the individualism that Protestantism promoted. Furthermore, the fact of De Joux's explicit link between his religious conversion and political developments in Europe emphasized the connection that Vatican supporters maintained between religious and political identity. That is, through conversion, not only did De Joux support the religious ideology of the Catholic Church with his condemnation of the destructive force of the French Revolution, but he, like most Vatican supporters, condoned the politics of the Old Regime. Thus his words suggested a national vision in which conversion to Catholicism and a return to the Old Order are presented as interdependent and intertwined issues.

In conjunction with excerpts of De Joux's letter, the writer reporting his conversion story explained that Protestant converts to Catholicism, more frequent and more important than those from other religions, were a great comfort to the Catholic Church. It was an end, the journalist concluded, to the grievances produced by the Reformation, when Catholics suffered from "the ungrateful defections that have torn so many children from her breast for the past three centuries."[9] Like Bresciani, Manzoni, and the Inquisition officials that directed the Labani and Cavalieri trials, the pervasive imagery is one of Catholic youth, the next generation of leaders, who are being denied their right to be raised within the arms of the Church. With these words, the journalist reaffirms the Catholic community that De Joux had lauded so unquestionably in his letter. In so doing, both writers, De Joux and the journalist, exhort their readers to share the same ideology, to become members of the Catholic "civilization" they together extol.

De Joux's conversion resulted in the conversion of various family members, including his daughter. She too wrote a letter explaining her motives for conversion, which appeared in a later volume of both the *Giornale* and the *Memorie*.[10] Thus the young De Joux, like her newly converted father, was able to espouse her pro-Vatican beliefs and emphasize the differences between Catholicism and Protestantism to both a private audience—her sister, to whom the letter is addressed—and to a public audience, the readers of the journal that published her letter. This rendering public of a private letter reflected the accessibility and clarity of the convert's newfound personal beliefs, further illuminating the positive qualities of the Catholic community and its adherents. In addition, in the letter that De Joux's daughter pens, the young woman—with her father undoubtedly in mind—alludes to the inspiration of other converts. That she attributes her decision to convert in part to the letters of other converts not only emphasizes the genuineness of their conversions but marks her letter as a part of this process, a contribution to future conversions. The author's conversion thus becomes more complete, since, by voicing her hope that her letter will in turn lead others to change their religious practice, the convert defines herself as a would-be converter, proof of the authenticity of her newfound religious beliefs.

With regard to the reasons for her conversion to Catholicism, the younger De Joux provides readers with two criticisms of Protestantism: its lack of history, and hence, presumably, the authority and authenticity of Catholicism, and the infighting among many practitioners "regarding various subjects of their religion."[11] She takes issue with both the very foundations of Protestantism and the religion in its present conception as well, making two statements clearly in step with the beliefs of Vatican supporters. In his novel, Bresciani openly echoes these beliefs regarding the fractious nature of Protestantism when he writes that Romans saw the divine and human power of religious and civil authority "annihilated by a frenzy of political and moral liberty, the bitter fruit of the Protestant principle of *private authority*," the private nature of which, Bresciani ultimately concludes, led to anger, rebellion and revolution.[12] These beliefs are reiterated decades later in an article on Protestantism that appeared in *L'Araldo*, another Catholic newspaper, in which the writer expresses his antipathy for Protestantism: "[Protestantism] devastated horribly the order established for so many centuries. And is that a good or an evil? Scholars demonstrate it to be the gravest evil, since to place faith under the state is truly to lie."[13] The Catholic press thus sought to demonstrate how Catholicism was essential to societal order by portraying the Catholic Church as "truly liberal, conservative, great, sublime, glorious . . . the reflection of the spirit of God" in the face of a "sectarian spirit [that] was pagan, Voltairian, and consequently arbitrary, crazy, violent, tyrannical, destructive, mean-spirited, base, shameful."[14] The belief that Catholicism provided a unified, incorruptible presence was contrasted with the present era of turmoil, which many Catholic supporters believed began with the Protestant Reformation.

The Protestant convert Carl Ludwig von Haller exemplifies these sentiments in a letter to his family, in which he announces and explains his reasons for converting: "The world is divided between Christians united around the common center of the seat of Saint Peter on the one hand, and the evils and anti-Christian laws on the other. These two sides alone fight one another because they are the only ones organized."[15] That Haller's letter reached a large audience is proven by the reactionary writers who turn to it in their discussions of Catholicism and Protestantism. Bresciani, for example, cites Haller's letter in *L'Ebreo di Verona* in his denunciation of the secret societies: "Note what Haller declares in his letter to his family, 'The organization of the secret societies gave me a presentiment of the Catholic religion long before I embraced or even studied it.'"[16] By specifying that Haller's letter is directed to his family, Bresciani emphasizes its intimate nature; by sharing these ideas with his audience, however, and thus turning that which was private public, he applies the convert's words regarding the Protestant and Catholic communities to a more general understanding of the ideologies of these respective religions.

It appears from Haller's letter that the author himself knew that his conversion would be a matter of public discussion and speculation: "From my private discourses, and from public voices, you must have become aware of my inclination towards the Catholic Religion . . . no one forced me, and I was not pressed into it by anyone; it is the natural result of a good heart, healthy reasoning, and of the particular grace of God."[17] With these words Haller addresses both a private and a public audience and immediately sets out to counter any thoughts that he might have been coerced into converting. That his first words regarding his conversion reflect its noncoercive nature is also noteworthy. As we saw in the trial narratives of earlier chapters, one of the greatest fears of the Catholic Church was to be accused of forcibly converting individuals; genuine conviction had to accompany a convert's entry into Catholic society or the well-being of that society was at risk. In addition, like the De Joux family's conversion letters, Haller's words act as an instrument, circulated from one reader to the next, that sought to develop the opinions of his readership.[18] By possessing Haller's text, the reader absorbs his words and his ideas, enabling the circulation of Haller's words to become a means of shaping the minds of the public to whom they were directed.

Also similar to the De Joux father and daughter, Haller used his confessional letter to expound upon the ideological problems of Protestantism and how Catholic practice resolved these issues. Thus, for example, he explained how barren Protestantism was as a religion, and how, when speaking with Catholic clergymen, "I could not not admire their spirit of charity, their resignation in the midst of all the offences, and I dare to say it again, their enlightenment and profound knowledge."[19] The enlightenment of the clergy thus replaced the Age of Enlightenment ideals, and Haller's words echoed earlier texts we have examined: the charity of the clergy, the reasonable doctrine of the Catholic Church, and the wisdom of its leaders. Similarly, in an open letter that Antonio Ulrico, duke of Brunswich and Luneburg, published upon his conversion from Protestantism to Catholicism, the convert discusses his decision to convert as evidence that the Catholic Church was the only place where true justice reigns: "The Catholic [religion] seems to me at first sight the true one, since she is professed by the entire world, and preserves the nature of her unity; whereas the evangelical religion generates in me vigorous doubts regarding its veracity."[20] Again, the predominant idea was a vision of Catholic unity in contrast to the Protestant splintering connected to the Revolution. Upon concluding this conversion story, the author, like many Catholic journalists, concludes by emphasizing the dominance and justness of the Catholic Church and by naming family members who had been inspired to convert as well. In this case, Ulrico's return to the Church, and his arguments, led to the conversion of his daughter.[21]

Like the letters of conversion that Bresciani created for his characters, the accessibility of the letters of Protestant converts enables the Catholic press's reading public, through the act of reading, to participate in the conversionary act of the letter writer. That is, these letters serve as connective tissue between the letter writer, the addressee of the letter, and finally the reading public, who, by means of the journalist-narrator, can celebrate the conversion in a public forum. Thus the De Joux letters, like those of other Protestant converts, lend an intimate and personal tone to the articles that include them, while the journalist's narrative further empowers their words. Janet Altman notes that letters define themselves "in terms of polarities such as portrait/mask, presence/absence, bridge/barrier. These polarities guarantee the letter's . . . recognizable dimensions of thematic emphasis and narrative potential."[22] By allowing the public to read these letters, the journalist and the letter writer empower expressions of belief that celebrate the unity and authority of Catholic identity. Furthermore, by presenting these ideas in the form of a letter from the convert himself, the journal permits the reader a glimpse at private revelation. For example, in Pietro De Joux's letter, readers learn of his thought process as he begins to reject Protestantism. In this sense, the use of the letter as personal testimony lends it a persuasive character that other types of writing might not have. And finally, that which Altman refers to as "narrative potential" defines the ease with which letter writing and reading, both acts that revolve around possessing the text, empower the rhetoric and ideology expressed in the letter and elucidates their use in the Catholic press.

This confessional quality is particularly significant if one considers the history behind confession. Peter Brooks notes that confession was linked to the ecclesiastical courts and the Holy See's increased efforts, which began as early as the Fourth Lateran Council of 1215, to fight heresy. To this end, the Catholic Church developed a doctrine within which the heretic was obliged to admit to his heresy in order to save his soul and preserve the purity of the Church.[23] The journalistic confessions of converts such as De Joux function in a similar manner: first the convert speaks of the falseness of the religion he had previously practiced, and then he describes the truths of Catholicism and the ideology of the Catholic Church that convinced him to convert. Early confessions took place in front of judges and the larger community. Similarly, when private letters of confession are published—and thus publicized—conversion stories such as that of De Joux occur within a private sphere as well as before the public community. Access to such private letters on a large scale emphasizes to readers of the Catholic press a sense of the community that they represented. As Benedict Anderson notes, the act of newspaper reading on a wide scale links together members of one community. The simultaneity of such reading, he writes, serves as reassurance that "the imagined world is visibly rooted in everyday life." Print—that is, writing set up for mass consumption—he continues, becomes a means for "linking fraternity, power and time meaningfully together."[24] Through its visual and textual power, and through the shared act of reading, newspapers thus define a sense of community. I would submit that the publication of conversion letters functions within this framework. That is, not only did the Vatican ensure that the new convert sealed his membership in his newly adopted community by allowing, indeed encouraging, conversion letters to be published; by reading these letters, society defined itself through the conversionary act of the writer. That conversionary acts appeared regularly within the press further empowered Catholic identity by repeatedly linking together the community with the fraternity inherent in a shared religious experience.

Aside from encouraging Catholic identity to both a private and public audience, letters from new converts provided Catholic writers and editors with the means to depict Protestant conversions to Catholicism as numerous and ever increasing. In so doing, they reflected Catholic leaders' efforts to persuade their readers of the possibility of a Christian unification that went beyond the borders of the peninsula—the ultimate response to revolution and the Italian unification movement. This desire for the unification of Christendom was still expressed as late as the 1850s, after many European countries had established more liberal governments and minority religions had received civil and political rights. Particularly striking was a report on England and the allegedly overwhelming number of conversions occurring in this Protestant country: "By now Protestantism turns to its end in England. . . . This is not our imagination deprived of any foundation, but it is a truth that results clearly from the facts. . . . England is the queen of the seas; her conversion will be the conversion of the world, the triumph of the Church."[25] The Irish potato famine of 1845 had indeed resulted in the emigration of the greatest number of Irish Catholics to England in the nineteenth century; nonetheless, British Catholics remained a small, relatively unprivileged minority.[26] Despite these facts, however, Church supporters still spoke of converting Protestants and of winning back the countries who had defied the Catholic Church centuries earlier by turning to Luther and the Protestant Reformation.

In his ironically entitled work *Le Bellezze del Protestantismo proposte alle gioie degli italiani*, published in 1876, Father Antonino Maria Di Jorio cites extensively from several letters Haller wrote regarding his conversion. That which Di Jorio appreciated most was the convert's belief that society and religion were inseparable. To this end he cited one letter in which Haller wrote that the aftermath of the French Revolution had produced the moment of greatest crisis ever to occur and that it had persuaded him to convert. Not only did such upheaval inspire Haller's conversion, but the new convert, much to Di Jorio's delight, reported that the political upheaval of the nineteenth century initiated many conversions: "Conversions have never been so frequent and as bright as ours. You will see much more notable examples than mine, and I could cite some of them to you, from sovereign princes and scholars of this world to workers, even to Protestant ministers."[27] Like the newspaper story that suggested the conversion of all of England, Haller's comments suggested Catholic victory and continuity as a result of the upheaval of revolution. In sum, he suggested that many Europeans welcomed a society in which Catholic leaders maintained both temporal and religious power over a citizenry unified by Catholic ideology.

Underlying these triumphant views of Catholicism, however, was a fear that Protestantism was gaining popularity universally and might even spread to the Italian peninsula. The possibility of Protestantism being practiced at the heart of Catholic territory appeared to be a real, albeit unjustified, fear of many Vatican leaders. Gioachino Ventura, another Catholic intellectual, went so far as to define Catholicism as the defining aspect of Italian identity. To this end, he reasoned that if Protestantism were to take root even in part of Italy, the country would lose its sense of nationality. As he explained, "Without Catholicism, one would already have been speaking the French or German language, from the Alps to Cape Lilibeo, for a long time."[28] Instead, Ventura gave Catholicism the responsibility of introducing "well-intended" liberty into Europe—presumably ill-intended liberty was that which Protestants, Jews, and atheists fomented: "Correctly understood, modern liberty is the daughter of Catholicism and the Church. That is, under their influence the various political constitutions of all of the European states were formed."[29] That true liberty could only be found within the Church was a view often espoused by Vatican leaders. Here, however, Ventura went one step further: he attested to the political contribution of Catholicism, both as a unifying cultural force on the peninsula and as that which should be the driving force behind modernizing political governments elsewhere in Europe. To claim responsibility for such modernization enabled him to denounce the powers of Protestantism in the modernization of such countries as England, France and Germany, further emphasizing Catholicism as the true Christianity and empowering the Vatican as an Italian and pan-European leader.

His fearful suggestion that Protestantism would ruin the foundation of Italian society reflected the principal motivation behind the publication of Protestant conversion stories as well. That is, while Ventura alluded to this fear in a published work, Vatican officials countered the widely perceived threat of the spread of Protestantism with conversion stories that argued the opposite, namely that numerous conversions *to* Catholicism were a happy reality. The subject was, however, discussed at length in the private letters that passed between Vatican clergymen and leaders. Thus, while the letters of Protestant converts proving Catholic hegemony and the weakening of Protestantism were being published, very different letters were arriving at the Vatican regarding the matter of Protestant belief, particularly in Northern Europe. Indeed, a striking disparity distinguishes the journalistic representations of the victory of Catholicism and the reports that were arriving from the Vatican's representatives abroad. For example, a report delivered to Pope Gregory XVI, entitled *Nota sullo stato attuale della religione Cattolica nella Germania Centrale*, suggested that Catholicism was losing its popularity dramatically in the regions of Bavaria, Prussia, and Saxony. In Bavaria, the Protestant population was negligible at the turn of the century, but by the time this report was written, Protestants represented a significant portion of the population, with ever more Protestants arriving because of newly constructed Protestant churches; in Prussia, the number of Catholics was small, and they were persecuted by the local populace, compelling many of them to convert to Protestantism; and in Saxony, despite the presence of a Catholic king, the local population was almost completely Protestant, and, the report concluded, there was no chance that Catholicism would spread there in the future.[30]

The Vatican fear that Protestantism would spill over onto the Italian peninsula appears to be exaggerated, particularly if one considers that as late as 1848, when minority religions living in Piedmont were emancipated, no substantial Protestant communities existed in Italy aside from a small Waldensian community in Western Piedmont. Before 1848, however, when, as a minority religion, Protestants were denied civil and political rights, diplomatic pressures from Prussia and England, allies of the Piedmont government, prevented any severe discriminatory measures against Italian Protestants.[31] Documentation from the Inquisition archives suggests that Vatican fears of a Protestantizing influence on the peninsula resulted from its own weakening power and the allies that this small community had behind it. Significantly, it appears that some Vatican officials also feared an alliance between Protestant powers abroad and Italian Jewish communities, particularly those located within the Papal States.

One report that caused great consternation on the part of Vatican officials in this regard involved a Jew from Ancona, Flaminio Terni, who traveled to Britain in 1832, converted to Unitarianism, and had been living freely in Rome—outside the ghetto, that is—since his return to the peninsula. The Father Inquisitor of Ancona drafted a letter to the pope regarding this troubling situation and suggested that Terni's conversion papers were proof of an alliance between the Jews and the Unitarians. The letter reflected the suspicion with which Vatican officials viewed minority religions, and it suggested that they viewed both Jews and Protestants as subversive supporters of revolution and upheaval.[32] Taken together, the message contained in this confidential correspondence contrasts significantly with the letters published in Catholic journals; indeed these confidential letters undoubtedly compelled Vatican officials to portray a very different version of the facts in newspapers that supported Catholic hegemony. That is, Vatican supporters countered the pessimistic news contained in clergymen's private reports by making public a different kind of private letter, namely the confessions of converts available for public consumption.

Finally, centering Protestant conversion articles on conversionary letters held implications for the narrative style of the story itself. That is, by concentrating almost exclusively on exclamations of victory for Catholicism, by adhering closely to the words of converts and the letters they wrote, and by using these letters as proof that Catholicism was relevant in modern discussions of national identity, these newspaper stories gave no space to the drama or suspense that conversion often engendered. In the conversion narratives examined in earlier chapters, the denouement of the story occurred with the conversion of the central figure(s). When De Joux's daughter converted, however, while readers learn of some of the "motivations" behind her conversion, we know nothing of the moment itself. Had she had a religious revelation like Alphonse de Ratisbonne? Or had her decision to convert been the culmination of a long journey of introspection? Similarly, her father is said to have converted in Paris. Did he, like some say of Manzoni, enter a church on a whim, only to be drawn into the beliefs espoused there? In part, this lack of dramatic narrative was due to the fact that the central component of the story was a letter written by the convert. These letters were less a confessional moment of introspection than a means to publicize their decision, and the Catholic journals that published them did so as a means to lend to the authenticity of the conversion and to further attest to Catholic hegemony.

In the Catholic press, the drama of the moment of conversion is suppressed, and in its place readers receive heartfelt, if rather dull, letters that the converts wrote explaining their own conversions. In this sense, the letters that appeared in the press contrasted starkly with those of Bresciani's novel, where letters were surrounded by a fictionalized narrative that highlighted the drama that conversion might entail. The letters by Protestant converts published in newspapers, however, had no such embellishments—further proof, perhaps, of the truthfulness of the story being reported. Indeed, while the converts undoubtedly wrote these letters, the vocabulary they chose, and the arguments they made, so closely mirrored the official rhetoric of Vatican leaders on the subject that the text became an almost mechanical repetition of Vatican perceptions of Protestantism and Catholicism. Journalists reported a high number of conversions to prove through repetition of an "individual" event rather than a spectacle that Catholicism was regaining the supremacy that the Protestant Reformation had once threatened. Such an explanation would explain why, when one newspaper reported the conversion of thirty thousand Greeks to Catholicism—one of the few conversion stories regarding Greek Orthodox—the story warranted only a few lines. No letters were quoted, and no fanfare made of the event, despite the large numbers involved.[33]

If one contrasts Protestant conversion stories with the conversion stories of Jews in the same period, there are notable differences. The former are more numerous, and while they are factual, by including personal letters they often contain the voice of the convert himself. In contrast, Jewish narratives are lengthier. Rather than being factual accounts, the stories are filled with suspense and dramatic sensationalism. And unlike their Protestant counterparts, the narrative contains few direct citations attributable to the convert. One example that illustrates these differences is the conversion story of a German Jew that appeared in the *Memorie di religione di morale e di letteratura* in 1822. Rather than announcing the fact of the conversion and including a letter written by the convert himself, the journal relates a more detailed story about the young, talented Rabbi Weil, the head of a small Jewish community in Germany. The post for head rabbi of Maastricht, Netherlands becomes available and, despite his youth (he is under thirty years of age) and lack of experience, he applies. Against all odds, but reflecting his great intellect and maturity, the young Rabbi Weil wins the post. Already the stage is set for a dramatic story: the description of the young rabbi winning a prestigious and public position encourages readers to envision—or even invent—ideas regarding his character and identity.

Several years pass, and "our" rabbi protagonist is walking the streets of Maastricht when he encounters a Catholic procession. As the Holy Sacrament draws near, Rabbi Weil tries to withdraw, but instead finds himself physically compelled to kneel before the procession. One can guess the rest of the story: in an epiphany reminiscent of the Ratisbonne story, Weil converts. Furthermore, his conversion is so heartfelt, he feels compelled to convince his congregation to do so as well: "Jesus, whom our Fathers rejected," he is quoted as saying to the congregation, "is the true Messiah, and our salvation lies only with him: I unite myself to him; if you wish to follow me, you will find the same salvation."[34] The heightened drama of the story, his status among Jews, his youth and intelligence, the competition he must face down, and then, in sudden brilliant climax, his realization of the truth of Catholic doctrine all lend themselves to a suspenseful and compelling story. While the words he utters, the only words attributed to him, are similar to those of Protestant converts—both seek to convert other nonbelievers (and readers), after all—the rabbi does not seek to explain his conversion or place it in a political context. This conversion story is not based on motivations but on suspenseful revelation, as readers see depicted in the story: Rabbi Weil cannot escape the procession and instead finds himself falling to the ground in a spontaneous recognition of the Catholic faith. Rather than discussing the recent history of the French Revolution, Weil's reference to Jesus draws on the history and truth of the New Testament, beliefs that Protestant converts did not need to acknowledge to readers. By urging his congregants to follow him, he seeks to validate Catholicism as the "chosen" religion that follows Judaism and replaces it.

The differences in narrative voice are the result of divergent attitudes on the part of the Vatican toward Jewish and Protestant conversions to Catholicism. One reflection of this difference is the much larger space granted to Protestant voices in the text of their stories; they reiterate the words of Catholic leaders, and they are cited at length as a result. Jewish converts largely lose their voice when they convert; press stories tell about them but rarely quote them directly, and when they do, the citation is brief and indirect. Another distinction that surely contributes to differences in narration is the actual experience of conversion. Over half of the Protestants who converted return to their former religious practices. Indeed, if one counted the soldiers who converted to marry and the artists who converted to gain a permit to work in the region—two groups who often went back to their former religious practices—then abjuration hovered around seventy percent.[35] For Jews, however, conversion was generally an irreversible process, as seen with the Labani story. After baptism, the new convert was strictly forbidden contact with members of his former community, as well as family members; he was required to change his name and cut himself off from any means of support he would have had otherwise.

Thus the laws of conversion that aimed more directly at attempting to break ties with the Jewish convert's former life were not pursued with Protestant converts. In addition, there were the religious differences between Jews and Protestants: Protestants were baptized and believed in the authenticity of the New Testament and in this sense were already within the Christian community; Jews did not and were outside the Christian community. As such, they were on the one hand more threatening to Catholic identity than Protestants, and on the other their existence helped sharpen the papal definition of national belonging, which demanded the Other in order to define itself. As Homi Bhabha notes, "Nationalism . . . seeks to represent itself in the image of the Enlightenment and fails to do so. For Enlightenment itself, to assert its sovereignty as the universal ideal, needs its Other."[36] Ultimately, the conversion story of the rabbi was a story of conquest; the ultimate embodiment of Otherness had been conquered. As such, the story of his conversion depicted the values associated with "consensus, a common culture of shared understandings, and deeper, more vital ethics."[37] In other words, the conversion of the Jew enabled Catholic writers to establish the values they associated with a Catholic homeland, the Papal States.

While the Inquisition movement was initially established to respond to the Protestant threat, the motivation changed depending on the political atmosphere of the era.[38] In the nineteenth century, despite continued news coverage of conversions to Protestantism and concern regarding its spread, Vatican officials focused more on the threat of revolution and political upheaval than on the battle against Protestant "heresy." And, while Protestants received some of the blame for revolutionary sentiments, no minority religionists were more closely associated with revolution than the Jews. Letters that arrived at the Inquisition office from Vatican supporters, from both laypeople and clergymen, reflected this bias and illuminated the Vatican desire to eliminate social and economic ties between Jews and Christians. In 1839, for example, the Father Inquisitor of Rome received a letter from the Sant'Uffizio of Ancona that voiced his support for the continued enforcement of Inquisition law, particularly in light of the threatening political changes of the day; it was clear that Vatican officials were watching events such as the emancipation of minority religions across Europe with great concern. More specifically, the Ancona clergyman writes of the great demoralization of the Christian community because of its close contact with the Jews, who, he claims, have reported to foreign newspapers of their power within the Papal States. The Jews, he concludes, are much like the liberals: both use their connections against the government.[39]

The letter emphasizes the suspicion with which reactionary clergy regarded the Jewish community of the Papal States despite its small size. In addition, it ties Jews to revolutionary "liberals," portraying the former as not simply religiously subversive but, in the face of the unity sought by the Holy See, politically divisive as well. As such, the letter underscores the discomfort that the Vatican felt at the possibility that Italian unification might lead to emancipation and equal rights for minority religions. Finally, the letter, written five years before the news article that was censored out of *L'Artigianello*, anticipates almost all the complaints that Vatican leaders voiced about that story, suggesting why Jewish conversion stories were becoming more prevalent in the Catholic press. That is, the Jews, as supporters of emancipation and revolution, represented the most pressing threat against a wholly Catholic society. By advocating and publicizing their conversion stories, the Holy See and its supporters sought to reiterate and substantiate the Catholic nature of Italian culture.

From the Vatican's perspective, the fact that *Il Povero*, published within the Papal States, managed to print an article that the Vatican had officially censored, was a harbinger of greater troubles to come. No case made this drama more apparent than the controversial conversion of the six-year-old Jewish boy from Bologna, Edgardo Mortara. In June 1858, papal police removed Edgardo from his parents' home in Bologna on the grounds that a Christian maidservant—illegally employed, no less—had baptized him years before, when he had fallen—according to her, at least—deathly ill. Bologna, still part of papal territory in 1858, was ruled by Inquisition law, according to which a baptized child could not be raised by non-Catholic parents. Thus the Mortara child was brought to a special monastery where his conversion was to be completed.

In the hopes that the boy be returned to them, the Mortara family constructed a case to present to the pope that highlighted the irregularities of the boy's conversion. They claimed that little Edgardo had never fallen seriously ill, and that he was simply suffering from a childhood illness when the maid baptized him. To further support their arguments, they sought to prove that the servant, Anna Morisi, was an untrustworthy woman of ill repute and named witnesses who would attest to her promiscuity. In addition, they argued that they had never consented to the conversion, and that it thus violated the paternal rights of Edgardo's father. And finally, in case all these arguments failed and the baptism was deemed valid, they argued that the child should still remain with his parents, as natural law dictated. In response to these arguments, the Church countered that, while a child could not be baptized without parental consent, the baptism was still valid if it was executed and that Morisi performed the sacrament correctly. In addition, they claimed that according to Inquisition law, the "acquisitive right" of the Church was of a higher order than natural or paternal law, and thus the baptized child should not be returned to his biological parents. And finally, they argued that the validity of Edgardo's baptism meant that the Church had the right to remove the child from "the danger of apostasy" to which he would be exposed in his parents' home.[40]

The details surrounding the case have been thoroughly researched, and it is not my aim here to further explore these historical facts.[41] The conversion story of Edgardo is particularly relevant to the present discussion, however, because of the attention it gained in the press. The narrative drama of the story, and the conflict between modern, secular ideology and religious law that it reflected, attracted the attention of politicians, journalists, clergymen, and even Pope Pius IX himself, not to mention the public at large, which followed news of the case avidly. Each party had a different perspective, and the facts of the Mortara affair largely depended upon who was narrating the story. Thus, for example, despite representing different points on the political spectrum, the revolutionary Giuseppe Mazzini, Prime Minister Camillo Cavour, and even the conservative King Victor Emmanuel supported the claims of the

Mortara family, pushed by their shared desire to undermine papal rule. References to the case can even be found in Giuseppe Garibaldi's historical novel, *I Mille*, in which the vehemently anticlerical Garibaldi taunts the Church for its efforts at conversion, describing Edgardo Mortara as the little boy "stolen from Jewish parents by the priests in order to make a Catholic out of him."[42] Portrayals such as this one ignited antipapal protests on the part of Jews and secular nationalists, both of whom called for the civil emancipation of Jews living under papal rule and the end to papal temporal rule.

Vatican officials, who considered the case to be of an ecclesiastical nature, regarded secular and Jewish protests as meddlesome—proof that the post-French revolution ideology was a threat to their authority. Officials found it particularly odious that an ecclesiastical issue had been taken up by so many secular newspapers and by writers who were, in their view, merely interested in arousing the passion of their readers. Most significant for our discussion, the story also generated a wave of correspondence among Vatican leaders as they discussed the Mortara case and the public disclosure they deemed appropriate on the subject. And despite the wide array of scholarship on the Mortara affair, no work has thoroughly examined the relationship between the correspondence and press that helped formulate and publicize the Vatican's attitudes on the case. The documentation that comprised both private communiqués and public discourse cannot be ignored, however, since the language used to recount the affair, like the narrative content itself, reveals the relationship between legal forms, cultural identity, and even nationalist sentiment among Vatican leaders. In other words, the Vatican correspondence and publications on the Mortara affair manifested ethical, legal and political values that reflected their vision of the state; perspectives that papal leaders expressed in their personal correspondence were made official and public in Catholic journals.[43] As we will see, the so-called facts of the story were quickly submerged and corroded, replaced by fictional stories of miracles that proved the boy's Catholicism. Catholic stories depicted Edgardo's parents as Jews who broke the law and were deserving of little sympathy for the loss of their son, and ultimately these journals advocated a defense of the Inquisition legal system that enabled the Vatican to redefine Edgardo as a son of the Church.

While the main focus of this section will be an exploration of Vatican correspondence and its relationship to Catholic press stories regarding the Mortara Affair, the text upon which antipapal writers based their story should not be overlooked, particularly since the Vatican struggled to counter this narrative for the duration of the time that the story remained in the press. I refer here to the documents that the Mortara family submitted to the Vatican in their attempt to regain their son. This testimony, known as the *Pro-Memoria*, became the basis for many versions of the story published in antipapal newspapers:

> Seeing armed forces in the house filled [Edgardo] with wonder and fear that soon changed to terror when he learned that they were looking for him. And he asked anxiously what misdeed he had committed, but the only response he received were the desperate tears of his loved ones. . . . When finally in the midst of the relentless wails of his family, Edgardo was torn away, sobbing and convulsive, his childish imagination adding to the great pain with the horrible suspicion that he was being dragged away to have his head cut off.[44]

The story of papal police knocking at the door of the Mortara home in the middle of the night, taking a little boy from his bed with no explanation to him or his helplessly terrified parents, bore suspense and drama that ignited liberal passions and antireligious sentiment. In addition, the description of Edgardo's cries and his fear, expressed in childlike terms, of having his head chopped off, provided a powerful narrative of the abuses of power that secular nationalists believed the Holy See wielded with its temporal control. The secular and Jewish press immediately used these details against the Vatican, denouncing papal actions as a "kidnapping" of the young boy, and in so doing employing a term that the Vatican had used against the Jewish community in earlier times, as seen in the Cavalieri affair.

Upon receiving the Mortara family's petition for the return of their son, Cardinal Secretary of State Antonelli dispatched instructions across the world on how to refute their arguments. The archives contain letters that Antonelli sent off to papal representatives in Austria, Germany, Portugal, Spain, Belgium, France, Switzerland, Brazil, Panama, Columbia and Mexico, as well as to many nuncios on the Italian peninsula. The letters all date from the end of October to early November, about four months after papal police removed Edgardo from his parents' home and shortly after the Mortaras' *Pro-Memoria* had begun to spark stories in the secular press and the earlier counterstories in the Catholic press; the struggle for public opinion and the battle against the secular press had begun.[45]

Following these initial instructions, Antonelli received and sent out various kinds of letters regarding the affair, from reports on the secular press to details of meetings with foreign diplomats. With regard to the former, for example, a papal nuncio to Germany wrote to warn Antonelli about the press there, writing that German periodicals were controlled almost entirely by Jews. He expressed his concern that these journals would take advantage of the current situation and use it against the Holy See to the best of their abilities, particularly since the Jews were "in alliance as they are with all parties hostile to the Church."[46] A similar letter arrived from the archbishop of Madrid acknowledging receipt of Antonelli's instructions. He described the French and Belgian press as "ruthless and rabid" and known even before the Mortara affair as being anti-Catholic. In Madrid, too, he wrote, there were papers "that delight in injuring Rome and advocating hatred for the august head of the Church."[47] Propapal newspapers, he reported, remained relatively silent regarding the affair and only wrote the occasional article. The archbishop included a copy of *La Monarqua Española*, which contained a two-column article on the Mortara affair that he deemed "quite praiseworthy."[48] The director of this newspaper is, he explains, "a monarchist and antiparliamentarian, and he believes that the fundamental principle of the monarchy is Catholicism."[49] The paper's political ideology thus defined its religious orientation and determined its acceptability in the eyes of the Holy See.

Even on the Italian peninsula and within the Papal States, Antonelli had trouble controlling the information available to the public. One Vatican official, writing from Naples, thanked Antonelli for his letter regarding the Mortara affair, stating that it would be useful because of the notoriety the case had gained: "The enemies of the [Catholic] Religion," he writes, "have found ground that is most favorable for them."[50] A member of the papal police in Bologna also wrote Antonelli, warning him of the critical articles being published in a French newspaper. He asked the cardinal to consider forbidding sale of the periodical in the Papal States.[51] In his response, Antonelli lauded the envoy for his views, although he judged it imprudent for the Church to carry out such a drastic measure.[52] Undoubtedly the realistic Antonelli knew—as *Il Povero* had earlier demonstrated—that it would be impossible to censor all the negative press regarding the Mortara affair. At the same time, however, or perhaps as a result of this new reality, the Mortara case came to mean more than simply the welfare of one little boy; for the Church, possession of Edgardo was a means to regain a symbol of the future of the Church, to prove its legitimacy and the power of Inquisition law within the Papal States.

The challenge of spin control did not end with the secular and Jewish press; much to the consternation of Vatican officials, a French clergyman, Abbot Delacouture, criticized propapal newspapers for misrepresenting the case of Edgardo. Delacouture presented one of the greatest threats to the Catholic news stories: himself a Catholic leader, he doubted the very truthfulness of their narratives. Thus, for example, he asked how a journal could reasonably claim that statements of faith and proselytization could come from a little boy who was not yet seven years old. He asked, too, how believing Catholics could support a ruling that took children away from their biological parents and still explain the commandment of obeying and honoring one's parents. In the eyes of Vatican officials, Delacouture's arguments were contentious, if not downright heretical. "Stories and counterstories," Delgado notes, "to be effective, must be or must appear to be noncoercive. They invite the reader to suspend judgment, listen for their point or message, and then decide what measure of truth they contain."[53] From the Vatican's perspective, Delacouture's question deconstructed the reality that propapal narratives, and the letters behind them, had carefully built. The French abbot showed, as Delgado states, how readers could believe in unjustified cruelty and exclusion; in effect, he uncovered the coercion and bias that papal newspapers hoped to hide with their supposedly neutral, yet authoritarian, commentaries.

Antonelli wrote the nuncio in Paris at the end of October 1858 to warn him of a critical letter that Delacouture had published in the French Catholic journal *Debats* addressing the Mortara affair and to ask for a background check of the Abbot.[54] Over the next few months the nuncio sent reports on the French troublemaker: Delacouture was withdrawn, he wrote; and while his conduct never provoked comment, he was animated by a "French spirit."[55] The patriotism of the clergyman suggested that he was more connected to French ideals of liberty than Vatican standards of piety. When Delacouture published a booklet expressing his opinions of the Mortara Affair, the nuncio reported to Antonelli, "He always speaks with great satisfaction of the uses, liberties, and maxims of the Gallic Church, to which he is extremely attached, and he hurls himself with furor against the followers of Roman doctrines."[56] Delacouture's actions were striking because he placed into doubt the dominant values of the Vatican. Indeed, he went so far as to examine the Mortara affair from the perspective of the victim, despite belonging to the papal community, and he challenged readers to question the power the Vatican used in this case.

The desire to counter claims such as Delacouture's, not to mention those of antipapal voices, that questioned the legitimacy of the Vatican's actions was the driving force behind a second type of correspondence among Vatican officials, namely letters that developed into articles published in propapal newspapers. Thus, for example, in a letter to the papal representative in Milan, Antonelli included an article that he wished to appear in a propapal Milanese newspaper. The article once again reflected the Vatican's desire to ensure that newspapers published its point of view and, in so doing, demonstrated just how deeply involved Antonelli was in coordinating the official Vatican portrayal of the affair. Similarly, the Vatican nuncio to Germany, whose anti-Semitic comments regarding the German press echoed those made about *Il Povero*, had a direct link to the propapal *Gazzetta Ufficiale di Vienna* and regularly contributed to this newspaper. Indeed, his connection to the Austrian journal illustrates the frequent collaboration between the Catholic press and the Vatican, particularly when the Vatican was under scrutiny, as was the case with the Mortara Affair. In this period, it was the nuncio's task to keep the *Gazzetta*'s editors informed about developments regarding the Edgardo story. And yet this job appeared to be a double-edged sword: while the archbishop could help shape the articles—and he noted that the paper treated the Mortara affair with great delicacy—the editors, much to the archbishop's dismay, used his participation to advertise their story as the "*publication of the Roman See.*"[57] The Viennese journal, like other pro-Vatican newspapers, sought to sell itself as the word of the Holy See; the Vatican, however, was reluctant to give the paper this title, undoubtedly not wishing to show how clergymen influenced journals not directly connected to the Holy See.

In another letter sent to Antonelli, a clergyman included a draft of an article that supported the Church's actions. Significantly, the author explained that while he had written the article, he pretended to be a journalist when sending the piece to the newspaper to "avoid any suspicion of the influence of the Roman Court."[58] Such an explanation suggests the lengths to which Vatican officials resorted to ensure that the public received their version of the story. Indeed, in this sense, the communiqué expressed the desire of many clergymen to convey to the public an "official" version of Edgardo's story, reflecting Vatican desires to simultaneously gain popular support and exert spin control as the case gained notoriety. By writing a propapal article but attributing its authorship to a disinterested party, this clergyman hoped to establish a widely accepted propapal version of the story by which the public would judge the case.

Similarly, in an article that arrived at the Inquisition Tribunal in the hopes that Antonelli would have it published anonymously, Edgardo was quoted as promising that he would return to his family, "When I am grown up in order to convert daddy and mommy."[59] The article lauded the Mortara maidservant for baptizing Edgardo, whom she believed was going to die, and drew a parallel between Edgardo and Christ. Edgardo's recovery from his illness was miraculous—"like Moses at the hand of the daughter of Pharaoh"[60]—and was the result of his baptism. While the comparison between Edgardo and Moses might be interpreted as proof of their Jewishness, the writer hastened to correct this conclusion: "Who was Moses if not the prophetic image of Jesus Christ?"[61] It was from Moses, after all, that the Church took on its baptismal customs, and thus it was particularly apt that Edgardo be compared to him.

By drawing a parallel between Moses and Jesus, the journalist rendered a typological argument that suggested that conversion to Catholicism and acceptance of the New Testament perfected Judaism and the figures of the Hebrew Bible. In so doing, the author not only advocated Edgardo's conversion but also suggested that the history of the Jews was incomplete without conversion to Catholicism. As Michael Ragussis notes in his discussion on the culture of conversion, conversion was viewed here "as a kind of completion, or refinement, of one's religious education, a new stage in one's religious development."[62] While the journal to which the writer hoped his article would be sent is not specified, the fact that he sent his article to the Vatican's secretary of state, who would then send it on to an appropriate journal, again reflects how closely the Vatican monitored and developed its version of Mortara story.

In his memoirs, Edgardo also described the commotion that the secular and Jewish communities made over his removal, writing that "for six months this violent and impassioned polemic continued, in which all the enemies of the papacy and the Roman Church arranged a meeting."[63] Among these so-called "enemies," Edgardo named the Jewish community of Piedmont, which organized a campaign against the pope and the Roman Catholic Church. That Edgardo viewed the Jewish community as an enemy and that he remembered with disdain the commotion that his parents and the Jewish community created on his account reflected how successfully the justice system of the Papal States had redefined Mortara's attitudes toward the Jewish community from which he came, and the Catholic one that he ultimately embraced.

Finally, the archives contain letters that report on exchanges between the Vatican and other political powers regarding the Mortara affair. Thus, for example, in a letter that the papal nuncio to Paris wrote to Secretary of State Antonelli, the diplomat reported on his meeting with the French minister of foreign affairs. The French minister's message to the Vatican appears to have been particularly pointed: he complained of the rising public discontent that the Vatican's actions regarding the Mortara affair sparked in France and Europe more generally and warned that many had urged the French government to take advantage of the fact that its troops were stationed in Rome to forcibly return the child to his parents.[64] In addition, he asked that, if the Vatican could not return the child, then at the very least it could publish an article in a Roman newspaper explaining its actions to the public. In response, the nuncio first chided the French diplomat for the sympathy he expressed for the Mortaras. The Mortara parents, he argued, "should not inspire such interest and such compassion."[65] They were, he reasoned, the cause of their own misery, since they broke the law by hiring a Catholic woman to work for them. In other words, the Mortaras themselves had created the circumstances that led to the removal of their child.

In keeping with this absence of sympathy, other clergymen responded to accusations that the removal of Edgardo was barbaric with proof of the uncivilized nature of the community from which Edgardo had been taken. Not only did this include suggestions that the Mortaras had themselves caused their son to be taken from them by breaking the law; many clergymen even went so far as to expound upon the barbarism of Jewish rites such as circumcision and the uncivilized nature of non-Christian communities. For example, one Vatican official defended the Church's removal of Edgardo by stating that "the *civilized* world is nothing but the Christian world, which has always existed with this law [that is, of raising and educating Christians in a Christian environment]."[66] The Church, by definition the heart of civilization, could never have permitted the acts individuals accused it of committing. This identification of the civilized world with the Christian world embodied the problem of identity of non-Christian communities, since they lay by definition outside this conception of "civilized." Thus the Jewish community represented a group of uncivilized outsiders, dangerous because of their non-Christian identity. Such descriptions helped reinforce a national Catholic identity on the peninsula by stressing the Otherness of alien populations such as, in this case, the Jews.[67]

Second, and in response to the French diplomat's request for a public explanation of the Vatican's actions, the nuncio explained that, for the time being at least, the Vatican preferred to remain silent with regard to the affair. Following the polemical publicity the case had received in the secular press, he explained, the Holy See was not interested in rendering a public account of its role; to do so would provide "the appearance of subjecting [the Vatican] to their [that is, the public's] judgment. And thus, either it was better that the Holy Father kept silent, or, if he still desired to speak, or to have someone speak in his name, he would do it in a dignified manner, and would choose other means, such as, for example, that of a letter and an instruction to the bishops of the Pontifical State, or to other authorities."[68] The conversation displays the constant battle between the Vatican and foreign diplomats over defining and separating private from public, ecclesiastical from secular. And, while officials discussed the affair at length among themselves, this letter suggests that in the early months following the removal of Edgardo from his parents' home, the "official" voice of the Vatican was largely a silent one.

Indeed, years after Edgardo had been taken from his parents' Bologna home, Cardinal Camillo Tarquini wrote of the event and sought, like the newspaper articles examined below, to counter accusations of kidnap. Like the Paris nuncio, he emphasized that his description was by no means an apology for the Church's actions in the case; rather, he writes, it was an explanation that would prove that the Church acted within its rights with regard to the Mortara affair. The Church, he explains, is responsible for all baptized children, and therefore it was obligated to remove a child who lives with "insidious" nonbelievers: "Such is the case with [Edgardo's] parents, and thus from their hands [the Church] must do its utmost to free him."[69] Thus he describes the "extraction" of Edgardo from his Bologna home as liberation rather than kidnapping.

On August 17, 1858, about two months after Edgardo was removed from his family's home, one of the earliest propapal articles on the affair was published in the pro-Vatican Roman newspaper *L'Armonia della religione colla civiltà*. The story's eye-catching title, "L'Ebreo di Bologna e le bombe di Giuseppe Mazzini" ("The Jew of Bologna and the Giuseppe Mazzini's Bombs"), recalled Bresciani's novel, drawing a parallel between Edgardo and Aser, the novel's converted hero.[70] Indeed, not only did the title remind readers of Aser and his conversion story; Bresciani devoted an entire chapter to Mazzini in his *L'Ebreo di Verona*, writing that Mazzini was "as atrocious as the terror which his name inspires."[71] In addition, Pius IX's initial open-mindedness toward liberalism changed after his encounter with Mazzini, and he soon became convinced that liberalism was a threat to the Church just as the French Revolution had been in the past.[72] Clearly the journalist sought to remind readers of this terror in an article that responded to secular press stories of the Mortara affair. And, while the story was published two months before Antonelli began monitoring the Vatican response to the affair extensively, it in no way undermined the silence with which the

Vatican had initially reacted to the secular and Jewish stories on the case. Indeed, in some ways, the article strengthened this line of defense; while purporting to write on the affair, the author never mentions the Mortaras or their son by name, referring vaguely to the "*ebreo di Bologna*" instead. And, while he explains that his newspaper had not written up the story earlier because they wanted to gather all the facts, he provides no details about the case. In so doing, the journalist denies narrative space to the story, maintaining the silence that Vatican diplomats encouraged in their letters:

> Why, when so much space is dedicated to the Jews' request, why cannot two lines be found that tell us something of the uprisings tried in La Spezia, of the bombs imported by Mazzini, and of many other things which grip, or have gripped, people with great fear? . . . Why do you [that is, the secular newspapers and their journalists] not busy yourselves with the *actual* mistakes that have been committed in our home? If instead . . . of being the lawyer to the Jews of Bologna, you occupied yourselves a little bit with *our* affairs, of *our* people, and with *our* property which is threatened from time to time by bands of marauding criminals and revolutionaries.[73]

Rather than focus on the Mortara affair, the author excoriates liberal newspapers for reacting to Jewish cries of injustice and, at the same time, ignoring the plight of Catholics. With his emphasis on the word "actual," the author suggests that Mazzini's bombs are real problems, whereas the Mortara case has yet to prove that it is an issue at all. Furthermore, by placing together Mazzini's actions and those of the Jewish community on behalf of Edgardo, the author implies a connection between the Jewish letter writers and the Mazzinian revolutionaries, suggesting that cries of injustice of the former are baseless and that the latter are common criminals. Both groups create chaos and uproar, and both threaten the peaceful existence of innocent Catholics. Thus the "nonproblem" of Edgardo is contrasted to the very real problems of terror and suffering that result from Mazzini's bombs. In addition, the writer's continual use of the word "our" emphasizes the us-versus-them mentality between the hegemonic world of papal supporters and those who are not considered members of this social group.

While failing to narrate Edgardo's story, the journalist successfully reminds his readers of the Catholic community's relationship with the Jewish population in its midst.[74] That is, the Jews were a distinct and easily identifiable community, one that was separated even physically by the existence of the ghetto. Indeed, the Jews were so separate that the writer seemed unwilling to sympathize with the harsh blow that Inquisition law had dealt the Mortara family. Thus, while the journalist openly recognized the suffering of the boy's parents, he insisted that the Church was not to be criticized for its role in the affair; indeed it was obliged to act as it did: "It is legal, reasonable, provident, beneficial, even though it cost many tears to a mother, unhappy only because she does not know the truth and fate of her son."[75] The nuncio to Paris had explained to the French foreign minister that the Mortara family did not deserve sympathy; in this article, readers are exposed to similar sentiments. The application of Inquisition law and its reflection of the hegemony of the Vatican overrides any compassion that Vatican supporters might have had toward the Mortaras.

Richard Delgado defines the "official" story, or the majority or stock story, as he calls it, as one that "the institution collectively forms and tells about itself. . . . It stresses stability and the avoidance of risks. . . . [It] emphasizes certain 'facts' without examining their truth."[76] The *L'Armonia* story, like those of other Catholic papers and writers, actively works to silence various details within the story they narrate.[77] That this paper initially tried to avoid any details of the case whatsoever exemplifies this suppression. With continued coverage of the case, however, and growing international protest regarding the Vatican's actions, as reported in letters to Antonelli, the Catholic press found itself forced to respond. Their second wave of stories seeks above all to remind papal supporters, the dominant group, "of its identity in relation to outgroups, and provide it with a form of shared reality in which its own superior position is seen as natural."[78] To this end, when in mid-October *L'Armonia* published more details on the Mortara affair, the journalist presents his article as the "official" story of the case by claiming that he learned its details from a trustworthy witness, who nonetheless goes unnamed. The most striking aspect of the story is the description of Edgardo's removal from his family's home. The Catholic press, bent on exonerating the Vatican from accusations of kidnap, tries to present narratives that make Edgardo's conversion appear noncoercive, an event that the boy himself desired.

In so doing, the journalist attempts to rewrite the story the Mortaras presented in their *Pro-Memoria*. Instead of a narrative of terror and tears, the journalist claimed that when Edgardo was taken from his parents' home,

> he went with extraordinary happiness, and as soon as he put a foot across the entryway of the house [of Catechumens], he saw a Madonna Addolorata;

> and turning to the person who had brought him there, he asked: "Why does she cry?"
>
> "She cries," the caretaker responded, "because the Jews are in discord, nor do they wish to recognize her Divine Son."
>
> "So," added the young boy, "she cries for my father and mother!" These are the first words uttered by the child as soon as he entered the house.[79]

Finally, the Catholic press's "official" version of the Mortara affair has some of the drama and emotive quality that readers saw in the earlier, more traditional Jewish conversion story of the German Rabbi Weil. Edgardo's happiness at being in the House of the Catechumens counters accusations of a traumatic "kidnap." Similarly, attention is drawn away from questions surrounding the boy's conversion with his implied desire to convert his parents. Indeed, just as Weil was depicted as a man torn between two communities, his Jewish congregation and the Catholic procession, in Edgardo's story there exists a tangible struggle between the actions of the Church and the response of the Jewish and secular communities, with Edgardo depicted as choosing the former over the latter. Also as in the case of Weil's conversion story, readers are reminded of the New Testament with the vision of the Madonna who wept for the Jews who denied the divinity of her son. Indeed, these words also reflect the lack of sympathy that the Vatican and Catholic press maintain toward the Mortara family. That is, Momolo and Marianna weep and suffer because they, like the Jews of Jesus' time, do not recognize the Christian nature of their own son. And finally, like Weil, who was literally struck down by his realization of the truth of Church ideology, the miraculous story of Edgardo is that of a boy who inherently projects his Catholic identity from the moment he is free to express his "true" self.

The *Civiltà Cattolica* reported a somewhat different story. In this version, Edgardo cried throughout the trip from Bologna to Rome, asking for his parents. When a policeman placed a cross around his neck and wanted him to kiss it, Edgardo cried harder, saying he wanted his Jewish *mezuzah* instead. Upon entering the House of the Catechumens, however, Edgardo was told of his Christian identity, and the change in his behavior was immediate. The journal explained this behavioral change as an effect of conversion: he appeared extremely happy to be raised and educated in Christian environs, and he sought the protection of his new father, Pope Pius IX. "'I am baptized,' he said with greater wisdom and exactness than a child; 'and my father is the Pope.'"[80] Thus the journal countered claims that the Vatican had stolen Edgardo from his Jewish family by re-creating the family unit: Edgardo had a new father, the pope, and a new mother, the Catholic Church. To reinforce this newly invented family structure, the article depicted Edgardo as reversing his earlier pleas to return to his parents; instead he begged that he never have to be exposed to their apostasy again.[81] Such words are remarkably similar to those that Church officials presented to counter the arguments of the Mortara's *Pro-Memoria*. In that response, an official letter from the Inquisition Tribunal, they asserted that Edgardo could not be returned to the Mortara household because of the "danger of apostasy" that the Mortaras presented. Finally, the story comments on Edgardo's wisdom and maturity—unusual in a boy his age. Indeed, it is a unique facet within the genre of conversion narrative, where generally the Jew (one need only think of Aser)—urban, educated, rich—submits to the instruction of a Catholic child—young, naïve, pious. In the Edgardo story, however, the young, naïve boy already possessed the intellectual and Catholic piety of a mature individual. And thus Catholic portrayals of his conversion story attested to the predestined nature of his conversion and how it proved his Catholic identity.

The nature of Edgardo's conversion was addressed in yet another version of the story where Edgardo, happy to be in the House of the Catechumens, learned of the possibility that his baptism might not be valid. Upon hearing this news, he asked, "If that woman [i.e., the servant, Anna Morisi] made a mistake, could they rebaptize me?"[82] Edgardo's expressed desire to be Catholic, his wish to convert if the initial baptism was invalidated, provided further evidence to Catholic readers of the little boy's inherently Catholic identity. In other versions of the story, the extent of Edgardo's Catholic beliefs was further proven during two visits with his parents after he was taken into Vatican custody. One story related how happy Edgardo was at the prospect of seeing his father—happy, the article explained, because the visit provided an occasion to convert Momolo. Edgardo's Catholic beliefs are thus proven genuine by his desire to convert others. Another version recounted how, in his first visit to see his son, Momolo was accompanied by the secretary of Rome's Jewish Community, Rabbi Sabatino Scazzocchio. After the meeting, the article described Edgardo's supposed reaction to Scazzocchio's request for a kiss: "If that man comes one more time with my father and wishes to kiss me, I will take out an image of the Madonna and I will say to him: kiss this!"[83] The fact that the secretary was a rabbi is emphasized in the story. That Edgardo found him particularly odious and that he wished to convert him stressed Edgardo's Catholic integrity and reassured readers that Edgardo had no interest in returning to the Jewish community.

Distressed at the Catholic versions of the affair, Edgardo's father, Momolo Mortara, wrote letters to the editors of both *L'Armonia* and the *Civiltà Cattolica* in an attempt to clarify matters and relate his version of the story. To the former journal, he wrote trying to convince the editors to allow him to provide further details of his meeting with his son: "I limit myself now to beg you to include in one of the upcoming issues the following report . . . to put forward other facts that are equally truthful and eloquent." The editor-in-chief of *Civiltà Cattolica*, Father C. M. Curci, responded to a similar letter that Momolo sent that journal: "Most Esteemed Sir: I thank you for the kindness of sending me new information on the well-known affair. But since in your letter you broadened the question beyond the three enclosed facts, my work does not permit me to continue an epistolary discussion that would not be brief."[84] Curci's letter is one of the few available from the editors of the *Civiltà Cattolica*, since the journal's archives do not permit researchers access to the private correspondence of its editors or writers. And, while the "three facts" that Curci refers to are not specified, the letter reflects a clear lack of interest on the part of the journal most closely associated with the Vatican in hearing a version of the story that deviates in any way from its own. That these details—"new information" as Curci himself admits—would have been provided by one of the primary actors in the story appears not to have been a compelling reason; quite possibly the Catholic press simply did not want to portray any aspect of the Mortaras' relationship with their son that would have evoked the sympathy of its readers.

Indeed, to limit the sympathy readers felt for his biological parents, a later article that appeared in the *Civiltà Cattolica* reported on a meeting between Edgardo and his mother, Marianna. When Marianna saw her son—their first meeting since Edgardo had been taken from Bologna—she immediately tore a medallion of the Virgin Mary from around his neck, "[saying], 'You are a Jew, and a Jew you must die'; 'And I,' responded the little boy, 'out of respect I was quiet; but however many times she said this to me, I repeated in my heart: I am Christian by the grace of God, and Christian I wish to die.'"[85] Not only is Marianna portrayed as sacrilegious in this scene; her motherly love is overtaken by a morbid and even sinister desire: her son should die rather than become a Christian. As was done with Ricca in the Labani affair, the *Civiltà Cattolica* portrays Edgardo's mother as preferring death for her child rather than conversion. In contrast, when Edgardo states the same words, substituting "Christian" for "Jew," a sense of martyrdom—Christian martyrdom—tinges his response; even at his young age he is willing to think of his own mortality in terms of his beliefs, and he is well aware of how they contrast with and contradict those of his mother.

The *Civiltà Cattolica* article also seeks to counter claims that the Jewish and secular press put forth that suggested that the Vatican's removal of Edgardo was a violation of paternal and natural law. To this end the journalist makes an analogy between the Vatican struggle to maintain and extend its power and the European battles to extend their territories through colonialization. Thus, he argues, if a parent believes that taking a young man from his home and sending him to battle in the colonies conflicts with paternal law, the government would respond that the laws of paternity are overridden by national interests. Similarly, the writer continues, the interests of the state and of Catholic law override the interests of the Mortara family, justifying the removal of Edgardo to the Catechumens.[86] Significantly, the argument reformulates the ideology of conversion in terms of a national, Catholic identity. That is, the journalist's analogy between taking a young Italian man to fight in the colonies, and taking a young Jewish boy into the Church draws a parallel between colonial—that is, racial—conquest and religious conversion.[87] Just as colonial efforts seek to dominate "uncivilized" minority populations, the writer suggests that Church efforts to conquer religious minorities, portrayed as similarly savage, are equally acceptable. Conversion in this context should therefore be understood as conquest, and the Vatican's interest in prevailing in the Mortara case reflects its desire to insist upon the Catholic identity of the land it ruled.

The threat to papal territory was further aggravated when, in June 1859, the Austrian troops responsible for protecting papal rule over the city of Bologna were driven out of the city; a year after papal forces took Edgardo away, a provisional civil government was established. In mid-November of that same year, Luigi Carlo Farini, the newly appointed governor of Romagna, abolished the Tribunal of the Holy Inquisition in the region.[88] And a month later, in response to a letter that Edgardo's grandfather wrote Farini asking for the return of his grandson, Farini ordered the arrest of those behind Edgardo's removal. Responding to the pervasive culture of conversion within the Papal States, the first antipapal tribunal sought to undo one of the aims of Inquisition law and papal culture. On January 2, 1860, the Father Inquisitor of Bologna, Father Pier Gaitano Feletti, accused of ordering Edgardo's removal from his family's home, was arrested; the first major trial in the newly secular territory of Romagna was tied to a conversion story, and the charge, kidnapping, was precisely that which the Catholic press tried to disavow with its stories.

Indeed, a mirroring effect can be seen between Feletti's trial and the Mortara affair, as well as between other conversion stories discussed earlier. When Farini abolished the Inquisition Tribunal for which Feletti worked, he declared it "incompatible with civilization, with the common principles of public law."[89] His denunciation of the tribunal as uncivilized echoes earlier Church proclamations of the uncivilized nature of secular power and reflects the greater debate of the degree to which secular or religious law defines civilization in a broad sense and Italian civilization in particular. In addition, just as Edgardo and other Jews "extracted" from the ghetto were forcibly taken in the middle of the night, Father Feletti was arrested in the early hours of the morning. He himself testifies how:

> At about 2:30 in the morning of January 2, I was surprised in my bed by various police agents and guards. I dressed as quickly as I possibly could and was taken from my bedroom to a room of my residence, where a police inspector . . . declared that I was under arrest. After that they began to interrogate me, declaring that I was guilty of an assault on public tranquility because of the seizure that I ordered of the boy Edgardo Mortara, son of the Jew Mommolo.[90]

The accusation regularly leveled at Jews of disturbing the peace and promoting civic disorder is now leveled against Feletti. Furthermore, as the trial proceeded, and much to the consternation of Feletti's court-appointed lawyer, Francesco Jussi, the crime for which Feletti was being tried escalated from an assault on public tranquility to kidnapping, to the violent removal of Edgardo from his family, to an abuse of power.[91] The court scene is rich in irony: clergymen previously accused Jews of being willing to kidnap, or even kill, their own children before giving them to the Church, and now a leader of the Church was being accused of precisely this crime. Finally, just as the hegemonic Catholic Church pursued and effectuated trials against minority populations in its midst, now the newly empowered civil government sought to try a representative of the politically disempowered Vatican.

While numerous questions were asked of Feletti regarding the Inquisition Tribunal, he refused to answer, explaining that he was bound by oath to remain silent on all matters pertaining to the tribunal. The prosecutor's argument that such allegiances had no value in newly secular

Bologna were to no effect; Feletti held his ground. With regard to the Mortara affair, however, Feletti willingly described the boy's departure for Rome, testifying that the boy allowed the papal police to calmly lead him away:

> Removing the child to the carriage away occurred without any uproar. . . . It is true that Agostini [the policeman who accompanied Edgardo] also told me that he quieted him with sweets and toys, but he assured me that every time they stopped in some place, the boy sought to go to Church. With regard then to the oral exchanges, I believe much more in what was written by the Rome officials of the Supreme [Ecclesiastical Authorities] than in the depositions made by the father and mother of the little boy.[92]

Similarly, Feletti retold the story of Edgardo's meeting with his parents in Rome:

> Once they arrived in Rome, Edgardo's parents, together with the Rabbi of Rome, were permitted to speak with their son. These three did all they could . . . to persuade the boy to return with them. But he, all by himself . . . knew how to protect himself from his father's, his mother's, and the Rabbi's temptations. He told them that he was Christian and that he wanted to live and die as a Christian.[93]

Like the Catholic journals' rendition of the story, Feletti indicates that Edgardo, while exhibiting some of the behavior befitting a six-year old, also demonstrated a religious fervor that could only be the result of his Catholic conversion. This sanctity was further proven, according to Feletti's testimony, when the boy met his parents, during which his piety, maturity, and tranquility again illuminated the boy's inherently Catholic identity.

Feletti's account is significant for several reasons. First, it enables him to corroborate many of the details that the Catholic press put forward and to question openly the Mortaras' version of the story. Second, by recounting the story himself, he exploits the case's narrativity. He does so to promote Catholic identity, regardless of the fact that the Inquisition tribunal had been abolished. Thus, even though he is purportedly disempowered, Feletti, much like Rector Colonna before him, finds a way to perpetuate the ideology of the Church and to expand a culturally Catholic identity for readers avidly following the trial. In so doing, he further manages to silence the Mortara narrative about their son. Ironically, despite his political and personal disempowerment, his ability to silence the narrative of his opponents invokes the same relationship between storytelling, power, and truth that existed in the times of the Inquisition tribunal.

In his defense of a man the prosecution had portrayed as an overzealous power-monger, Feletti's lawyer emphasizes the version of the story that the Inquisitor narrated:

> [Father Feletti] felt inspired to render glory to the Maker of the universe after the grace that he saw infused in that little boy of such a tender age, for his impassiveness at the sight of the *carabinieri* [police] and his admirable tranquility at the separation from his family, for his patience, for his, I would say, almost enjoyment of the trip, as Marshall Agostini confirms and swears to. [Father Feletti] was reminded of what others have already said or written of the extraordinary intelligence of this little child, of the very rational display of his mental faculties, of his attention in learning, of his piety in observing customs while preserving his continual, entire affection for his parents.[94]

With its reference to "that which others have said or written," Jussi's statement reflects the pervasive nature of the coverage of the Mortara affair. In addition, Jussi carefully draws for his listeners and readers (a script of the proceedings was widely published following the trial) a Catholic portrait of Edgardo as a little boy of extraordinary intelligence who, far from being torn from the bosom of his family, happily and voluntarily joined the Catholic community. Finally, he entices his readership with a description of the most emotionally charged aspects of the conversion narrative, namely the miraculous transition in Edgardo upon being allowed to join the Catholic community. All these details are proof of his client's righteous behavior and justify his carrying out the orders of the Inquisition Tribunal in Rome.

At the same time, however, Jussi operates with the awareness that he is defending Feletti before an audience that opposes the temporal rule of the Church and that is sympathetic to the plight of the Mortara family. Consequently, rather than portray the Mortara parents as detestable individuals who wanted to steal away their child, and perhaps even kill him before allowing him to be raised as a Catholic—accusations that Feletti himself puts forth in his interrogation—the lawyer expresses his empathy with Marianna, stating that "as I think of the pain of that poor mother, tears come before words that can describe it."[95] Unlike the many letters and articles that articulate an antipathy toward the Mortara family and a lack of compassion for the loss of their son, Jussi's discourse expresses sympathy and pity for their situation—all the while, of course, maintaining Feletti's innocence. To justify Feletti's actions, Jussi explains that the bishops of the Inquisition Tribunal and the Church's head, Pope Pius IX, make all the tribunal's decisions. He even notes that, contrary to the current accusations against Feletti, "public opinion of those days never spoke in this way, and it never entered anyone's head to attribute that action to Father Feletti; all the newspapers said as much; regardless of their color they always referred to the Holy Congregation of Rome and to the Sovereign Pontiff."[96] As Jussi seeks to persuade a tribunal made up of antipapal magistrates, he emphasizes that the removal of Edgardo, whether depicted in Catholic, Jewish, or secular journals, had been attributed to the Inquisition Tribunal and not to the actions of any single man.

On April 15, after Feletti had spent over three months in prison, the judges convened to read their verdict on the case. They were well aware of the implications of the case: First was the question of whether the civil government could apply its law retroactively and punish a man for enforcing the law of the time. Second was the fact that, even if one could prove Feletti's guilt, condemning and jailing him would surely result in a confrontation with the Holy See, which was already seething at the fact that one of its representatives was standing trial. Despite Pius's opposition to the civil government they supported, the politicians of Romagna sought to portray themselves as respectful sons of the Church, and such a verdict would certainly not help their cause.[97] Like the Tuscan officials in the Labani affair, these civil leaders found themselves caught between the desire and obligation to serve the interests of their citizens, the promotion of their own personal identification as Catholics, and the need to maintain some sort of relationship with the neighboring Papal States. Thus it is not surprising that the grounds for the arrest of Father Feletti were found to be insufficient and the former Inquisitor was ordered released from prison.[98]

The narrative power and persuasive rhetoric that the Catholic press and Vatican supporters employed in their depictions of the Mortara affair reflect the dramatic potential that conversion stories held more generally for a growing readership. In this chapter, I have suggested that the private correspondence that passed between Vatican officials provided a significant commentary on their desire to maintain control over the press in the Papal States—a concern that was exemplified in the failed attempt to suppress the *Il Povero* story and, later, in the letters regarding press coverage of the Mortara affair. On the public front, by designating a central role to conversion narratives in the press, Catholic news stories sought to counter the antipapal articles of the secular press.

That is, in response to this latter threat, propapal newspapers published conversion stories as "proof" of the vitality, relevance and conquests of the Catholic Church in an era when secularism was on the rise and papal authority was being challenged. Although these stories spoke of the conversions of both Protestants and Jews to Catholicism, the former religious identity of these converts provided the basis for different archetypal conversion stories. Protestant conversion narratives, such as that of De Joux, were portrayed as a kind of "return" to the original religion—a final answer for the upheaval that the Protestant Reformation produced. In contrast, Jewish conversion stories, as Rabbi Weil's story suggested, often followed the example of Paul and narrated a turn to Catholicism that was the result of an epiphany; the distinct religious beliefs of Jews, particularly their rejection of Jesus (a key difference between them and Protestant converts), meant that their conversion stories related a dramatic about-face as they rejected their former beliefs and community and accepted the tenets of Catholicism.

Nowhere is the combination of private letters and public stories more compelling than in the narratives surrounding the Mortara Affair. The story of Edgardo, and the audacious (in the eyes of Vatican leaders, at least) suggestion on the part of secular and antipapal leaders that Edgardo be returned to his biological parents, and hence to the Jewish community, brings us back to the motto with which this study began—*If this is true, let us go immediately to the ghetto and make ourselves Jews.* The motto, spoken by papal supporters and repeated by the cardinal secretary of state of that time, expressed the unfeasibility of a conversion story that worked in reverse; nothing, that is, denoted absurd impossibility more than the image of a Catholic transforming into a Jew. The Pope's vehement insistence that Edgardo remain a Catholic reiterated this belief to a new, not to mention more many, generation of readers. In addition, the Vatican's immovable stance regarding Edgardo's future displayed the unwillingness of papal leaders to enter into a meaningful dialogue with supporters of politically modern, secular governments. In this sense, the reactionary attitudes adopted for this one conversion narrative reflected a larger reality, one that the stories of the Inquisition tribunal of earlier decades invoked as well: rather than seeking a solution to the church-state question, Pius IX chose the road of Catholic absolutism. In so doing, he guaranteed that the future relationship between Vatican followers and supporters of Italian unification, like the question of religious versus national identity itself on the peninsula, would remain a thorny, unresolved matter for years to come.

Conclusion

In 1861, not long after Feletti's release, the secular Kingdom of Italy was established on the Italian peninsula; the pope managed to maintain temporal control only of Rome and the lands surrounding it. Like the trial of Bologna's Inquisitor, this latest blow to papal hegemony simply illustrated to Pius IX and Vatican supporters the many evils of revolution, modernization and secular government. In an attempt to enforce Inquisition law in the last remnant of the Papal States, Rome's Jews were still forced to live in the ghetto and forbidden to employ Christian servants; the boundaries crossed in the controversial article of Andreuccio and Antonio had yet to touch Rome. Similarly, the archives of Rome's House of the Catechumens show that conversions continued to occur, even if in drastically reduced numbers.[1] In 1864, Pius IX responded definitively against the newly established secular governments of Europe with his encyclical *Quanta Cura*, accompanied by his *Syllabus of Errors*, a list of the errors produced by modern advances in the political, social, and scientific worlds. Pius IX's edicts reflected his determined attempt to cling to the temporal power jeopardized by the revolutions sweeping across Europe, just as they reflected the germination of a reactionary political line already visible in the early nineteenth century. Most importantly, the *Syllabus* condemned many liberties that supporters of the revolution of 1848—and supporters of the French Revolution—had championed, including the freedom of religion and the separation of Church and State. Thus, the Vatican's efforts to fight secularism and other so-called "modernist" ideologies were an attempt to conquer the inroads that Italian unification had made on papal temporal power with decrees that deliberately excluded non-Catholic individuals or communities. For example, aside from declaring that non-Catholics could not attain eternal salvation, the pope forbade Catholics from disagreeing with papal claims of temporal control of the Papal States. Significantly, the Jesuits of the *Civiltà Cattolica* had long promoted the publication of a list like the *Syllabus*. Indeed, Giovanni Spadolini connects the establishment of the *Civiltà Cattolica* to the ideas contained in the *Syllabus*, and this connection is not surprising: Monsignor Gioacchino Pecci, who first suggested the *Syllabus* in 1849, on the occasion of the Provincial Council of Spoleto, was a Jesuit, and, while the idea for a *Syllabus* was not taken up immediately, the Jesuits had the idea for such a condemnation in mind when they established their journal: "*Civiltà Cattolica* managed to take the opportunity to include in the Bull . . . the 'explicit condemnation' of the errors of rationalism and semirationalism."[2] And so we appear to have come full circle. That is, we began this study in 1814, when Pius VII restored the Society of Jesus in the Papal States. Fifty years later, papal opposition to the ideals associated with the French Revolution, which led to the readmittance of the Jesuits, found further support within the ecclesiastical hierarchy of the Vatican. The reactionary Jesuit order that had contributed profoundly to the ideology of conversion on the peninsula finally saw their idea of a syllabus come to fruition.

In his discussion of the Church, Antonio Gramsci notes that the temporal and religious power of the papacy in Italy, typified by the assertions of Pius's *Syllabus*, contributed to the difficulty of conceptualizing or developing a secular Italian state. Unlike other countries, in which "national formation limited ecclesiastical function," in Italy Vatican representatives had both an economic and political role.[3] As a result of the political personality associated with Catholicism in Italy, writes Gramsci, "Italian Catholicism was viewed as a surrogate not only for the spirit of nationality and state but even as a worldwide hegemonic function, that is, as imperialistic spirit."[4] Temporal and religious control enabled the Vatican to use its system of beliefs to define a national ideology on the peninsula, even as it promoted its Catholic identity on a world stage as well. The conversion stories examined herein attest to this "imperialistic" vision of the Vatican: through their vocabulary of conquest, their persuasive rhetoric, their threatening stereotypes, and their legal power, the Vatican promoted an international cultural identity that was defined by Catholic belief; on the Italian peninsula, this cultural identity found expression through the culture of conversion, which attempted to ensure the Catholic identity of the citizenry at the center of Catholic civilization.

Pius IX himself expresses the problem of the simultaneously Italian and international identity of the Church in a letter he writes to a teenage Edgardo Mortara in 1867:

> You are very dear to me, my little son, for I acquired you for Jesus Christ at a high price. . . . Your case set off a worldwide storm against me and the apostolic See. Governments and peoples, the rulers of the world as well as the journalists—who are the truly powerful people of our times—declared war on me. Monarchs themselves entered the battle against me, and with their ambassadors they flooded me with diplomatic notes, and all this because of you. . . . People lamented the harm done to your parents because you were regenerated by the grace of holy baptism and brought up according to God's wishes. And in the meantime no one showed any concern for me, father of all the faithful.[5]

In his letter, Pius envisions himself as a universal father, fighting a "worldwide storm" of anti-Catholic sentiment. While these words reflect the international identity of the Church, it was the local power of Inquisition law in Bologna that enabled papal troops to remove Edgardo and bring him to the Catechumens. Thus the political power of the Church on the peninsula reinforced the hegemony of its religious ideology. This reinforcement can be seen in the very vocabulary Pius uses in his letter. While the note begins on an endearing and personal note, Pius goes on to describe his adoption of Edgardo with vocabulary typical of the Inquisition, namely that of acquisition. Pius's purchase of Edgardo, encapsulated in his words "I acquired you for Jesus Christ at a high price," portrays the boy's conversion and transfer to Rome as a conquest similar to the territorial colonialization of other nineteenth-century powers. While such a conquest could only occur on a local level, because it required the implementation of Inquisition law, it had implications for local and universal Catholic identity, since the boy's "regeneration," as Pius calls it, like that of the protagonists of the trials and novels investigated earlier, marks a rejuvenation of Catholic ideals and beliefs in a new generation. These conversion stories were told for a variety of different audiences: from the general public to which the novels and newspapers were directed to Church officials to whom the letters and trial documentation was addressed. The official nature of all of these genres binds them together: all of them were written by Christians, for Christians, and they were meant to redefine and reinforce that which made them Christian. Ironically, enforcing this official vision of Christian identity was carried out through writing about Jews and acting upon Jewish bodies—proof that the boundary between self and Other is very fine indeed.[6]

Thus, in the face of threats to its power, the Vatican viewed the conquest of conversions, or "acquisitions," as fundamental for ensuring the Catholic identity of its lands, and even of extending religious identity beyond these lands. In their promotion of such conquest, Catholic leaders, legislators, novelists, and journalists followed similar paths: all express the prejudices and fears that directed papal policies of the nineteenth century, and all promote conversion as the elaboration of a cultural initiative that responded to the political fears of the Vatican. Not only were the French Revolution and the subsequent unification of Italy the contexts in which this effort took place; the "imperialist" hegemony of the Vatican on the peninsula enabled Vatican leaders to use the political and religious upheaval brought about by the conflict as a stimulus for a return to a culturally and socially Catholic society.

Epilogue

The complicated relationship between Church and state during the Risorgimento has serious ramifications for Italian and Vatican politics in the twentieth century, when religious difference and issues of nationhood took on new, more perilous meanings to which the Vatican was forced to respond. In 1870, Italian troops took Rome, leading Pius IX to barricade himself within the Vatican; soon thereafter he forbade Catholics from participating in the political life of the new Italy, as electors or as candidates. Following the *Syllabus of Errors*, this last act once again illustrated Pius's vehement opposition to the establishment of a unified Italy with Rome at its center. Fifty years later, however, relations between the Vatican and the Italian state that surrounded it seemed to be on the mend: Benito Mussolini, eager to legitimize his rule and gain support at home and abroad, appeared particularly willing to negotiate with Church leaders. For its part, the Vatican, leery of nineteenth-century liberalism, and still bitter over the loss of much of its land and temporal power, viewed the rise of authoritarian governments quite favorably, believing that these one-party leaders would better serve the interests of the Church. Mussolini, for example, was opposed to communism, deemed a worrisome threat by Vatican leaders, and he appeared disenchanted, to say the least, with other liberal, socialist groups that were critical of the Church. In 1929, officials signed the first treaty between the Holy See and the Italian state, providing evidence of the appeal that the Vatican saw in Mussolini's government. Among other things, these Lateran Accords required that Italy recognize the area of the Vatican City State as a separate entity. In addition, the Italian government declared Roman Catholicism the official religion of the state and made religious education in public schools compulsory; in return, the Vatican recognized the Italian state with Rome as its capital.

The Lateran Accords reflected the unique relationship between the Vatican and the nation that surrounded it, and the closeness of those ties continued well after this treaty was ratified. During World War II, for example, Vatican diplomats, most of whom were Italian by birth, assumed, as Susan Zuccotti notes, "a right to intervene with government officials, making suggestions as well as requests, to a much greater extent than with representatives of other nations. They were assured that they would be received and respected, if nothing else."[1] That is not to say that the relationship between Mussolini's government and the Holy See did not have its problems. Shortly after the Lateran Accords were ratified, Mussolini ordered attacks to be carried out against members of Catholic Action, an umbrella organization of youth groups, charity organizations, and schools. In response, Pius XI issued his encyclical *Non abbiamo bisogno (We Do Not Need)*, on June 29, 1931. However, the condemnation contained in the encyclical was limited in scope; rather than providing a unilateral denunciation of fascism, Pius XI spoke out against only those actions that threatened the Church and its organizations.

Similarly, when Mussolini passed racial legislation in Italy in 1938, the Vatican did not protest the new restrictions against Italy's Jews, despite Pius XI's opposition to Nazi racial policies, as expressed in his 1937 encyclical entitled *Mit Brennender Sorge (With Burning Concern)*. Indeed, even this encyclical, striking because of its condemnation of racism and because of the fearlessness with which the pope criticized Hitler's abrogation of the concordat that both countries had signed, contains no reference to or denunciation of anti-Semitism.[2] As far as Italy is concerned, the reason behind this lack of condemnation seems quite clear; the racial legislation that Mussolini instigated in Italy was startlingly similar to the Vatican's own restrictions against Jewish inhabitants of the Papal States before 1870. Indeed, Mussolini pursued anti-Jewish legislation that advocated a separation between Jewish and Catholic communities that, before the unification of Italy, the Vatican had pursued. Thus, while the Church disagreed with the Nazi perception of Jewish faults based on race, Church doctrine viewed Jews as problematic because of their religious beliefs and threatening because of their past support for the French Revolution—still remembered—and their supposed present support for Communism and Bolshevism. These sentiments are reflected in a letter that the Vatican diplomat to the Italian government, Father Pietro Tacchi Ventura, reported to Cardinal Secretary of State Luigi Maglione regarding the former's attempts to limit Italian racial laws: "I took care not to call for the total abrogation of [the racial laws] which, according to the principles and the traditions of the Catholic Church, certainly have some clauses that should be abolished, but which clearly contain others that have merit and should be confirmed."[3] Thus, while Mussolini's racial motivations for such legislation—like those of other fascist leaders—might have conflicted with Catholic ideology, the end result, namely a separation and exclusion of Jews from the general community, appealed to many clergymen, and the Vatican protested racial laws only insofar as they impinged upon ecclesiastical powers and jurisdiction.

The Vatican's silence in the face of the racial laws in Italy (and numerous other European countries) was only one aspect of its problematic response to the events surrounding World War II. A second, perhaps more troubling element of the Vatican response to racial legislation was the fact that the correspondence of Vatican representatives, be it addressed to secular leaders or to fellow clergymen, regularly adopted Nazi racial vocabulary. Most relevant for our discussion here, this rhetoric often related to the issue of religious belonging and conversion. Thus, for example, Vatican diplomats regularly differentiated between so-called Mosaic Jews, referred to as "non-Aryans," and Jews who converted to Catholicism, or "non-Aryan Catholics." In January 1941, for instance, the apostolic nuncio in Bucharest, Andreas Cassulo, wrote Maglione requesting help for converted Jews, complaining that these "non-Aryan Catholics" were subjected to the same laws as Jews "because of the race to which they belonged."[4] Similarly, the Vatican representative in Slovakia, Monsignor Giuseppe Burzio, wrote Maglione regarding the situation of "non-Aryan Catholics" in that country, explaining that if the Vatican did not help them emigrate, this "category of Jews" would endure the same fate as Mosaic Jews.[5] In November 1942, the nuncio in Berlin, Cesare Orsenigo, informed Maglione of new laws directed against "non-Aryans" in Germany, complaining that the new law demanded the deportation not only of "non-Aryans" but also of "converted non-Aryans," and Catholics married to "non-Aryans" of either category.[6]

In part, the Aryan vocabulary with which Vatican representatives refer to converts and Jews alike reflects the Church's desire to maintain strict neutrality during the war. That is, the Vatican felt it impossible to protest on Jews' behalf because Jews were viewed as enemies of Germany; any protest on their behalf would therefore be viewed as an act of hostility. The Church's acquiescence to Germany's position with respect to the Jews, and the Vatican's regulation of their behavior in response to German demands for strict neutrality, resulted in the Vatican assimilating

German attitudes and judgments.[7] I would submit that the Holy See attuned its response to such a degree that it acquiesced to arguments produced by Nazi sentiments even when not dealing directly with the German government, as demonstrated by its indiscriminate use of Aryan vocabulary. Thus the Church's fascist vocabulary is a result of the Vatican desire to maintain its neutrality, a diplomatic stance it insisted upon lest its own interests be threatened. These interests are reflected linguistically by the differentiation between "Catholic non-Aryans" and "non-Aryans" more generally, since writers and readers are reminded that, despite their non-Aryan status, as Christians the former should still receive certain religious and social freedoms denied the latter. By accepting the Nazis' categorization of inferiority, the Church hoped to maintain its relationship with Germany; by singling out converts, it hoped to effectuate legislative changes with regard to issues that involved Church jurisdiction, which at times included speaking out on behalf of converted Jews.

The problematic use of Aryan rhetoric is further complicated by the historians who edited the volumes of correspondence in which these letters appear.[8] In the lengthy introductions that accompany each of these volumes, these editors regularly fail to distinguish between Jews and converted Jews. This time, however, the discrimination works in the opposite direction: the editors call both Jews and Jewish converts to Catholicism "Jews." Thus while the wartime diplomats sought to distinguish non-Aryan Catholics from non-Aryans more generally—suggesting, at least, a shared religious association with the former—the editors seek to obfuscate the Catholic identity of Jewish converts by avoiding mention of their adopted religion entirely. This vagueness enables the editors to claim that the Vatican helped many "Jews" during the war, while the letters point to the fact that they aided mainly Jewish converts and that they did so not simply out of a sense of altruism but because as Catholics these individuals fell under the jurisdiction of the Church. Thus they challenged the racial laws against converts as much as a symbol of ecclesiastical freedom as a means of helping. For example, in the introduction to volume six, the editors state that the appeals that the Vatican representative to Italy, Father Tacchi Ventura, made to Mussolini regarding Italy's anti-Jewish laws lessened the country's racial policies against Jews. The documents suggest, however, that Tacchi Ventura's protests were made on behalf of converted Jews, and the protests were voiced largely because Church officials chafed at the idea that secular legislation could regulate social issues formerly in the Church's domain. Later on in the same introduction, the editors write that during the period from 1939 to 1940, the Holy See helped about 2,000 individual Jews. Only afterwards do they clarify that these individuals were "Jews who had become Christians" or "half-Jews."[9]

Here we find a striking dichotomy. While Vatican wartime diplomats sought to differentiate between non-Aryans and non-Aryan Catholics in an attempt to help the latter and denote them as different from "regular" non-Aryans, Vatican editors sought to collapse the two categories into one: "Jews." In both instances, the references to converted Jews suggest that the Vatican did not recognize these individuals as equals. In both cases, too, the word used to refer to Jews and converted Jews reflects political considerations on the part of the writers. During the war, differentiating between non-Aryans and non-Aryan Catholics was an indication of the Vatican's desire to distinguish between individuals whom the Nazis had branded *en masse* as racially inferior. The postwar reference of the Jesuit editors to "Jews" was part of the Vatican response to accusations put forth against precisely these actions, or inactions, during the war. As Father Blet, the one still-surviving member of the editorial team, states in his book, the editors were appointed to their task as a means of formulating a response to the accusations brought against Pius XII.[10] Thus, while the Jesuit editors would prefer readers to believe that their work represents an objective selection of Vatican wartime correspondence, Blet's statement reflects the fact that their work was a politically defensive measure that the Vatican took to respond to its critics.

And the debate regarding this subject has been reignited recently. In late February 2003, after years of negotiations and arguments, the Vatican began to open the archives of Pius XI to scholars (the archives of Pius XII, the wartime pope, are still off-limits). Among the first documents released was the letter of a well-known Jewish convert to Catholicism, Edith Stein, who wrote Pius XI in 1933 asking him to intervene on behalf of Europe's Jews and to speak out publicly against Nazism. Stein had converted to Catholicism in 1922 and in 1933 entered the Carmelite convent in Cologne, Germany. The Nazis arrested her in August 1942, and she died in Auschwitz several weeks later. Her death, deemed martyrdom by the Vatican, led to her beatification in 1987 and sainthood in 1998. Angela Ales Bello, a scholar of Stein, explains that Stein never denied her Jewish birthright, viewing the relationship between Judaism and Christianity as one of continuity rather than rupture: "For her—Christians can never disassociate themselves from the Jews," explains Bello.. "That association," concludes journalist Luigi Accattoli, "was critical for her 'martyrdom.'"[11] The Vatican's support for

Stein's beatification thus recalls the powerful allusions to Pauline Christianity we saw in many nineteenth-century narratives.

In addition, the release of her letter serves as a reminder not only that the Vatican was receptive to pleas for help leading up to and during World War II but also that Catholics, like others, suffered at the hands of Nazis. Stein herself, in her letter to Pius XI, wrote, "The war against Catholicism takes place stealthily and by less brutal means than against Judaism, but no less systematically."[12] Vatican supporters have suggested that their institution has fallen victim to a liberal conspiracy since the French Revolution, as seen in nineteenth-century Vatican correspondence, the Catholic press, and even novels such as that of Bresciani; these suggestions multiplied after the Holy See lost its temporal power in 1870, and the recent wave of criticism against the Vatican's wartime activities has led some Vatican supporters to publicly speak out against similarly unjust attacks simply meant to malign the Church.[13] Stein's letter reiterates this view with her warning of the threat to Catholicism, providing the Vatican with a further defense against its detractors.

Finally, the Vatican's decision to make Stein's letter public not only reminds readers of a powerful modern conversion story but underscores the Vatican's rejection of racially based anti-Semitism, since Stein is a saintly church figure (Santa Teresa Benedetta della Croce) regardless of her Jewish birth. Disclosing her letter thus emphasizes the difference between the Church-instigated, theologically based anti-Judaism of earlier centuries—attitudes displayed in the nineteenth century as well, as illustrated herein—and the racially based anti-Semitism of the twentieth century. In other words, like its 1998 text *We Remember: A Reflection of the Shoah*, the Vatican seeks to mitigate its responsibility for the atmosphere of hatred against European Jews that led to the Holocaust.[14] Regardless, however, of the letters the Vatican chooses to publish from its archives, and in spite of the editors' adjustments in their commentary to earlier wartime documentation, the racial vocabulary Vatican officials adopted during the war reflected at the very least a linguistic acceptance of the Nazi mentality, just as Vatican "anti-Judaism" of earlier centuries led to a passive acceptance of fascist racial laws. Ultimately, these two factors make the boundaries between two originally separate forms of intolerance—Church-instigated anti-Judaism and racially based Nazi anti-Semitism—less distinct. The Vatican's latest response to the ethical implications of its wartime diplomacy and rhetoric simply illustrates how deeply the politics of conversion and the question of religious and political identity continue to resonate today.

Notes

Chapter 1

1. Anne Fremantle, ed., *The Papal Encyclicals in their Historical Context* (New York: New American Library, 1956), 120.
2. Bartolommeo Cardinal Pacca, *Memorie storiche del ministero de' due viaggi in Francia e della prigionia nel Forte di S. Carlo* (Rome: F. Bourlie, 1830), 252–53. Unless otherwise indicated, all translations are mine.
3. Pacca, 253.
4. It is difficult to say for certain how many Jews lived in the Papal States in this period. In 1842, the number hovers at about 12,700 Jews in the entire Papal States out of a general population of about 2,900,000, making Jews a mere 0.4 percent of the population. For Jewish population statistics, see Ermmano Loevinson, "Gli israeliti della Stato Pontificio e la loro evoluzione politico sociale nel periodo del Risorgimento Italiano fino al 1849," *Rassegna Storica del Risorgimento* 4 (1929): 768–803; for general population statistics, see B. R. Mitchell, ed., *The International Historical Statistics Europe, 1750–1993*, 4th ed. (New York: Stockton, 1998).
5. Patricia Wald, *Constituting Americans: Cultural Anxiety and Narrative Form* (Durham, NC: Duke University Press, 1995), 2.
6. Cited in Giovanni Miccoli, *Fra mito della Cristianità e secolarizzazione* (Casale Monferrato: Marietti, 1985), 26–27.
7. Robin West, *Narrative, Authority, and the Law* (Ann Arbor: The University of Michigan Press, 1993), 5.
8. For a discussion of *italianita* (Italian-ness) see Giulio Bollati, *L'Italiano: Il carattere nazionale come storia e come invenzione* (Turin: Einaudi, 1984), 3–13.
9. The very word "convert," from the Latin "convertere" signifies this change: "To turn about, turn in character or nature, transform, translate, etc." *Oxford English Dictionary*, 1991 ed.
10. Richard Weisberg, *Poethics: And Other Strategies of Law and Literature* (New York: Columbia University Press, 1992), 72.
11. Stephen Greenblatt coined the phrase "cultural poetics" to define this relationship between literature and society in his essay "Towards a Poetics of Culture," in *The New Historicism*, ed. H. Aram Veeser (London: Routledge, 1990), 1–14. Also see Stephen Greenblatt, "Invisible Bullets: Renaissance Authority and its Subversion," *Glyph* 8 (1981): 40–61.

12. For further discussion of the theories and development of the interdisciplinary study of law and literature, see Peter Brooks and Paul Gewirtz, eds., *Law's Stories: Narrative and Rhetoric in the Law* (New Haven: Yale University Press, 1996).
13. Peter Brooks, *Reading for the Plot: Design and Intention in Narrative* (New York: Vintage Books, 1984), 61.
14. Robert A. Ferguson, "Untold Stories in the Law," in *Law's Stories: Narrative and Rhetoric in the Law*, ed. Peter Brooks and Paul Gewirtz (New Haven: Yale University Press, 1996), 89.
15. On a more personal note, these archives opened at a time when a new initiative began to open even more recent Vatican archival material to the public. I refer here to the efforts of the International Catholic Jewish Historical Commission, a group of six scholars that was appointed in November 1999 (by the Vatican and a Jewish liaison group) and assigned the task of reviewing the Church's published archival material relating to World War II in the hopes of, eventually, turning to undisclosed documentation. I acted in the capacity of researcher for this group, and it was largely because of my work in this more modern period of Vatican politics, a subject I shall return to briefly at the end of this book, that I became interested in archival resources more generally and those of the Vatican in particular.
16. Natalie Zemon Davis, *The Return of Martin Guerre* (Cambridge, MA: Harvard University Press, 1983), 4.
17. Paul established the Congregation of the Inquisition, also known as the Roman Inquisition and Holy Office, during the time of the Protestant Reformation. Its task was to maintain the correct doctrine of faith for the Church and to examine erroneous or false doctrines. While initially focused on the danger of the Reformation, the Inquisition tribunal's focus changed depending on that which the Holy Office viewed as new or imminent threats to Catholicism. I shall return to this issue in Chapter 2.
18. John C. Hawley, "Making Disciples of All Nations," in *Historicizing Christian Encounters with the Other*, ed. John C. Hawley (London: Macmillan, 1998), 6. For a discussion on boundaries in the nineteenth-century city, also see Peter Stallybrass and Allon White, *The Politics and Poetics of Transgression* (Ithaca, New York: Cornell University Press, 1986).
19. This term is used by Nelson Moe in his discussion of Vincenzo Gioberti. See Nelson Moe, *The View from Vesuvius: Italian Culture and the Southern Question* (Los Angeles: California University Press, 2001), 112–20.
20. Stallybrass and White note that the boundaries of the nineteenth-century city were generally denoted along terms of high and low, rich and poor, clean and dirty. The mapping of the city along these lines repeated "the discourse of colonial anthropology. With regard to papal cities, this division was also made along religious and moral lines: moral Christian versus immoral Jew" (Stallybrass and White, 127).
21. Archivio della Congregazione per la Dottrina della Fede (hereafter referred to as ACDF); Santum Officiium (hereafter referred to as S. O.), Stanza

Storica (hereafter referred to as St.St.). TT.2.n.17. *Edito sopra gli ebrei* (Rome: Stamperia della Rev. Camera Apostolica, 1775), 6–7.

22. For further discussion of how the marriage market affected conversion rates, as well as more general statistics regarding the conversion of Jewish men and women, see Luciano Allegra, "Modelli di conversione," *Quaderni Storici* 78 (1991), 901–15.
23. For a discussion of this subject, see Maria Faust Maternini Zotta, *L'Ente comunitario ebraico: la legislazione negli ultimi due secoli*, Pubblicazioni della facoltà di giurisprudenza della università di Trieste, vol. 27 (Milan: Giuffrè Editore, 1983), 60–83.
24. ACDF, S. O., St.St., BB.5.i.
25. When Napoleon freed the pope from his exile, he handed Pius VII only the lands of Rome and Trasimeno. As Cardinal Wiseman recorded, "The ability, perseverance, and admirable tact of Cardinal Consalvi," who was sent to the Congress of Vienna in an attempt to win back some of the pope's former holdings, "won [the richest and fairest of his provinces] back." Nicholas Cardinal Wiseman, *Recollections of the Last Four Popes and of Rome in their Times* (New York: Joseph F. Wagner, 1858), 86.
26. Clement reluctantly agreed to suppress the Jesuit order after coming under much pressure to do so by the courts of France, Spain, Portugal and Naples, all of whom viewed the Jesuits' highly visible missionary work and their supposed power in the royal courts as dangerous to their own authority.
27. For an extensive discussion of the fall of the Jesuits, see Owen Chadwick, *The Popes and European Revolution* (Oxford, UK: Clarendon, 1981), 346–90.
28. See Giovanni Miccoli, *Fra mito della cristianità e secolarizzazione: studi sul rapporto chiesa-società nell'età contemporanea* (Casale Monferrato: Marietti, 1985), 22–23.
29. Manfred Barthel, *The Jesuits*, trans. Mark Howson (New York: William Morrow and Company, 1984), 234. For a detailed history of the Society of Jesus, also see William V. Bangert, S. J., *A History of the Society of Jesus* (St. Louis: The Institute of Jesuit Sources, 1972).
30. This agenda ultimately led to the founding of the Jesuit newspaper *Civiltà Cattolica*, which, as Manfred Barthel writes, "set standards for backward thinking and sheer reactionary wrong-headedness that prevailed until the third decade of the present century" (Barthel, 239). I will explore the foundation and content of this journal more thoroughly in a subsequent chapter.
31. ACDF, S. O., St.St., BB.5.i. Undated letter.
32. See Miccoli, *Fra mito della cristianità e secolarizzazione*, 80–87.
33. CH. De Montalembert, *Histoire de Sainte Elisabeth de Hongrie Duchesse de Thuringe (1207–1231)*, Paris 1841, XII. *Miccoli*, *Fra mito della cristianità e secolarizzazione*, 46–47.
34. Daniele Menozzi, "Tra riforma e restaurazione," *Storia d'Italia, La Chiesa e il potere politico dal Medioevo all'età contemporanea*, vol. 9, ed. Giorgio Chittolini and Giovanni Miccoli (Turin: Einaudi, 1986), 778. Also, for further discussion of this hardening political line of the Catholic Church, see Mario

Rosa, "Tra tolleranza e repressione: Roma e gli ebrei nel '700," *Italia Judaica: Gli ebrei in Italia dalla segregazione alla prima emancipazione*, Atti del II Convegno internazionale, Tel Aviv 15–20 giugno 1986 (Rome: Ministero per i beni cultura e ambientali, Ufficio centrale per i beni archivistici, 1989), 81–98.

35. These numbers mark a significant increase from the number of converts at the end of the eighteenth century. During the pontificate of Pius VI, and despite the famous proselytization efforts of the then rector of the Catechumens, Rovira Bonet, on average only six people were baptized a year in the years immediately following the French Revolution. See W. H. de Collenberg, "Le baptême des juifs à Rome de 1614 à 1798 selon les registres de la 'Casa dei Catecumeni,'" *Archivum Historiae Pontificiae* 26 (1988): 119–294; and Marina Caffiero, "'Le insidie de' perfidi giudei'. Antiebraismo e riconquista cattolica alla fine del settecento," in *La questione ebraica dall'illuminismo all'impero (1700–1815)*, atti del convegno della Società Italiana di Studi sul secolo XVIII, ed. Paolo Alatri and Silvia Grassi (Naples: Edizioni Scientifiche Italiane, 1994), 194. Also, Attilio Milano notes that the House of the Catechumens in Rome received the baptism of 116 men and 80 women during the years 1813–1869, which includes the years of the present examination. While he does not specify, one can assume that Milano is only referring to the baptism of Jews. See Attilio Milano, *L'impari lotta della Comunità di Roma contro la Casa dei catecumeni* (Città di Castello: Tip. Unione arti grafiche, 1950), 5.
36. Archivio della Casa dei Catecumeni, Rome (hereafter referred to as ACC), Catecumeni neofiti 181, *Liber Battizzatorum Neophitorum Ven. Domus Cathecumen de Urbe, 1759–1826.*
37. Ermanno Loevinson, "Gli israeliti della Stato Pontificio," 784.
38. ACDF, S. O., St.St., BB.5.k, *Edito sopra gli ebrei*, 7.
39. David Kertzer, *The Pope against the Jews* (Knopf: New York, 2001), 54.
40. His conversion story will be discussed in a later chapter.
41. ACDF, S. O., St.St., CC5.l.
42. ACDF, S. O., St.St., BB.2.d. Pesaro, 1815.
43. For a discussion of antisemitism around Easter time, see Stallybrass and White, 54–5.
44. For further discussion, see Joshua Trachtenberg, *The Devil and the Jews: The Medieval Conception of the Jew and its Relation to Modern Antisemitism* (New Haven: Yale University Press, 1943).
45. ACC, Catechumeni neofiti 183, *Libro di Ebrei, e Turchi venuti nella Pia Casa de' Catechumens*, 1814–1824, 12.
46. ACDF, S. O., St.St., TT.3.b.9. Pesaro, November 2, 1823.
47. Maria Paiano, "Il dibattito sui riflessi dell'antisemitismo nella liturgia Cattolica," *Studi Storici* 41, no. 3 (July–September 2000): 658.
48. For discussion of these negotiations, see Nicholas Davidson, "The Inquisition and the Italian Jews," *Inquisition and Society in Early Modern Europe*, ed. Stephen Haliczer (Croom Helm: London, 1987). In addition, Mario

Rosa discusses the oscillations between tolerance and repression with regard to the Jews of various eighteenth-century pontificates in his *Tra tolleranza e repressione.*

49. For further discussion, and a series of important documents on the subject, see Ermanno Loevinson, "Gli israeliti della Stato Pontificio."
50. ACDF, S. O., St.St., CC.4.c.
51. *Canne* refers to a measurement. Three hundred *scudi* refers to a monetary sum the offender was forced to pay. ACDF, S. O., St.St., BB.5.k, *Edito sopra gli ebrei*, 6.
52. ACC, Catechumens neofiti 183, *Libro di Ebrei, e Turchi*, 18.
53. ACC, Catechumens neofiti 183, *Libro di Ebrei, e Turchi*, 18.
54. *Ratto della Signora Anna del Monte trattenuta à Catecumeni tredici giorni dalli 6 fino alli 19 maggio anno 1749*, ed. Giuseppe Sermonta (Rome: Carucci editore, 1989).
55. Robin West, *Narrative, Authority, and the Law*, 1–2. See also John Brannigan, *New Historicism and Cultural Materialism* (New York: St. Martin's, 1998).
56. Richard Delgado, "Storytelling for Oppositionists and Others: A Plea for Narrative," *Michigan Law Review* 87 (August, 1989): 2313.

CHAPTER 2

1. Archivio della Casa dei Catecumeni, Rome (ACC), Catecumeni neofiti 181, *Liber Battizzatorum Neophitorum.* The exact date of the baptism is October 9, 1804.
2. Indeed, according to the turn of the century historian Giuseppe Marcotti, Tivoli converted for the sole purpose of obtaining a job, although no records in the archives provide proof of this claim. Marcotti, 253.
3. For further discussion of the rules restricting converts, particularly Jewish converts, see Allegra, "Modelli di conversione," 901–15. As he points out, conversion was often tied to the marriage market, and, because Jewish converts were forbidden any contact with the Jewish community, they were wholly dependent on the House of the Catechumens for financial support.
4. While Livorno was certainly a haven in comparison to the Papal States, it should be noted that Livorno was more reactionary than the rest of Tuscany; while in Florence and Pisa, for example, Jews lived outside the ghetto, in Livorno they still lived within its walls. There were requests to move out, but one of the governor's closest advisers was an anti-Semitic priest by the name of Martolini, who argued that having Jews move out of the ghetto would lead to mixing with the general population, and the results would be disastrous. Marcotti, 255.
5. The name appears with different spellings throughout Vatican documentation: Cavaliere, Cavaglieri, Cavagliere. I have maintained the spelling most

frequently used, Cavalieri. In addition, the reader will note that while I generally refer to Tivoli by his preconversion name, I refer to Cavalieri by his postconversion name. I do so in large part because, while the legal documentation calls the case against Tivoli the "Labani Affair," they generally refer to the man in question as Tivoli rather than Labani. In contrast, similar legal documents refer to Cavaliere as such rather than as Manganetti. Why Tivoli is called by his non-Christian name is not discussed, although it is undoubtedly linked to his identity as an apostate Jew.

6. For a discussion of conversion as conquest, see Michael Ragussis, *Figures of Conversion: "The Jewish Question" and English National Identity* (Durham: Duke University Press, 1995), 171–72.
7. Indeed, as Ernesto Galli della Loggia notes, the Church in Italy was able to sustain itself precisely because of "popular religiosity" that it discovered and encouraged. By popular, he suggests that the Church had an extraordinary capacity of organization to bring attention to even the poorer strata of society. This capacity to establish a relationship with the masses meant that the Church was "the *only* Italian institution with a strong base and popular content . . . in the communal Italian experience Christianity . . . is a motive and pretense of unity." *L'identità italiana* (Bologna: Il Mulino, 1998), 50–51.
8. R. Po-Chia Hsia, *Trent 1475: Stories of a Ritual Murder Trial* (New Haven: Yale University Press, 1992).
9. ACC, Catecumeni neofiti 181, *Liber Battizzatorum Neophitorum.* In his discussion of converts, Ermanno Loevinson notes that converts were always referred to as such, even years after baptism occurred, as a means of ensuring the humility of the convert. In addition, they did so because this title carried over to police reports so that the police would know to keep a special eye on these individuals. This may have been another reason that Tivoli is constantly referred to as the "apostate." See Loevinson, "Gli israeliti della Stato Pontificio," 786.
10. Archivio della Congregazione per la Dottrina della Fede (ACDF), Santum Officiium (S. O.), Stanza Storica (St.St.), BB.2.c. Tuscany, June 20, 1814.
11. The meaning of the term "citizen," or "cittadino," has changed with the advent of nationhood, and hence I would like to clarify the use of the terms "subject" and "citizen" used herein. In Tuscan documentation, "cittadino" suggests any inhabitant of the duchy. Indeed, as the *Grande Dizionario della Lingua Italiana* notes in its definition of the term, "During the French Revolution, [it was] a common noun that came to refer without distinction to all people, to indicate the impartiality of the law." (*Grande Dizionario della lingua italiana*, vol. 3, 1st ed.) Not surprisingly, in the lands of Tuscany that remained under Napoleonic control, this definition was maintained in much of the documentation examined in this chapter, and the general usage of the word meant that it applied to both Jewish and Catholic inhabitants of the duchy. In contrast, papal representatives, who did not recognize the changes wrought by the French Revolution, maintained an older, pre–French Revolution definition of the term, when it meant simply "he who is part of the

population of a city" or "he who lives in a city" (*Grande Dizionario della lingua italiana*, vol. 3, 1st ed.) Jews, who did not live freely within the city and did not possess the civic rights and privileges of Catholic inhabitants of a city, are clearly not included in this designation, as the documentation cited herein reflects. To differentiate between Catholic and Jewish inhabitants of the Papal States, I therefore refer to Catholics as "citizens," a term the documents of the day often employ (albeit not with the modern connotation of this word) and Jews as "subjects," as often they were referred by papal officials.

12. ACDF, S. O., St.St., CC.3.f.
13. ACDF, S. O., St.St., CC.3.f.
14. ACDF, S. O., St.St., CC.3.f.
15. ACDF, S. O., St.St., CC.3.f.
16. ACDF, S. O., St.St., CC.3.f. Ferrara, May 30, 1821.
17. ACDF, S. O., St.St., CC.3.f. Ferrara, 30 May 1821.
18. ACDF, S. O., St.St., CC.3.f. Ferrara, October 3, 1821.
19. ACC, Catecumeni neofiti 183, *Libro di Ebrei, e Turchi*, 3–6.
20. Daniele Menozzi refers to the conversion stories of Protestants to Catholicism, suggesting that their conversions were viewed by the Church as victory against a destruction of the social order brought on by the Revolution but started by Luther and the Reformation. I would extend this battle to include Jewish conversion narratives. For further discussion, see Menozzi, *Tra riforma e restaurazione.*
21. ACC, Catecumeni neofiti 183, *Libro di Ebrei, e Turchi* 3–6.
22. ACC, Catecumeni neofiti 183, *Libro di Ebrei, e Turchi* 3–6.
23. ACC, Catecumeni neofiti 181, *Liber Battizzatorum Neophitorum.* This is not the only case Colonna records. In 1806, for example, only two years after Tivoli appeared in the Catecumen registry, Colonna records the story of a Muslim convert—one of only five converts that year—who was captured and enslaved by a papal vessel in 1805. The young man was brought to the port of Civitavecchia, where he, much like Jochanan, if we are to believe the rector's story, voluntarily approached the rector and asked to convert. The boy took the name Fortunato, and converted under Colonna's instruction. Several years later, in 1821, the number of Muslim converts grew further: out of a total of 15 converts, four were Muslim. The writer of the Catechumens registry explains that the increase was the result of an Armenian Catholic merchant working in Constantinople, who bought these Muslims as slaves and brought them to the peninsula. One fell ill in Trieste while they were traveling, and a priest who accompanied the group thought she should be baptized. She lived, however, and soon her fellow Muslims appear to have been converted as well.
24. ACDF, S. O., St.St., BB.2.c. Livorno, May 23, 1814.
25. ACDF, S. O., St.St., BB.2.c. Livorno, June 13, 1814.
26. ACDF, S. O., St.St., BB.2.c. Rome, June 1814.

27. James Shapiro, *Shakespeare and the Jews* (New York: Columbia University Press, 1996), 14.
28. Shapiro, *Shakespeare and the Jews*, 15.
29. Archivio dello Stato di Firenze (hereafter referred to as ASF). Presidenza del buongoverno 1814–1848, Affari Comuni (hereafter referred to as PAC), Parte Prima, Filza 14, 488. Livorno, June 13, 1814.
30. John Brannigan, *New Historicism and Cultural Materialism* (New York: St. Martin's, 1998), 64. Also see Greenblatt, "Invisible Bullets."
31. "MERDA PER il Dio de Cristiani / Guilotina P. LI. Ebrei Catechumeni / Alla Lanterna li Ministri / che promuovano l'Idolatria." ACDF, S. O., St.St., CC.3.f.
32. "I sudditi dello Stato Pontificio." Sonnetto: Scandelizzati da bestial governo / Che ci rode e ci affligge in ogni parte / Siam costretti a bramar che Bonaparte / D'Sant Elena torni o dall'Inferno, / Se' condannati siam a un male eterno / Dalle profane o dalle sacre carte / Ci regga almen colui che adoprò l'arte / D'aver per fin la innopotenza a scherno. / Che allor potremo dir, se questa legge / Irreta a sdegno, e alla vendetta il cielo [. . .] che ci governa, e regge. / Ma che sotto la scorta del vangelo / Fatto lupo il pastor divori il gregge / Tanta empietà ci fà restar di gelo. There is a parenthetical phrase, here marked by brackets, that is illegible in the original text (ACDF, S. O., St.St., CC.3.f).
33. Samaja "La Situazione degli ebrei nel periodo del Risorgimento." *Rassegna Mensile d'Israele* 23, nos. 7–9 (July-Sept. 1957): 298–309; 359–71; 414–21.
34. Cited in Samaja, 360.
35. Wald, *Constituting Americans*, 307. I draw here on Wald's formulation and use of the terms cultural and national identity.
36. As Marchiò wrote accusingly, the couple was "too well informed by *some national of theirs employed by the same [Livornese police force]* . . . " ASF.PAC, Parte Prima, Filza 14, 488. Livorno, June 5, 1814 (emphasis in the original).
37. ASF.PAC, Parte Prima, Filza 14, 488. Livorno, June 21, 1814.
38. It should be noted that while D'Arco expresses some typically anti-Semitic ideas in his work, he also recognizes that many of these attributes come about precisely because Jews are separated from the community at large.
39. See Francesco Gambini, *Dell'Ebreo Possidente* (Turin: Stamperia Pane, 1815) and *Della cittadinanza giudaica in Europa* (Turin: Tipografia di G. Pomba, 1834). For further discussion, see Franco della Peruta, "Gli ebrei nel Risorgimento fra interdizioni ed emancipazione," *Storia d'Italia, Gli ebrei in Italia: dall'emancipazione a oggi*, vol. 11.2 ed. Corrado Vivanti, (Turin: Einaudi, 1997), 1135–67.
40. ASF.PAC, Parte Prima, Filza 14, 488. Livorno, June 5, 1814.
41. ASF.PAC, Parte Prima, Filza 14, 488. Livorno, June 5, 1814.
42. ASF.PAC, Parte Prima, Filza 14, 488. Livorno, June 6, 1814.
43. ASF.PAC, Parte Prima, Filza 14, 488. Livorno, June 6, 1814.
44. ASF.PAC, Parte Prima, Filza 14, 488. Florence, June 6, 1814.

45. ASF.PAC, Parte Prima, Filza 14, 488. Florence, June 14, 1814. The same news was sent to the governor of Livorno on June 16, 1814.
46. Alessandro Roveri, *La Santa Sede tra rivoluzione francese e restaurazione: Il cardinale Consalvi, 1813–1815* (Florence: La Nuova Italia, 1974), 144.
47. ACDF, S. O., St.St., CC.3.f. Ferrara, May 30, 1821.
48. George Mosse, *The Culture of Western Europe: The Nineteenth and Twentieth Centuries (*Boulder, CO: Westview, 1988), 90–91.
49. ACDF, S. O., St.St., CC.3.f. Ferrara, 3 October 1821.
50. ACDF, S. O., St.St., CC.3.f.
51. ACDF, S. O., St.St., CC.3.f.
52. Marace's testimony made no reference to or connection between his sudden dismissal and the case at hand, nor did Marchiò mention the connection. Instead, the latter, upon sending the trial testimony to Cardinal Pacca several days later, happily noted that the testimony of a Jew would surely strengthen the Vatican's case in the eyes of the Tuscan government. ACDF, S. O., St.St., BB.2.c. Livorno, July 22, 1814.
53. ACDF, S. O., St.St., BB.2.c.
54. ACDF, S. O., St.St., BB.2.c. Florence, August 30, 1814.
55. Archivio della Communità Ebraica di Livorno (hereafter referred to as ACEL), Filza D, 71. Livorno, June 17, 1814.
56. ASF.PAC, Parte Prima, Filza 14, 488. Livorno, June 18, 1814. Accusations of poisoning were one stereotype that served as a weapon against the Jewish community well after this case. Laws that separated the two communities, from not hiring Christian servants to not eating food prepared by a Jew, were all established with the aim of saving Christians from death by poison. See Nino Samaja, "La Situazione degli ebrei nel periodo del Risorgimento," *Rassegna Mensile d'Israele*, "La Situazione degli ebrei nel periodo del Risorgimento." *Rassegna Mensile d'Israele* 23.7–9 (July-September 1957): 298–309; 359–71; 414–21.
57. ACDF, S. O., St.St., BB.2.c. Livorno, June 20, 1814.
58. ACDF, S. O., St.St., BB.2.c. Livorno, June 20, 1814.
59. ACDF, S. O., St.St., BB.2.c. Rome, June 25(?), 1814.
60. We see illustrated here the parallel between the position of the European Jew and the colonial subject. There is a significant body of literature on Orientalism, colonialism, and the European Jew. In particular, see Daniel Boyarin, *Unheroic Conduct: The Rise of Heterosexuality and the Invention of the Jewish Man* (Berkeley: University of California Press, 1997) and *Orientalism and the Jews*, ed. By Davidson Kalmar and Derek J. Penslar (Waltham, MA: Brandeis University Press, 2005). In Tudor Parfitt's essay entitled "The Use of the Jew in Colonial Discourse" that appears in this collection, for example, the author notes that Jewish ancestry was thought to explain the ancestry of many of the peoples whom European colonizers met upon their conquest of new lands. Thus the relationship between colonial subject and Jew is brought even further together (51–67).
61. See, for example, Po-Chia Hsia, *Trent 1475*, 105–13.

62. ACDF, S. O., St.St., BB.2.c. Livorno, June 20, 1814.
63. Daniel A. Farber and Suzanna Sherry, "Telling Stories Out of School: An Essay on Legal Narratives," *Stanford Law Review* 45 (April, 1993): 827.
64. ACDF, S. O., St.St., CC.3.f. Ferrara, May 30, 1821.
65. ACDF, S. O., St.St., CC.3.f.
66. "Such news [of the baptism], once it arrived, resulted in her great agitation. In this state of things, I strongly believed in soliciting verbally the official participation of the resolution assumed to that effect, that no mishap could happen both with regard to stealing the baby and with regard to the flight of the mother." ACDF, S. O., St.St., BB.2.c. Livorno, August 11, 1814.
67. ACDF, S. O., St.St., BB.2.c. Livorno, June 20, 1814.
68. ASF.PAC, Parte Prima, Filza 14, 488. Florence, August 30, 1814.
69. ACDF, S. O., St.St., CC.3.f. Ferrara, May 16, 1823.
70. ACDF, S. O., St.St., CC.3.f. Ferrara, June 13, 1823.
71. ACDF, S. O., St.St., CC.3.f. Ferrara, June 13, 1823.
72. ACDF, S. O., St.St., CC.3.f. Ferrara, June 23, 1823.
73. ACDF, S. O., St.St., CC.3.f. Ferrara, June 13, 1823.
74. ACDF, S. O., St.St., CC.3.f. Ferrara, June 13, 1823.
75. Paula Hyman notes that despite the extraordinary efforts and resources the Church expended in pursuing conversions, "Italian Catholic society did remarkably little with the converts."(8–9) The fates of Cavalieri and Tivoli are unknown, but the very fact that they seem to drop out of view confirms Hyman's suggestion that the Church's interest is in the conversion itself and not in the future well-being of the converts.
76. This was proven at the first Vatican council, which was organized in 1869–1870 by Pius IX, when theologians elaborated on the idea of the Church as 'societas perfecta.' See Giovanni Miccoli *Fra Mito della Cristianità e secolarizzazione* (Casale Monferrato: Marietti, 1985), 71, *Fra* For further discussion of the relationship between Europe and Christianity, see Aylward Shorter, *Toward a Theology of Inculturation* (London: Cassell Publishers, 1988).
77. Sander Gilman and Steven Katz, eds., *Antisemitism in Times of Crisis* (New York: New York University Press, 1991), 2.
78. ACDF, S. O., St.St., TT.3.b.15.
79. Cited in Pickering 76. Susan Zickmund, "Approaching the Radical Other: The Discursive Culture of Cyberhate" in S. G. Jones, ed., *Virtual Culture: Identity and Communication in Cybersociety* (London: Sage, 1997).
80. Pickering, 68.
81. For a thorough discussion of reactionary attitudes within the Vatican from the return of Pius VII through the reign of Pius IX, see Daniele Menozzi, *La chiesa cattolica e la secolarizzazione* (Turin: Einaudi, 1993).
82. For a thorough discussion of medieval views of Jews, see Joan Young Gregg, *Devils, Woman and Jews: Reflections of the Other in Medieval Sermon Stories* (Albany: SUNY Press, 1997), 169–235.
83. See Miccoli, *Fra Mito della Cristianità e secolarizzazione.*

84. Peter Brooks, "The Law as Narrative and Rhetoric," *Law's Stories: Narrative and Rhetoric in the Law*, ed. Peter Brooks and Paul Gewirtz (New Haven: Yale University Press, 1996), 17.
85. Peter Brooks *Reading for the Plot: Design and Intention in Narrative (*New York: Vintage Books), 1984, 216.
86. This term is coined in the title of Brooks and Gewirtz, eds., *Law's Stories: Narrative and Rhetoric in the Law.*

Chapter 3

* This phrase comes from Michael Ragussis, *Figures of Conversion. "The Jewish Question" and English National Identity* (Durham: Duke University Press, 1995), 49.

1. In his work *Alessandro Manzoni. Reminiscenze* (Milan: 1892), Cesare Cantù confirms this version of the story, as does R. Barbiera…*Il Salotto della Contessa Maffei* (Milan: 1895). Giovanni Visconti Venosta gives a similar account in his *Ricordi di gioventù* (Milan: Cogliati, 1906). Cristoforo Fabris, in his *Memorie manzoniane* (Milan: 1901), recounts a similar story. Finally, while Giuseppe Giusti does not mention the occasion of Napoleon's wedding, he also attests to fireworks and the crowds of Paris as the reason that Manzoni found refuge in St. Roch. Cited in Piero Fossi, *La conversione di Alessandro Manzoni* (Florence: La Nuova Italia Editrice, 1974), 75.
2. Barbiera, 268.
3. For further discussion of Manzoni and the issue of agoraphobia, see Massimo Riva, *Malinconie del moderno: Critica dell'incivilmento e disagio della nazionalità nella letteratura italiana del XIX secolo* (Ravenna: Longo Editore, 2001), 115–35.
4. Roch, much like Father Christopher in *I Promessi Sposi*, ministered to those afflicted with the plague. Although Roch eventually contracted the disease himself, he miraculously recovered, similar to the protagonist of Manzoni's novel, Renzo, to whom I shall return.
5. Numerous scholars have discussed the stories of Manzoni's conversion. For an excellent overview of many of these stories, see Fossi, 75–78, and John Lindon, "Alessandro Manzoni and the Oxford Movement: His Politics and Conversion in a New English Source," *Journal of Ecclesiastical History* 45, no. 2 (April 1994): 297–318. Umberto Colombo also refers to several of these stories in his essay, "I silenzi del Manzoni," *Otto/Novecento* 9, no. 1 (1985): 41–72. In addition, they are discussed in Emma Pistelli Rinaldi, "Il cosiddetto 'miracolo di san Rocco' nella conversione del Manzoni," *Italianistica* 14, no. 3 (1985): 433–57; and in Francesco Ruffini, "La 'conversione' del Manzoni," *Manzoni: Testimonianze di critica e di polemica*, ed. Giorgio Bárberi Squarotti and Marziano Guglielminetti (Florence: G. D'Anna, 1973),

39–44. And finally, they receive attention in Cesare Angelini, *Con Renzo e con Lucia (e con gli altri). Saggi sul Manzoni* (Brescia: Morcelliana, 1986).

6. Davide Norsa, *Pensieri d'un cattolico* (Prato: Guasti, 1850), 6.
7. Norsa, 6.
8. G. Giorgini (Vittoria's husband), letter to Carlo Magenta, 1876, in *Manzoni intimo*, vol. 2, ed. Michele Scherillo (Milan: U. Hoepli, 1923), 257.
9. Lindon, 316–17; John Henry Wynne to Edward Moore, December 9, 1882.
10. Kenneth Stowe, *Alienated Minority: the Jews of Medieval Latin Europe* (Cambridge, MA: Harvard University Press, 1992), 13. For further discussion of Pauline conceptions of conversion, also see Marina Caffiero, *La nuova era: miti e profezie dell'Italia in Rivoluzione* (Genoa: Marietti, 1991). Also see Alan F. Segal, *Paul the Convert: the Apostolate and Apostasy of Saul the Pharisee* (New Haven, CT: Yale University Press, 1990). The Gospels also speak of Christianity as the extension and fulfillment of the Hebrew Scriptures, although Paul connects this association much more clearly to his own Jewish background.
11. Renato Moro, "L'atteggiamento dei cattolici tra teologia e politica," *Stato nazionale ed emancipazione ebraica*, ed. F. Sofia and M. Toscano (Rome: Bonacci Editore), 313. On this subject, see also Giovita Scalvini, *Foscolo, Manzoni, Goethe*, ed. Mario Marcazzan (Turin: Einaudi, 1948), 209–37.
12. Lynn Gunzberg briefly refers to these stories, and to Manzoni's conversion, in her work *Strangers at Home: Jews in the Italian Literary Imagination* (Berkeley: University of California Press, 1992), 59.
13. John Gatt-Rutter, "When the Killing Had to Stop: Manzoni's Paradigm of Christian Conversion," *The Italianist* 10 (1990): 9. Gatt-Rutter's essay concentrates on defining the pattern of conversion that can be found in Manzoni's novel, and in this sense, the objective of his essay is quite different from my own study.
14. Manzoni met Henriette on a trip he took with his mother to Lake Como. For a thorough treatment of his early years, see Mario Sansone, *Manzoni Francese (1805–1810): Dall'Illuminismo al Romanticismo* (Rome: Laterza, 1993). For a complete biography of Manzoni, see Natalia Ginzburg, *La famiglia Manzoni* (Turin: Einaudi, 1994). A briefer biographical overview, as well as an overview of Manzoni's writing, can be found in Francesco De Sanctis, *Storia della letteratura italiana. Dall'Ottocento al Novecento* (Turin: Einaudi, 1991).
15. Undated letter to Fauriel, believed to have been written in October, 1807, *Carteggio di Alessandro Manzoni*, vol. 1, eds. Giovanni Sforza and Giuseppe Gallavresi (Milan: U. Hoepli, 1912), 118.
16. Alessandro's mother not only sanctioned the marriage; she herself had turned to Calvinism following the death of Imbonati and even had plans to become a nurse in the largely Protestant city of Geneva. See G. G. Orelli's letter to Davide and Regula Orelli, February 12, 1808, *Carteggio*, vol. 1, 138–9.

17. In 1821, Eustachio Degola authored an unedited work entitled *Sulla conversione degli ebrei*, in which he refers to the Pauline belief that Jews will find salvation through conversion to Christianity. These beliefs appear remarkably similar to Manzoni's own thoughts on conversion, as discussed in the next section of this chapter. For further discussion of this work, see Caffiero, *La nuova era*, 80–96.
18. Eustachio Degola, *Eustachio Degola, il clero costituzionale e la conversione della famiglia Manzoni*, ed. Angelo de Gubernatis (Florence: G. Barbèra, 1882), 481. Count Somis to Abbot Degola, June 28, 1810.
19. *Eustachio Degola*, 509. In a letter Tosi received from Henriette five days later, on March 27, 1811, he must have been immensely pleased to read that, just as he wished, she had distanced herself substantially from her parents: "I will tell you nothing of my parents, except that they seem to be more foreign than ever, especially since I had a small discussion with my mother about religion, when, thank God, I spoke with all the warmth that the subject demanded." *Eustachio Degola*, 510.
20. Indeed, John Lindon alludes briefly to the "method" employed by these clergymen, noting that scholars have yet to seriously examine it. Lindon, 308. For further discussion of Henriette's conversion, also see Caffiero, *La nuova era*, 121–22.
21. *Eustachio Degola*, 489–90. Tosi to Degola, August 5, 1810.
22. I return to a comparison of conversions of Jews and Protestants to Catholicism in chapter 5.
23. *Eustachio Degola* 503–4. Henriette to Degola, December 16, 1810.
24. *Eustachio Degola* 520–23. Henriette to Degola, March 28, 1813 and March 16, 1815.
25. Ragussis, 2.
26. See, for example, his letter of August 12, 1810 to Degola. *Eustachio Degola*, 491–93.
27. This belief was reflected in a letter Degola sent Tosi when the Manzoni family left Paris for Milan. In the note, Degola mentioned the care the newly converted Henriette required and the spiritual assistance given Manzoni's mother; he made no mention of Manzoni himself, however, and in doing so suggested that Manzoni was not a potential candidate for conversion. The letter, dated May 30, 1810, to Tosi, appears in *Carteggio*, vol. 1, 208–9.
28. *Carteggio*, vol. 1, 236–37. Tosi to Degola, August 26, 1810.
29. Cited in Lindon, 309.
30. Vittorio Spinazzola, *Il libro per tutti: saggio sui "Promessi Sposi"* (Roma: Editori Riuniti, 1983), 10.
31. Carlo Dionisotti, *Manzoni and the Catholic Revival* (Oxford: Oxford University Press, 1974), 12.
32. According to Giovanni Visconti Venosta, the clergyman who discovered the relationship between Manzoni and Marco Coen was told to reorder Manzoni's manuscripts and correspondence after the author's death, unlike

the other men who wrote memoirs detailing Manzoni's conversion and their own. Among these documents, he discovered hundreds of letters from men and women, including Coen, who wrote Manzoni "as if to a saint, saying that his writings had put faith, peace, hope in their souls." Venosta, 595.

33. Fossi, 185. Unfortunately, I could not find the originals of either Coen's or Manzoni's letters. Fossi reprinted Manzoni's two letters to the young man, the first of which alludes to two letters that Coen had sent him previously. Ettore Bonora also discusses this correspondence in *Manzoni e la via italiana al realismo* (Naples: Liguori Editore, 1989), 91–107. Also see his essay, "Ancora sulla lettera a Marco Coen," *Giornale storico della letteratura italiana* 102, no. 521 (1986): 27–43.
34. Fossi, 193–4.
35. Typological readings mean that the Old Testament is read as prefiguring the stories of the New Testament. As the Vatican itself wrote recently, "Typological interpretation consists in reading the Old Testament as preparation and, in certain aspects, outline and foreshadowing of the New." "Notes on the Correct way to Present the Jews and Judaism in Preaching and Catechesis in the Roman Church," written by the Vatican's Commission for Religious Relations with the Jews, 1985, and cited in James Shapiro, *Oberammergau* (Vintage Books: New York, 2000), 94.
36. Fossi, 194.
37. Giovanni Miccoli, "Santa Sede, questione ebraica e antisemitismo fra Otto e Novecento," in *Storia d'Italia, Gli ebrei in Italia*, Vol. 11.2, ed. Corrado Vivanti (Turin: Einaudi, 1972), 1394–95. Miccoli cites a pamphlet entitled *Il figlio di Maria un fratello di più*, in *Continuazione delle memore di religione di morale e di letteratura*, vol. 13 (Modena, 1842), 89–147, which speaks of Ratisbonne's conversion. Another example can be found in *Lettera di Giacomo Forti à suoi genitori israeliti per la sua conversione dal giudaismo alla fede cristiana*, in *Annali delle Scienze Religiose*, 18, no. 53 (Rome, 1844): 3–12.
38. For further details, see *Conversione miracolosa alla fede cattolica di Alfonso Maria Ratisbonne, avvenuta in Roma nella Chiesa dei PP. Minimi in S. Andrea delle Fratte. Tratta dai processi autentici formatisi in Roma nel 1842* (Roma: G. Cesaretti, 1864). Also see René Laurentin, *20 janvier 1842, Marie apparaît à Alphonse Ratisbonne*, vol. 1–2 (Paris: O.E.I.L., 1991).
39. This visit is well documented in Lindon, 298.
40. Dionisotti, 15. Igino Giordani also writes of Catholicism in England in his *I grandi convertiti* (Rome: Apollon, 1945), 121–84.
41. Lindon, 316–7.
42. Thomas William Allies, to an unidentified correspondent, July 23, 1847, *Journal in France in 1845 and 1848, with Letters from Italy in 1847 of Things and Persons concerning the Church and Education* (London: 1849), 124.
43. At the same time, however, he was well aware of Napoleon's ambitions and his keen interest in military glory and power. As Carlo Dionisotti notes, "Manzoni had little regard for Roman law, even less for the political and

military achievements of ancient Rome. He could not fail to see that Napoleon was following the same path." Dionisotti, 6.

44. Dionisotti, 6.
45. Norsa, 27.
46. Manzoni describes Protestantism in terms similar to Norsa. The Protestants, writes Manzoni, "lay down a principle from which they remove the consequence, which is destructive of the principle itself. They want free interpretation, and it is upon this that they would like to establish their unity." See Giuseppe Borri, *I colloqui col Manzoni* (Bologna: Zanichelli Editore, 1929), 202.
47. Norsa, 33.
48. Manzoni expresses similar visions of fratricide in his poem *Il conte di Carmagnola*. For further discussion of the nationalist and Catholic themes of the poem, see Alberto Banti, *La nazione del Risorgimento* (Turin: Einaudi, 2000), 133–39.
49. These attributes are generally associated with Romanticism, and they certainly mark a change in the direction of Manzoni's writing. The question of whether Italian Romanticism existed (Gino Martegiani, an Italian student of German Romanticism famously claimed in 1908 that it did not exist) is beyond the scope of the present discussion. I use the term *Romanticism* to refer to a specific historical period—a conventional label for those who considered themselves to have Romantic attributes or defined themselves as "Romantics." For examples of Manzoni's early writing, see *Poesie di Alessandro Manzoni prima della conversione*, ed. Alberto Chiari (Florence: Felice Le Monnier, 1947). For a discussion of Manzoni's relationship to Romanticism and neoclassicism, see Francesco De Sanctis, *La scuola cattolico-liberale e il romanticism a Napoli*, ed. Carlo Muscetta and Giorgio Candeloro (Turin: Einaudi, 1953), 353–59.
50. For further discussion of the relationship between Manzoni's religious conversion and his writing, see Filippo Puglisi, *L'Arte del Manzoni* (Rome: Edizioni Studium, 1986).
51. The rejection of pagan mythology should thus be considered a crucial aspect of *PS*. For further discussion, see Lucienne Portier, "La conversion d'Alessandro Manzoni et son refus de la mythologie," *Revue des Etudes Italiennes* 10 (1964): 92–100.
52. Cited in Giovanni Carsaniga, "The Age of Romanticism (1800–1870)," *The Cambridge History of Italian Literature* (New York: Cambridge University Press, 1996), 429.
53. For further discussion of Manzoni's identification with modernity, see Ezio Raimondi, *Letteratura e identità nazionale* (Milan: Mondadori, 1998).
54. For an interesting discussion of this issue and an overview of Manzoni's work more generally, see Giulio Bollati, *L'Italiano: Il carattere nazionale come storia e come invenzione* (Turin: Einaudi, 1983), 3–13.
55. Spinazzola, 308.
56. Fossi, 192.

57. In 1817, Manzoni began the composition of the only other completed hymn, *La Pentecoste*.
58. Salvatore Nigro, *Il Primo ottocento: l'età napoleonica e il risorgimento* (Rome: Laterza, 1978), 39.
59. Tanto piacque al Signor di porre in cima / questa fanciulla ebrea. / O prole d'Israello, o nell'estremo / Caduta, o da sì lunga ira contrita, / non è Costei che in onor tanto avemo, / Di vostra fede uscita? / Non è Davidde il ceppo suo? Con Lei / Era il pensier dei vostri antiqui vati, / Quando annunziaro i verginal trofei / Sopra l'inferno alzati. / Deh! A Lei volgete finalemente i preghi, / Ch'Ella vi salvi come salva i suoi; / E non sia gente né tribù che neghi / Lieta cantar con noi: / Salve, o degnata del secondo nome, / O Rosa, o Stella ai periglianti scampo, / Inclita come il sol, terribil come / Oste schierata in campo." Alessandro Manzoni, *Il Nome di Maria*, in "Manzoni's *inni sacri* and *il cinque maggio*. A Translation," Joseph Tusiani, *Annali d'Italianistica* 3 (1985): 36–7. For a complete, annotated Italian version of the poem, see Alessandro Manzoni, *Inni Sacri*, ed. Franco Gavazzeni (Parma: Ugo Guanda Editore, 1997), 65–86. For a thorough analysis of the poem, albeit with little on the significance of Manzoni's biblical references, see Silvana Ghezzo, "Il nome di Maria nel *Nome di Maria* di Alessandro Manzoni," *Otto/Novecento* 4 (1983): 185–93.
60. Antonio Prieto, "La logica della sua conversione," *Manzoni Pro e Contro*, vol. 3, ed. Giancarlo Vigorelli (Milan: Istituto di propaganda libraria, 1975–1976), 261.
61. Robert Dombroski, "The ideological question in Manzoni," *Studies in Romanticism* 20, no. 4 (Winter 1981): 499. It should be noted that Manzoni's firm support of Christian values and the Catholic Church did not necessarily translate into absolute support of the pope; while it falls outside of the boundaries of our discussion here, it is noteworthy that Rome and the pope go almost unmentioned in Manzoni's novel, as opposed to the next work in this study, Bresciani's *L'Ebreo di Verona*. Opposed to papal temporal power, Manzoni believed that the sovereignty and moral authority of the pope would be guaranteed and better protected if the pope did not have any political power.
62. An excellent overview of the role of conversion in *PS* can be found in Brennan Wales, "Conversion in the *Promessi Sposi*—Coincidence and Disposition," *Queensland Dante Review* (1983–1986): 44–48.
63. In his article, John Gatt-Rutter explores these various paradigms, arguing that most of the characters end up as "positive phenotypes" of the conversion paradigm. He handily summarizes the conversion paradigm by outlining all the possible conversion combinations with a model. Gatt-Rutter, 34–35.
64. Alessandro Manzoni, *PS*, 279. All English citations are taken from Alessandro Manzoni, *The Betrothed and History of the Column of Infamy*, ed. D. Forgacs and M. Reynolds (London: J. M. Dent, 1997).
65. Lindon, 306. Luigi Colombo discusses this connection in his work, *. . . e non era più lago ma specchio del cuore . . . Scritti e discorsi di argomento*

manzoniano (Lecco: Comune di Lecco, 1985). For a thorough discussion of the *Innominato*, see Annette Leddy's essay, "The Conversion of Manzoni's L'Innominato or, the Repressed Catholic Consciousness of a Criminal," *Carte Italiane* 2 (1980–1981): 27–41. In addition, some space is devoted to his conversion in Angelini 111–15.

66. Manzoni, *PS*, 279.
67. Manzoni, *PS*, 337.
68. Riccardo Verzini, "Il sogno della giustizia non violenta," *I mondi impossibili: l'utopia*, ed. G. Barberi Squarotti (Turin: Tirrenia Stampatori, 1990), 175.
69. Manzoni, *PS*, 166.
70. Manzoni, *PS*, 258.
71. Angelo Marchese, "Il grande capitolo di Renzo," *Humanitas* 40, no. 1 (1985), 12.
72. Manzoni, *PS*, 166.
73. Ibid., 28.
74. Ibid., 35.
75. Ibid., 87.
76. Ibid., 187.
77. Ibid., 192.
78. Ibid., 186.
79. Ibid., 503.
80. Ibid., 504.
81. Ibid., 506. In his article, Lindon suggests that Manzoni's depiction of Father Cristoforo converting Don Rodrigo may also correspond to Wynne's rendition of Manzoni's conversion, in which the author converts in an unnamed church in Lyons. Lindon, 311.
82. Davide Albertario, "Il Giansenista ha messo alla luce il liberale," *Manzoni pro e contro*, vol. 1, ed. G. Vigorelli (Milan: Istituto propaganda libraria, 1974), 448.
83. "[Sì], quel Dio che nell'onda vermiglia/chiuse il rio che inseguiva Israele,/ quel che in pugno alla maschia Giaele/ pose il maglio ed il colpo guidò." Alessandro Manzoni, *Opere*, ed. Di Riccardo Bacchelli (Milan: Riccardo Ricciardi Editore, 1953), 77.
84. Mazzini also borrowed from Bible stories to envisage the formation of the Italian nation as a religious fact in and of itself and to this end developed "a religious, quasi missionary conception of literature as the embodiment in time of universal values (such as country, freedom, destiny)." See Carsaniga, 444. In his vision of Italy, however, no place existed for the pope or the Papal States. Indeed, to a certain degree Romanticism and secularism appeared to go hand in hand, and, just as the Enlightenment posed the greatest stumbling block for eighteenth-century Catholic culture, in the nineteenth century, the cultural contest for Catholicism lay in the rise of Romanticism. Thus, what is surprising about *Marzo 1821* is that Manzoni, a papal supporter, would be the author of such a work. Numerous other writers used biblical stories of the Israelites as an archetype that reflected

the cause of national liberation. In his essay on the subject, Bruno Di Porto discusses works of Verdi, Goffredo Mameli, Carlo Cattaneo, Niccolò Tommaseo, and Massimo D'Azeglio. See his essay, "Gli ebrei nel Risorgimento," *Nuova Antologia* 115, no. 3 (1980): 256–72. For further discussion of *Marzo 1821*, see Banti, 61.

85. Moses was denied entrance into the Promised Land because, while leading the Israelites through the desert, he defied God's instructions to obtain water from a rock by speaking to it; instead, in a moment of anger, he struck the rock.
86. When Davide Norsa set out on his journey, this is the direction that he too travels.
87. *PS*, chapter 31. The narrator explains how a soldier with the plague entered Milan and shortly thereafter fell ill, infecting those around him.
88. Manzoni, *PS*, 478.
89. Ibid., 524.
90. For a discussion of the movement on the part of the bourgeoisie to ally themselves with the clergy, see Dombroski, 499–500.
91. This vision of Catholicism and the New Testament as the replacement for Judaism and the Hebrew Bible is expressed succinctly in an essay written many years after *PS* by another Catholic intellectual, Roberto D'Azeglio. While D'Azeglio is more conservative than Manzoni, and the essay probably more melodramatic than Manzoni would have written, Manzoni would certainly have endorsed the ideas behind them: "The voice of God no longer thunders from Sinai, but from the Vatican, and men listen to it with equal reverence." Roberto d'Azeglio, "Pio IX e Roberto D'Azeglio," *L'Armonia* 13, no. 14 (1860): 53.
92. Dombroski, 500.
93. Regarding this subject, Dombroski brings up Manzoni's *Osservazione sulla morale cattolica*. In it, Manzoni does not try to defend the abuses of the papacy and clergy; rather, he defends the institution of the Church and views Catholicism as a unified, coherent moral code. Dombroski suggests that readers understand Manzoni's treatise as a response to the development of bourgeois liberalism in its most progressive forms; thus he does not oppose the human ends of liberal doctrine but tries to place them with in a Catholic framework.

Chapter 4

1. Cited in Alberto Banti, *La nazione del Risorgimento* (Turin: Einaudi, 2000), 136.
2. See Giovanni Vicini, *Giovanni Vicini: memorie biografiche e storiche* (Bologna: Zanichelli, 1897), 211. Vicini was appointed secretary general of the Cisalpine government after serving as president of the provisional

government of the Cispadane Republic in 1796. For further discussion of his work, see Lynn Gunzberg, *Strangers at Home: Jews in the Italian Literary Imagination* (Berkeley: University of California Press, 1992), 42–45. Even many anticlerical liberals, while not advocating religious conversion per se, did strive toward assimilating Jews into the greater community, and in so doing of eliminating the difference between Jew and Christian. For further discussion, see Andrew M. Canepa, "Emancipation and Jewish Response in Mid- Nineteenth-Century Italy," *European History Quarterly* 16. 4 (1986): 403–39.

3. The English citations are from Antonio Bresciani, *The Jew of Verona: An Historical Tale of the Italian Revolutions of 1846–9*, vols. 1–2 (Baltimore: John Murphy & Co., 1854) (translator unnamed).
4. Antonio Gramsci, *Selections from Cultural Writings*, ed. David Forgacs and Geoffrey Nowell-Smith, trans. William Boelhower (London: Lawrence and Wishart, 1985), 339. Gramsci cites Manzoni's supposed reaction to Bresciani's novel as further proof of Bresciani's terrible writing, attributing the citation to the diary of Margherita di Collegno. It should be noted, however, that in the biographical notes on Bresciani released by *Civiltà Cattolica*, a more positive response is attributed to Manzoni. Bresciani's memoirs state that when a woman asked Manzoni what he thought of the work, Manzoni responded, "The author of the *Jew of Verona* is the best writer in Italy." *Della vita e delle opere del p. Antonio Bresciani della C.d.G. Commentario* (Rome: Office of Civiltà Cattolica, 1869), CXI.
5. Bresciani's title is an ironic reference to the anti-Jesuit novel by Eugène Sue, *Le Juif errant*. The work, a favorite among Italian liberals, recounts the story of a Jesuit agent who schemes against the descendants of a persecuted Protestant to stop them from inheriting the latter's fortune. See A. Di Ricco, "Padre Bresciani: populismo e reazione," *Studi Storici* 22 (1981): 848.
6. Gunzberg, 61. Gunzberg's essay on *EV* gives a thorough overview of the story. However its focus, quite different from the discussion here, concentrates primarily on the historical context of the revolution of 1848 and, more specifically, the relationship between Mazzinian revolutionaries and Vatican supporters.
7. As a priest explains to the characters Bartolo and Polissena, true liberty is not freedom from Austrian rule but "that peace which is the fruit of a rational obedience to God, submission to the Church, and to legitimate authority." Bresciani, *EV*, vol. 1, 219.
8. Antonio Gramsci, *Selections from Cultural Writings*, 298.
9. The most well-known of these was the *Amicizia cristiana* of Turin, which opened to the public in 1817 and renamed itself *Amicizia cattolica*. The aim of the group was to encourage "buona stampa," or a positive representation of papal politics in the press. For further discussion of the *Amicizia cattolica*, see Gunzberg, 63–64. Aside from the *Amicizia cattolica*, several newspapers were established up and down the peninsula that sought to

reestablish the power of the Church and to redefine values that were believed to be disappearing from society. Among the most well-known of these journals were the *Enciclopedia ecclesiastica e morale* in Naples (1821–1822); the *Giornale ecclesiastico* in Rome (1825–1826), directed by the controversial French clergyman Jabalot; and *L'Amico d'Italia*, which was founded in Turin (1822–1829) by Cesare Taparelli d'Azeglio, brother of Massimo d'Azeglio. In addition, there were the *Memorie di religione, di morale e di letteratura* of Modena (1822–1830) and the *Giornale degli apologisti della religione cattolica* of Florence (1825–1827).

10. Curci was the same Jesuit clergyman whom Pius chose, along with Father Luigi Taparelli d'Azeglio, brother of the statesman Massimo, to publicly defend his decision not to support unification. In addition, Bresciani dedicates *EV* to him. As discussed in an earlier chapter, Pius VII had restored the Society of Jesus in 1814 as part of his effort toward rebuilding a religious presence on the continent after the collapse of the Napoleonic Empire. During the two hundred years that the Jesuits had been banned in the Papal States, they had nonetheless become well entrenched in the society of Catholic Europe and among Catholic colonies. For Leo XII, the Jesuits embodied a kind of Catholic internationalism that held great appeal. In addition, their Society represented values associated with the world prior to the French Revolution, a world to which Leo strove to return. Jesuits were particularly hated by many liberal thinkers because they represented the epitome of conservatism: "The general tendency of the Italian Jesuits toward a conservative kind of political thinking made them, in the eyes of many patriots, allies of Austria and enemies of national unity. No one wrote with more venom than Vincenzo Gioberti, who denounced the Society as the chief obstacle to the civic and religious salvation of Italy and to the harmonious fusion of religion and modern civilization." William V. Bangert S. J., *A History of the Society of Jesus (*St. Louis: The Institute of Jesuit Sources, 1972), 442.
11. Bresciani, highly critical of any such "progress," noted sarcastically that Pius' reputation as a moderate resulted in his election being an event "hailed by the [secret] societies a propitious occasion for the execution of their plans for the ruin of the Italian princes. . . . In fact, the Roman Pontificate, against which the hatred and rage of the impious had so long been exerted, instantly, on the elevation of Pius IX became the idol of Catholics, the envy of Protestants, and the admiration of Mahometans." Bresciani, *EV*, vol. 1, 56–7.
12. Riccards suggests that Pius was influenced by Gioberti's *Il Primato* initially. See Riccards, 13.
13. For a detailed discussion, see Riccards, 5–30.
14. Indeed, Bresciani not only cites the pope as speaking out in favor of the Austrians; in his novel he writes that the soldiers of the Roman National Guard who had been taken prisoner by Austria "everywhere proclaimed the kindness and courtesy generously shown them by the Austrians." Bresciani,

EV, vol.1, 378. Thus the Austrians are depicted as acting in the charitable way of Christians, just as the pope supports them as part of the Catholic people.

15. Banti, 138.
16. Rossi, who had been warned to stay away, was murdered on the steps of the council chamber in Rome. His murderer, Luigi Brunetti, was the son of a Mazzini supporter. His murder has often been compared to that of Julius Caesar, and in his praise of the assassination, Garibaldi also compares it to Caesar's death. Riccards, 16. In his novel, Bresciani regularly recalls ancient Rome and draws a connection between it and modern Christian society. In so doing, he tries to shape the memory of ancient Rome as the birthplace of modern Christian civilization, rather than as the birthplace of the modern Italian state. Revolutionaries like Garibaldi are clearly trying to use the comparison to Caesar as a means of tying themselves and a new, secular republic to the history of ancient Rome.
17. The journal, still printed today, became the most influential of all Catholic journals of the time, and circulation quickly rose from 4,200 to 12,000. Bangert, 441.
18. The two had met at Pius' papal inauguration, which Bresciani attended in Rome. At that time, the pope reportedly complimented Bresciani's writing, saying, "Know that I read all of your works and I like them very much. *You write quite well and with the great advantage of youth.* Continue to write, because you will make yourself very useful to Italy." Bresciani, *Opere del P. Antonio Bresciani della compagnia di Gesù*, Vol. 2 (Rome: Ufficio della Civiltà Cattolica, 1865), 152.
19. *Della vita e delle opere del p. Antonio Bresciani*, CX.
20. Pius was said to love the novel, and he purportedly approved the work before it appeared in *Civiltà Cattolica*, again providing evidence of the remarkably active role the pope had in the establishment and functions of this journal.
21. Cited in Florinda M. Iannace, *Conservatorismo cattolico in Antonio Bresciani* (Rome: Trevi editore, 1973), 79. In Modena in 1837, Bresciani also published a series of lectures that he had given a decade earlier under the title *Sopra il Romanticismo*. The roots of the anti-Romantic, anti-Risorgimento ideals that Bresciani exhibited as a writer can be found in his youth. Born into an impoverished noble family in Ala, Trento, in 1798, Bresciani twice witnessed the invasion and destruction of Trento, first in 1809 and again in 1813, by Napoleon's troops—memories that he recorded vividly in his later years. See Iannace, 10.
22. Owen Chadwick, *The Popes and European Revolution* (New York: Oxford University Press, 1981), 549.
23. Furious at his son's disobedience, Bresciani's father wrote the Austrian government complaining that his son had broken the law by traveling without a permit. Indeed, in an ironic twist that will become clear in the next chapter, Bresciani's father even claimed that his son had been kidnapped by the

Church. Ultimately, when Bresciani's father's letters to the Austrian government appeared likely to cause legal troubles for the young man, Pope Leo XII himself became personally involved, expressing his complete approval of Bresciani's arrival in Rome and of his affiliation with the Society of Jesus. In 1826, Bresciani finally gained his father's permission to enter the Jesuit order.

24. His desire to be sent abroad to represent the Church was never granted. In Rome, the pope entrusted the College De Propaganda Fide to the Jesuits, and Bresciani was appointed head of the college until 1848, when the Society of Jesus was forced to abandon their colleges and houses in their flight from Rome. Despite not being sent to carry out missionary work, Bresciani still maintained an interest in proselytization. In July 1840, he received a striking letter from the well-known author Silvio Pellico. In his letter, Pellico requests that Bresciani arrange to have a learned Catholic talk to a Rabbi who appears to be interested in converting to Christianity. Indeed, the rabbi appears to be considering a conversion to Protestantism, which is what prompted Pellico to ask for religious education from a Catholic clergyman. See Iannace, 123–24. In another example that Bresciani himself recounts, just after the pope had fled Rome for Gaeta, Bresciani manages to convert a woman who later became a nun. *Della vita e delle opere del p. Antonio Bresciani*, C–CXI.
25. Filippo Aminta, *L'ebraismo senza replica e sconfitto colle stesse sue armi* (Rome, 1823), VI.
26. "Charitate Christi," in *The Papal Encyclicals, 1740–1878*, ed. Claudia Carlen Ihm (Raleigh: The Pierian Press, 1990), 213.
27. Wiseman, 215.
28. Bresciani, *EV*, vol. 1, 42. Bartolo exemplifies the naïve citizen of Rome who was tricked into supporting the values of the Risorgimento. Initially, this likeable man advocates a Giobertian vision of a united Italy that is grounded on religious principles, and while he personally does not support the secret societies, he has friends who are members. However, once the wickedness of revolution and the impossibility of reforming liberal revolutionaries become apparent, Bartolo recognizes the power of the Church and the need to throw his complete support behind her. For further discussion, see Miccoli, *Fra mito della Cristianità*, 41.
29. Cited in Michael P. Riccards, *Vicars of Christ: Popes, Power and Politics in the Modern World* (New York: Crossroad Publishing, 1998), 5.
30. Shortly after he fled Rome, Pius tried to quell Garibaldi's men by excommunicating any supporter of the movement to end papal temporal rule. The excommunication went unheeded. After a Constitutional Assembly had been proclaimed and the Roman Republic established, the pope sought help from the Catholic powers of Europe—Austria, France, Spain and the Kingdom of the Two Sicilies—to reaffirm his political position. In early July 1849, French troops took Rome, defeating the troops of the Roman Republic. At

the same time, Austrian troops marched on cities throughout the peninsula, defeating republicans and reestablishing the rule of the Old Regime.

31. "Academies and universities resound with new and monstrous opinions," he writes, "and no longer secretly or obscurely do they attack the Catholic faith. . . . The lessons and examples of the masters thus pervert the youth . . . and the most frightful immorality gains and spreads." Cited in Anne Fremantle, ed., *The Papal Encyclicals in their Historical Context* (New York: New American Library, 1956) 128. In addition, among the notes of poet Giuseppe Gioacchino Belli, an undated reference to Pope Gregory (most likely from 1846, after the pope's death) was discovered that reiterates how unpopular this pope was: "A Papa Gregorio je volevo bene perche' me dava er gusto de potenne di' male." Belli employs similarly sarcastic language in a poem dedicated to the recently deceased pope, entitled *Er Papa bbon'anima*, Giuseppe Gioacchino Belli, *Sonetti*, ed. Giorgio Vigolo and Pietro Gibellini (Milan: Mondadori, 2000), LXXXVIII.
32. One only has to look, for example, at Eugen Weber's well-known work *Peasants into Frenchmen: the modernization of rural France, 1870–1914* (Stanford, CA: Stanford University Press, 1976), in which the author discusses the development of these different elements that coincided with the emergence of modern nationhood, to see the idea of circulation employed in another context. That is, in his discussion of statehood, Weber examines precisely the issues that I have mentioned above: young men gathering from all corners of the country to form the military; roads that connect different parts of the country, allowing for postal routes and for a greater number of people to travel; trains that allowed for more extensive traveling to other cities.
33. Benedict Anderson coined this phrase in his work, *Imagined Communities: Reflections on the Origin and Spread of Nationalism* (London: Verso, 1991).
34. Bresciani, *EV*, vol.1, 109.
35. For one example, see Gianfranco Legitimo, "Il padre Bresciani cento anni dopo," *Dialoghi: Rivista Bimestrale di Letteratura Arti Scienze* 10 (1962): 155–70.
36. Gunzberg, 68. Aser embodies the qualities of the Wandering Jew and of the wealthy, internationally known Rothschild family, whose wealth Bresciani undoubtedly disliked in particular, as one branch of the family had even bankrolled the bankrupt Vatican. For an excellent discussion of this relationship, see Francesco Barbagallo, "The Rothschilds in Naples," *Journal of Modern Italian Studies* 5, no. 3 (2001): 294–309.
37. Bresciani, *EV*, vol. 1, 84.
38. Gramsci, *Selections from Cultural Writings*, 299.
39. Bresciani, *EV*, vol. 1, 83.
40. Bresciani, *EV*, vol. 1, 48.
41. Gunzberg, 73–74.

42. For further discussion, see Silvio Furlani, *La politica postale di Metternich e l'Italia, Quaderni di storia postale*, vol. 8 (Prato: Istituto di studi storici postali, 1987).
43. Furlani, 20.
44. Bresciani, *EV*, vol. 1, 83.
45. Cited in Bernhard Siegert, *Relays: Literature as an epoch of the postal system*, trans. Kevin Repp (Stanford: Stanford University Press, 1999), 165.
46. Bresciani, *EV*, vol. 1, 140–41.
47. Richard R. John, *Spreading the News: the American Postal System from Franklin to Morse* (Cambridge, MA: Harvard University Press, 1995), 57.
48. Siegert, 53.
49. Bresciani, *EV*, vol. 1, 55.
50. For a detailed discussion of Ciceruacchio, see Fedele Clemente and Mario Gallenga, *Per servizio di nostro signore: strade, corrieri e poste dei papi dal medioevo al 1870, Quaderni di Storia Postale* 10 (Modena: Mucchi Editore, 1988). He is also mentioned in Attilio Milano, *Storia degli ebrei Storia degli ebrei in Italia* (Turin: Einaudi, 1992), 360.
51. Bresciani, *EV*, vol. 1, 55–56.
52. Clemente and Gallenga, 393.
53. Bresciani, *EV*, vol. 1, 371.
54. Reflecting this takeover, on June 30 the new minister of Finance, Lunati, writes the superintendent of postal services to compliment him for his comportment during the fiasco at the post office. He also mentions that the Vatican's newspaper censors had been eliminated (Clemente and Galenga 396). We shall return to this subject of newspapers, censorship, and the post in the next chapter.
55. Clemente and Gallenga, 400.
56. Janet Gurkin Altman, *Epistolarity: Approaches to a Form* (Columbus: Ohio State University Press, 1982), 185.
57. Even the word "convert," meaning to transform or change in character, points to the changes Aser and other converts of *EV* exhibit.
58. Bresciani, *EV*, vol. 2, 165.
59. Bresciani, *EV*, vol. 1, 101.
60. Bresciani, *EV*, vol. 2, 207.
61. "A war so savage and cruel had filled him with a remorse, which he sought to stifle in Italy; which had gnawed his heart insupportably during the excesses in Vienna, and which now in Hungary completely overcame him. Thenceforward, he resolved to break off all communication with the secret societies, the pestilence, the malediction, and the scourge of God upon our age." Bresciani, *EV*, vol. 2, 260.
62. Gunzberg, 80.
63. When the pope chose to flee to Gaeta, things were dangerous enough that one of Bresciani's parishioners came to beg that he leave the city, as a French invasion appeared imminent. According to Bresciani, her brother came to Bresciani's house in soldier clothes—he was in the Civic Guard—and took

Bresciani, who was wearing civilian clothes rather than priestly clothing, to his house and hid him. The story is echoed in the story of the priest who saves Aser, who was also rescued by a devoted follower during the revolution. Thus, in a certain sense, Bresciani posits himself as the priest that converts Aser, enabling to proclaim both a personal and more general victory of the Vatican over revolution.

64. Schwyz is also home to a large Catholic monastery, which is undoubtedly why Bresciani chose to have Aser go there.
65. Bresciani, *EV*, vol. 2, 328.
66. Gunzberg, 86.
67. Gunzberg, 69–70.
68. Bresciani, *EV*, vol. 1, 177.
69. Jessica Lang, "Circulating Bodies: Reading *Charlotte Temple* and Susannah Rowson," Unpublished essay, 2003.
70. For further discussion, see Furlani.
71. Bresciani, *EV*, vol. 1, 245.
72. Bresciani, *EV*, vol. 1, 247.
73. Bresciani, *EV*, vol. 1, 255.
74. Bresciani, *EV*, vol. 1, 146.
75. Bresciani, *EV*, vol. 1, 236.
76. Bresciani, *EV*, vol. 1, 276.
77. For further discussion of this theme in the *Bildungsroman*, see Franco Moretti, *Atlas of the European Novel* (London: Verso, 1999).
78. Bresciani, *EV*, vol. 1, 350.
79. Siegert, 31.
80. Bresciani, *EV*, vol. 1, 310.
81. Bresciani, *EV*, vol. 1, 312.
82. Bresciani, *EV*, vol. 1, 315. In this same section, Bresciani details the conversion of yet another character, this time an unnamed journalist who seeks help from a clergyman with the following words: "I am a writer for the press, by which I earned an abundant support, but as I had not yet abandoned my soul entirely to the spirit of evil, I have forsaken my occupation, for I was stricken with terror at the danger which I have been constantly incurring." Bresciani, *EV*, vol. 1, 314. Needless to say, the journalist denounces all printing presses in Italy and converts to the life of a pious believer.
83. *Civiltà Cattolica*, "Il giornalismo moderno e il nostro programma," 1, no. 1 (1850), 13.

CHAPTER 5

1. ACDF, S. O., St.St., TT.2.n.17. Ferrara, November 23, 1847.
2. ACDF, S. O., St.St., TT.2.n.17. Ferrara, February 10, 1848.

3. For further details, see Fabio Levi, "Gli ebrei nella vita economica italiana dell'Ottocento," in *Storia d'Italia. Gli ebrei in Italia, Dall'emancipazione a oggi*, vol. 11.2, ed. Corrado Vivanti (Turin: Einaudi, 1997), 1171–1210.
4. "Gli ebrei si devono rispettare," *Il Povero*, January 5, 1848: 402.
5. Carlebach, 38.
6. Indeed, if the articles related the conversion of a well-known aristocrat or community leader, they would be reprinted in other Catholic journals, demonstrating the lack of originality in both content and ideology that afflicted reactionary journals.
7. Robert Weisberg, "Proclaiming Trials as Narratives: Premises and Pretenses," *Law's Stories: Narrative and Rhetoric in the Law*, ed. Peter Brooks and Paul Gewirtz (New Haven:Yale University Press, 1996), 76.
8. G. Baraldi, "Lettere sull'Italia considerata riguardo alla Religione del Signor Pietro de Joux," *Memorie di religione di morale e di letteratura* 10 (1826): 251.
9. "Notizie ecclesiastiche sulla conversione del Principe d'Anhalt-Coethen, e del Ministro Le Joux," *Memorie di religione di morale e di letteratura*.10 (1826): 203.
10. "Lettera di Madamigella de Joux de la Chapelle a sua sorella. Per informarla del suo ritorno al seno della Chiesa cattolica, ed esporle i motivi della conversione sua," *Memorie di Religione, Morale e Letteratura* 10 (1826): 435. The letter also appeared in *Giornale degli apologisti della religione cattolica* 8 (1827).
11. "Lettera di Madamigella de Joux," *Memorie di Religione, Morale e Letteratura* 10 (1826): 435.
12. Bresciani, *EV*, vol. 1, 205.
13. "Cenno di un discorso," *L'Araldo* November 16, 1859: 366.
14. Gioacchino Ventura, *Lettere ad un ministro protestante ed altri scritti minori* (Naples, 1860), 12.
15. Miccoli, *Fra mito della cristianità e secolarizzazione*, 27.
16. Bresciani, *EV*, vol.1, 108.
17. Padre Antonino Maria Di Jorio, *Le Bellezze del Protestantismo proposte alle gioie degli italiani* (Naples, 1876), 340–42.
18. As Peter Brooks writes, "narrative discourse is never innocent, but always presentational, a way of working on story events that is also a way of working on the listener or reader." Peter Brooks, "The Law as Narrative and Rhetoric," 17.
19. Di Jorio, 340–42.
20. Di Jorio, 333.
21. Di Jorio, 333.
22. Altman, 185–86.
23. Peter Brooks, "Storytelling Without Fear? Confession in Law and Literature," *Law's Stories: Narrative and Rhetoric in the Law*, ed. Peter Brooks and Paul Gewirtz (Yale University Press: New Haven, 1996), 119.

24. Benedict Anderson, *Imagined Communities: Reflections on the Origin and Spread of Nationalism (*London: Verso, 1991), 35–36.
25. "Conversione d'Inghilterra," *L'Araldo* October 12, 1859: 331.
26. For further discussion, see Ian Machin, "British Catholics," *The Emancipation of Catholics, Jews and Protestants*, ed. Rainer Liedtke and Stephan Wendehorst (New York: Manchester University Press, 1999), 11–32.
27. Di Jorio, 343.
28. Ventura, 14–15. Lilibeo is the old name for the city of Marsala, on the Western coast of Sicily, facing the Libyan coast.
29. Ventura, 15–16.
30. ASV, Archivio Particolare di Gregorio XVI, busta 1, Fascicolo 1.2. *Nota sullo stato attuale della religione Cattolica nella Germania Centrale.*
31. For further discussion see Gian Paolo Romagnani, "Italian Protestants," *The Emancipation of Catholics, Jews and Protestants*, ed. Rainer Liedtke and Stephan Wendehorst (New York: Manchester University Press, 1999), 148–68.
32. ACDF, S. O., St.St., TT.3.b.15.
33. "Notizie Ecclesiastiche," *L'Araldo* October 12, 1859: 331.
34. "Conversione d'un Rabbino capo," *Memorie di religione di morale e di letteratura* 2 (1822): 473–4.
35. Allegra, "Modelli di conversione," 903.
36. Homi Bhabha, *The Location of Culture* (Routledge: New York, 1994), 141.
37. Delgado 2314.
38. For further discussion, see Edward Peters, *Inquisition* (New York: The Free Press, 1988), 112.
39. ACDF, S. O., St.St., TT.3.f.5. September 10, 1843.
40. ASV, Archivio Particolare di Pio IX, Oggetti vari, indice 1132 [Arch. Part. Pio IX, Oggetti vari], *Brevi cenni e riflessioni sul pro-memoria e sillabo. Scritture umiliate alla santità di nostro signore Papa Pio IX relative al battesimo conferito in Bologna al fanciullo Edgardo figlio degli ebrei Salomone e Marianna Mortara*, 3.
41. For the most recent, and perhaps most thorough, treatment of the Mortara Affair, see David I. Kertzer, *The Kidnapping of Edgardo Mortara* (New York: Vintage 1998).
42. Giuseppe Garibaldi, *I Mille* (Torino: Camilla e Bertolero, 1873), 165.
43. Weisberg, "Proclaiming Trials as Narratives" 63.
44. ASV, Segreteria di Stato, anno 1859, rubrica 66 (ebrei e scismatici), fasc.1, 129–30.
45. ASV, Segreteria di Stato, anno 1859, rubrica 66 (ebrei e scismatici), fasc.1, 88.
46. ASV, Segreteria di Stato, anno 1859, rubrica 66 (ebrei e scismatici), fasc. 2, 99–100.
47. ASV, Segreteria di Stato, anno 1859, rubrica 66 (ebrei e scismatici), fasc. 2, 103.

48. ASV, Segreteria di Stato, anno 1859, rubrica 66 (ebrei e scismatici), fasc.2, 103.
49. ASV, Segreteria di Stato, anno 1859, rubrica 66 (ebrei e scismatici), fasc.2, 104.
50. ASV, Segreteria di Stato, anno 1859, rubrica 66 (ebrei e scismatici), fasc.2, 80.
51. ASV, Segreteria di Stato, anno 1859, rubrica 66 (ebrei e scismatici), fasc.1, 10.
52. ASV, Segreteria di Stato, anno 1859, rubrica 66 (ebrei e scismatici), fasc.1, 72.
53. Delgado, 2415.
54. ASV, Segreteria di Stato, anno 1859, rubrica 66 (ebrei e scismatici), fasc.2, 84.
55. ASV, Segreteria di Stato, anno 1859, rubrica 66 (ebrei e scismatici), fasc.2, 90.
56. ASV, Segreteria di Stato, anno 1859, rubrica 66 (ebrei e scismatici), fasc.2, 91.
57. ASV, Segreteria di Stato, anno 1859, rubrica 66 (ebrei e scismatici), fasc.2, 99 (emphasis in the original).
58. ASV, Segreteria di Stato, anno 1859, rubrica 66 (ebrei e scismatici), fasc.1, 19.
59. ASV, Segreteria di Stato, anno 1859, rubrica 66 (ebrei e scismatici), fasc.1, 214.
60. Like Edgardo, who was saved from his illness as a small child, the Pharaoh's daughter saved Moses when he was an infant. ASV, Segreteria di Stato, anno 1859, rubrica 66 (ebrei e scismatici), fasc.1, 210. This is an article; on its cover is scribbled "quest'articolo non fu mandato alla stampa." The headline is: *Il Battesimo conferito al fanciullo ebreo Edgardo Mortara in Bologna da una serva bolognese nell'atto che il med. Era in procinto di morte ha fatto.*
61. ASV, Segreteria di Stato, anno 1859, rubrica 66 (ebrei e scismatici), fasc. 1, 210.
62. Ragussis, 47.
63. Cited in Masetti Zannini, "Nuovi documenti sul caso Mortara," *Rivista storica della chiesa italiana* 13.2 (1959): Appendice I, 265.
64. ASV, Segreteria di Stato, anno 1859, rubrica 66 (ebrei e scismatici), fasc. 1, 79–80.
65. ASV, Segreteria di Stato, anno 1859, rubrica 66 (ebrei e scismatici), fasc. 2, 85–6.
66. ASV, Segreteria di Stato, anno 1859, rubrica 66 (ebrei e scismatici), fasc.1, 65 (emphasis in the original.).
67. For further discussion of otherness in this context, see Edward Said, *Orientalism*, New York: Pantheon Books, 1978.
68. ASV, Segreteria di Stato, anno 1859, rubrica 66 (ebrei e scismatici), fasc.2, 87–88.

69. ASV, Segreteria di Stato, anno 1859, rubrica 66 (ebrei e scismatici), fasc.3, Camillo Tarquini, *Osservazioni fatte sul medi da altra mano sul giovane Mortara*. This citation is from an anonymous accompanying text, 35.
70. "L'ebreo di Bologna e le bombe di Giuseppe Mazzini," *L'Armonia della religione collà Civiltà*, August 17, 1858: 755–56.
71. Bresciani, *L'Ebreo di Verona*, Vol. 2, 81.
72. Mosse 254.
73. "L'ebreo di Bologna" August 17, 1858: 755.
74. For further discussion of these ideas of dominant "ingroups" and of "outgroups" and the stories they create, see Delgado 2411–41.
75. "L'Ebreo di Bologna," *L'Armonia della religione collà Civiltà*, October 6, 1858: 924.
76. Delgado, 2421–22.
77. When *L'Araldo*, a Lucca newspaper, published its first article on the case, it too brushed over the Mortara affair, moving instead to reminding readers of the hardships Catholics suffer the world over. "Edgardo Mortara," *L'Araldo della Pragmalogia Cattolica*, December 1858: 414–16.
78. Delgado, 2411.
79. "Notizie del giovanetto cristiano Mortara," *L'Armonia della religione collà Civiltà*, October 16, 1858: 959–60.
80. "Il piccolo neofito Edgardo Mortara," *Civiltà Cattolica* 9, no. 12 (1858): 390.
81. In similar testimony, *L'Armonia* records how Momolo tries to get the boy to return home to Bologna, saying to him: "Why don't you come with me? Have you perhaps forgotten the Commandments of the law of God: honor our father and your mother?" Edgardo is quoted as answering in the negative and deferring to the wisdom and power of his Church father rather than his biological one: "The Papa [Pope] knows the Commandments better than you and I; I will do that which my Papà [father] says. "Notizie del giovanetto cristiano Mortara," 960. The story, playing with the words *papà* ("father") and *Papa* ("Pope"), equates the former with the latter, and portrays Edgardo as not only deferring to his Church father, but as defining the pope as his true father.
82. "Edgardo Mortara," *L'Armonia della religione collà Civiltà* November 4, 1858: 1020.
83. "Edgardo Mortara," *L'Armonia della religione collà Civiltà* November 4, 1858: 1020.
84. Archivio Storico della Comunità Ebraica a Roma (henceforth ASCER), Caso Mortara.
85. "Il piccolo neofito Edgardo Mortara," *Civiltà Cattolica* 9, no. 12 (1858): 394. Similar stories appear in other Catholic journals. In one, Marianna is described as removing several medallions with saints on them from her son's neck, "giving him coins, and telling him that she had ordered a vest of gold for him, and other such tempting promises." Edgardo listened to her respectfully, but when she left, he dismissed the gifts, explaining that he

would receive better gifts in Paradise and adding that if she came to visit again, he would hide in order not to hear what she said. "Edgardo Mortara," *L'Armonia della religione collà Civiltà* November 4, 1858: 1020.

86. "Il piccolo neofito Edgardo Mortara," *Civiltà Cattolica* 9, no. 12 (1858): 415.
87. For further discussion on the relationship between conversion and conquest, see chapter 2.
88. Farini had already expressed his criticism of the Tribunal in a letter to Gladstone in 1856. See Luigi Carlo Farini, *La Diplomazia e la Quistione italiana: lettera di Luigi Carlo Farini al signor Guglielmo Gladstone* (Turin, 1856), 33.
89. Farini, 13.
90. Archivio di Stato di Bologna (henceforth ASB). Tribunale Civile e Criminale di Prima Istanza. Processo su il rapimento di Edgardo Mortara, n.52/1860, Coll. Torre C, piano II, scaf.23.
91. Francesco Jussi, *Difesa del Padre Pier Gaetano Feletti. Imputato come inquisitore del santo uffizio del ratto del fanciullo Edgardo Mortara davanti al tribunale civile e criminale di prima istanza in Bologna* (Bologna, 1860), 5.
92. Jussi, 50.
93. Jussi, 50.
94. Jussi, 27–28.
95. Jussi, 3.
96. Jussi, 11.
97. Kertzer, *The Kidnapping of Edgardo Mortara*, 241.
98. After his imprisonment, Church authorities thought it best for Feletti to move to Rome, which was still under papal control.

CONCLUSION

1. The director of these archives was extremely protective of this information, and thus I only managed to obtain statistics for certain years after 1866. In 1860, there were five baptisms, in 1861 through 1866 there were approximately four baptisms a year (Archivio della Casa dei Catecumeni, Rome [ACC], 184. *Liber III. Baptizatorum Neophytorum. Ven. Domus Catechumenorum de Urbe. A die VII Januari 1827 ad diem XXI Novembris 1887.*)
2. Giovanni Spadolini, "L'intransigentismo cattolico: dalla *Civiltà Cattolica* al *Sillabo*," *Rassegna Storica Toscana* 4 (1958): 314.
3. Antonio Gramsci, "Riforma e Rinascimento," *Il Risorgimento* (Rome: Riuniti, 1977), 14.
4. Gramsci, "Riforma e Rinascimento," 14.
5. Giuseppe Pelczar, *Pio IX e il suo pontificato*, vol. 2 (Turin: Libreria Berruti, 1910), 200. Cited in Kertzer, *Edgardo Mortara*, 260.
6. Bhabha, "Introduction," 4.

EPILOGUE

1. Susan Zuccotti, *Under His Very Windows: The Vatican and the Holocaust in Italy* (New Haven: Yale University Press, 2001), xiii.
2. For a thorough discussion of this encyclical, see Georges Passelecq and Bernard Suchecky, *The Hidden Encyclical of Pius XI*, trans. Steven Rendall (New York: Harcourt Brace & Co, 1997). Both Zuccotti and Kertzer, in *The Popes Against the Jews*, discuss the anti-Jewish laws in Italy and elsewhere in Europe, and both suggest a connection between Church-instigated anti-Judaism and racially based antisemitism. Here I am suggesting that an examination of the language of Vatican diplomats, particularly with regard to the subject of converts, provides further proof of this relationship. Neither the aspect of conversion or language—particularly that of the Vatican's World War II correspondence—has been explored thoroughly in past studies of theological versus racial anti-Jewish sentiment.
3. Pierre Blet et al., eds. *Actes et Documents du Saint Siège relatifs à la Seconde Guerre Mondiale*, vol. 9 (Vatican City: Libreria Editrice Vaticana, 1975), 433–34.
4. Pierre Blet et al., eds. *Actes et Documents du Saint Siège relatifs à la Seconde Guerre Mondiale*, vol. 8 (Vatican City: Libreria Editrice Vaticana, 1974), 73.
5. *Actes et Documents du Saint Siège*, vol. 8, 163. March 31, 1941.
6. *Actes et Documents du Saint Siège*, vol. 8, 708–9. November 7, 1942.
7. For further discussion see Giovanni Miccoli, *I dilemmi e i silenzi di Pio XII. Vaticano, Seconda guerra mondiale e Shoah* (Milan: Rizzoli, 2000).
8. In 1964, the Vatican responded to a controversy that had been sparked a year earlier, when Rolf Hochuth published his play, *The Deputy*, which harshly criticized Pope Pius XII's inaction during World War II. Pope Paul VI commissioned three Jesuit scholars (a fourth joined the group subsequently), who were allowed access to the otherwise closed archives containing the Church's wartime documents. These Vatican-appointed historians were assigned the task of compiling part of this archival material for publication. The result, eleven volumes of Vatican diplomatic correspondence known as the *Actes et Documents du Saint Siège*, was published over the next twenty years. The eleven volumes that comprised the work of these editors were unusual because they broke the customary Vatican standard of waiting a period of seventy years following the death of a pope before releasing documents relating to his pontificate.
9. Pierre Blet et al., eds. *Actes et Documents du Saint Siège relatifs à la Seconde Guerre Mondiale*, vol. 6 (Vatican City: Libreria Editrice Vaticana, 1972), 17.
10. Pierre Blet, S. J., *Pius XII and the Second World War*, trans. Lawrence J. Johnson (New York: Paulist Press, 1997), 1–2.

11. Luigi Accattoli, "Edith Stein: Santità, basta con il silenzio della Chiesa," *Corriere della Sera* February 19, 2003: 24.
12. Edith Stein, "'Il Silenzio Colpevole'," *Corriere della Sera*, trans. Brigida Pesce, February 19, 2003: 24.
13. See, for example, Margarita Marchione, *Pius XII: Architect for Peace* (New York: Paulist Press, 1999); Ronald J. Rychlak, *Hitler, the War and the Pope* (Columbus, MS: Genesis, 2000).
14. Commission for Religious Relations with the Jews, *We Remember: A Reflection of the Shoah* (Vatican City: Libreria Editrice Vaticana, 1998).

Bibliography

Archival Sources and Abbreviations

ACC Archivio della Casa dei Catecumeni Neofiti. Housed in the Archivio del Vicariato di Roma.

181. Liber Battizzatorum Neophitorum Ven. Domus Cathecumen de Urbe, 1759–1826.

183. Libro di Ebrei, e Turchi venuti nella Pia Casa de' Catechumeni, 1814–1824.

184. Liber III. Baptizatorum Neophytorum. Ven. Domus Catechumenorum de Urbe. A die VII Januari 1827 ad diem XXI Novembris 1887.

ACEL Archivio della Comunità Ebraica di Livorno.

ACDF Archivio della Congregazione per la Dottrina della Fede.

S. O. St.St. Santum Officiium, Stanza Storica.

ASB Archivio di Stato di Bologna. Tribunale Civile e Criminale di Prima Istanza. Processo su il rapimento di Edgardo Mortara, n.52/1860, Coll. Torre C, piano II, scaf. 23.

ASF Archivio di Stato di Firenze.

PAC Presidenza del buongoverno 1814–1848, Affari Comuni.

ASV Archivio Segreto Vaticano.

Archivio Particolare di Gregorio XVI.

Catecumeni—neofiti dimoranti in quel stabilimento, n.1438.

Fondo Pio IX, oggetti vari, "Mortara Edgardo—Intera Posizione," n. 1433.

Miscellanea di Carte Politiche o Riservate, anno 1858.

Segreteria di Stato, anno 1859, rubrica 66 (ebrei e scismatici), fasc. 1–2, 3.

ASCER Archivio Storico della Comunità Ebraica a Roma.

Caso Mortara

BAV Biblioteca Apostolica Vaticana, biblioteca Vali Ferraioli IV.

Works Cited and Consulted

Accattoli, Luigi. "Edith Stein: Santità, basta con il silenzio della Chiesa." *Corriere della Sera* February 19, 2003, 24.

Albertario, Davide. "Il Giansenista ha messo alla luce il liberale." In *Manzoni pro e contro*, Vol. 1., edited by G. Vigorelli, 443–62. Milan: Istituto propaganda libraria, 1974.

Allegra, Luciano. "L'anti-Semitismo come risorsa politica. Battesimi forzati e ghetti nel Piemonte del Settecento." *Quaderni Storici* 84 (1993): 867–99.

———. "Modelli di conversione." *Quaderni Storici* 78 (1991): 901–15.

Allies, Thomas William. *Journal in France in 1845 and 1848, with Letters from Italy in 1847 of Things and Persons concerning the Church and Education.* London, 1849.

Altgeld, Wolfgang. "German Catholics." In *The Emancipation of Catholics, Jews and Protestants*, edited by Rainer Liedtke and Stephan Wendehorst, 100–21. New York: Manchester University Press: 1999.

Altman, Janet Gurkin. *Epistolarity: Approaches to a Form.* Columbus: Ohio State University Press, 1982.

Aminta, Filippo. *L'ebraisimo senza replica e sconfitto colle stesse sue armi.* Rome, 1823.

Anderson, Benedict. *Imagined Communities: Reflections on the Origin and Spread of Nationalism.* London: Verso, 1991.

Angelini, Cesare. *Con Renzo e con Lucia (e con gli altri). Saggi sul Manzoni.* Brescia: Morcelliana, 1986.

Aubert, Rober, Alberto Maria Ghisalberti, Ettore Passerin d'Entrèves, and Pietro Pirri, eds. *Chiesa e stato nell'Ottocento.* Vol. 2. Padova: Editrice Antenore, 1962.

Balibar, Etienne, and Immanuel Wallerstein. *Race, Nation, Class: Ambiguous Identities.* London: Verso, 1991.

Balzofiore, Filippo. *Nelle solenni esequie celebrate per la gioventù romana al reverendo P. Antonio Bresciani.* Rome: Tipografia Forense, 1862.

Bangert, William V., S. J. *A History of the Society of Jesus.* St. Louis: The Institute of Jesuit Sources, 1972.

Banti, Alberto. *La nazione del Risorgimento.* Turin: Einaudi, 2000.

Baraldi, G. "Lettere sull'Italia considerata riguardo alla Religione del Signor Pietro de Joux," *Memorie di religione di morale e di letteratura* 10 (1826): 241–60.

Barbagallo, Francesco. "The Rothschilds in Naples." *Journal of Modern Italian Studies* 5, no. 3 (2001): 294–309.

Barthel, Manfred. *The Jesuits.* Translated by Mark Howson. New York: William Morrow and Company, 1984.

Barbiera, R. *Il Salotto della Contessa Maffei.* Milan, 1895.

Battista Gherardo D'Arco, Giovanni. *Dell'influenza del ghetto nello Stato.* Venice, 1782.

Belli, Giuseppe Gioacchino. *Sonetti.* Eds. Giorgio Vigolo and Pietro Gibellini. Milan: Mondadori, 2000.

Bhabha, Homi, K. *The Location of Culture.* New York: Routledge, 1994.

———. ed. *Nation and Narration.* New York: Routledge, 1990.

Blet, Pierre. *Pius XII and the Second World War.* Translated by Lawrence J. Johnson. New York: Paulist Press, 1997.

Blet, Pierre, Angelo Martini, and Burkhart Schneider, eds. *Actes et Documents du Saint Siège relatifs à la Seconde Guerre Mondiale*. 11 vols. Vatican City: Libreria Editrice Vaticana, 1975.

Bollati, Giulio. *L'Italiano: Il carattere nazionale come storia e come invenzione*. Turin: Einaudi, 1983.

Bonora, Ettore. "Ancora sulla lettera a Marco Coen." *Giornale storico della letteratura italiana* 102, no. 521 (1986): 27–43.

———. *Manzoni e la via italiana al realismo*. Naples: Liguori Editore, 1989.

Borri, Giuseppe. *I colloqui col Manzoni*. Edited by Ezio Flori. Bologna: Zanichelli, 1929.

Boyarin, Daneil. *Unheroic Conduct: The Rise of Heterosexuality and the Invention of the Jewish Man*. Berkeley: University of California Press, 1997.

Brannigan, John. *New Historicism and Cultural Materialism*. New York: St. Martin's, 1998.

Bresciani, Antonio. *Della vita e delle opere del p. Antonio Bresciani della C.d.G. Commentario*. Rome: Office of Civiltà Cattolica, 1869.

———. *L'Ebreo di Verona; racconto storico dall'anno 1846 al 1849*. 2 Vols. Milan: Ditta Boniardi-Pogliani di E. Besozzi, 1855.

———. *The Jew of Verona: An Historical Tale of the Italian Revolutions of 1846–9*. [Translation anonymous.] Vols. 1 and 2. Baltimore: John Murphy & Co., 1854.

———. *Opere del P. Antonio Bresciani della compagnia di Gesù*. Vol. 2. Rome: Ufficio della Civiltà Cattolica, 1865.

Brooks, Peter. "The Law as Narrative and Rhetoric." In *Law's Stories: Narrative and Rhetoric in the Law*, edited by Peter Brooks and Paul Gewirtz, 14–22. New Haven: Yale University Press, 1996.

———. *Reading for the Plot: Design and Intention in Narrative*. New York: Vintage Books, 1984.

———. "Storytelling Without Fear? Confession in Law and Literature." In *Law's Stories: Narrative and Rhetoric in the Law*, edited by Peter Brooks and Paul Gewirtz, 114–34. New Haven: Yale University Press, 1996.

Caffiero, Marina. *La nuova era: Miti e profezie dell'Italia in Rivoluzione*. Genoa: Casa Editrice Marietti, 1991.

———. "'Le insidie de' perfidi giudei'. Antiebraismo e riconquista cattolica alla fine del settecento." In *La questione ebraica dall'illuminismo all'impero (1700–1815). Atti del convegno della Società Italiana di Studi sul secolo XVIII*, edited by Paolo Alatri and Silvia Grassi, 183–207. Naples: Edizioni Scientifiche Italiane, 1994.

———. *Religione e modernità in Italia*. Rome: Istituti editoriali e poligrafici internazionali, 2000.

———. "Tra chiesa e stato. Gli ebrei italiani dall'età dei lumi agli anni della Rivoluzione." In *Storia d'Italia. Gli ebrei in Italia: Dall'emancipazione a oggi*, Vol. 11.2, edited by Corrado Vivanti, 1091–1134. Turin: Einaudi, 1997.

Camaiani, Pier Giorgio. "Castighi di Dio e trionfo della Chiesa. Mentalità e polemiche dei cattolici temporalisti nell'età di Pio IX." *Rivista Storica Italiana* 88, no. 4 (1976): 708–44.

Canepa, Andrew M. "L'atteggiamento degli ebrei italiani davanti alla loro seconda emancipazione. Premesse e analisi." *Rassegna Mensile di Israel* 43, no. 9 (1977): 419–36.

———. "Emancipation and Jewish Response in Mid- Nineteenth-Century Italy," *European History Quarterly* 16. 4 (1986): 403–439.

Cantù, Cesare. *Alessanro Manzoni. Reminiscenze.* Milan, 1892.

Carlebach, Elisheva. *Divided Souls: Converts from Judaism in Germany, 1500–1750*, New Haven: Yale University Press, 2001.

Carsaniga, Giovanni. "The Age of Romanticism (1800–1870)." *The Cambridge History of Italian Literature*, edited by Peter Brand and Lino Pertile, 397–456. New York: Cambridge University Press, 1996.

Castronovo, Valerio, Giuseppe Ricuperati, Carlo Capra. *La stampa italiana dal cinquecento all'ottocento.* Introduction, N. Tranfaglia. Rome: Laterza, 1976.

———. *La stampa italiana dall'unità al fascismo.* Rome: Laterza, 1973.

"Cenno di un discorso," *L'Araldo* November 16, 1859: 366.

Chadwick, Owen. *The Popes and European Revolution.* Oxford: Clarendon, 1981.

Chittolini, Giorgio and Giovanni Miccoli, eds. *Storia d'Italia, La Chiesa e il potere politico dal Medioevo all'età contemporanea.* Vol. 9. Turin: Einaudi, 1986.

Clemente, Fedele, and Mario Gallenga. *Per servizio di nostro signore: strade, corrieri e poste dei papi dal medioevo al 1870. Quaderni di Storia Postale.* Vol. 10. Modena: Mucchi Editore, 1988.

Colombo, Luigi. *. . . e non era più lago ma specchio del cuore . . . Scritti e discorsi di argomento manzoniano.* Lecco: Comune di Lecco, 1985.

Colombo, Umberto. "I silenzi del Manzoni." *Otto/Novecento* 9, no. 1 (1985): 41–72.

Commission for Religious Relations with the Jews. *We Remember: A Reflection of the Shoah.* Vatican City: Libreria Editrice Vaticana, 1998.

"Conversione d'Inghilterra," *L'Araldo* October 12, 1859: 331.

"Conversione d'un Rabbino capo," *Memorie di religione di morale e di letteratura* 2 (1822): 473–74.

Conversione miracolosa alla fede cattolica di Alfonso Maria Ratisbonne, avvenuta in Roma nella Chiesa dei PP. Minimi in S. Andrea delle Fratte. Tratta dai processi autentici formatisi in Roma nel 1842. Roma: G. Cesaretti, 1864.

Dante, Francesco. *Storia della "Civiltà Cattolica" (1850–1891). Il laboratorio del Papa.* Rome: Edizioni Studium, 1990.

Davidson, Nicholas. "The Inquisition and the Italian Jews." In *Inquisition and Society in Early Modern Europe*, edited by Stephen Haliczer. London: Croom Helm, 1987.

Davis, Natalie Zemon. *The Return of Martin Guerre*. Cambridge, MA: Harvard University Press, 1983.

De Cesare, R. *Roma e lo stato del Papa. Dal Ritorno di Pio IX al XX settembre*. Vol. 1. Rome: Forzani Editori, 1907.

De Sanctis, Francesco. "L'Ebreo di Verona." *Saggi critici*, edited by Paolo Arcari, 91–115. Milan: Treves, 1921.

———. *La scuola cattolico-liberale e il romanticism a Napoli*. Edited by Carlo Muscetta and Giorgio Candeloro. Turin: Einaudi, 1953.

———. *Storia della letteratura italiana. Dall'Ottocento al Novecento*. Turin: Einaudi, 1991.

Degola, Eustachio. *Eustachio Degola, il clero costituzionale e la conversione della famiglia Manzoni*. Edited by Angelo de Gubernatis. Florence: G. Barbèra, 1882.

Delacouture, A. *Roma e la opinione pubblica d'Europa nel fatto Mortara. Atti, documenti, confutazioni coll'aggiunta del diritto canonico e diritto naturale*. Turin, 1859.

Delgado, Richard. "Storytelling for Oppositionists and Others: A Plea for Narrative." *Michigan Law Review* 87 (1989): 2411–41.

Del Monte, Anna. *Ratto della Signora Anna del Monte trattenuta à Catecumeni tredici giorni dalli 6 fino alli 19 maggio anno 1749*. Edited by Giuseppe Sermonta. Rome: Carucci editore, 1989.

Della Pergola, Sergio. *Anatomia dell'ebraismo italiano: caratteristiche demografiche, economiche, sociali, religiose e politiche di una minoranza*. Rome: B. Carucci, 1976.

Della Peruta, Franco. "Gli ebrei nel Risorgimento fra interdizioni ed emancipazione." In *Storia d'Italia. Gli ebrei in Italia: dall'emancipazione a oggi*, col. 11.2, edited by Corrado Vivanti, 1135–1167. Turin: Einaudi, 1997. 1135–67.

———. "Le 'interdizioini' israelitiche e l'emancipazione degli ebrei nel Risorgimento." *Società e storia* 19 (1983): 77–107.

Di Jorio, Padre Antonino Maria. *Le Bellezze del Protestantismo proposte alle gioie degli italiani*. Naples, 1876.

Di Porto, Bruno. "Gli ebrei nel Risorgimento." *Nuova Antologia* 115, no. 3 (1980): 256–72.

Di Ricco, A. "Padre Bresciani: populismo e reazione." *Studi Storici* 22 (1981): 833–60.

Dionisotti, Carlo. *Manzoni and the Catholic Revival*. Oxford: Oxford University Press, 1974.

Dombroski, Robert. "The ideological question in Manzoni." *Studies in Romanticism* 20, no. 4 (Winter 1981): 497–524.

"Edgardo Mortara," *L'Araldo della Pragmalogia Cattolica* December 1858, 414–16.

"Edgardo Mortara," *L'Armonia della religione collà Civiltà* November 4, 1858, 1020–1021.

Fabris, Cristoforo. *Memorie manzoniane*, vol. 11.2. Milan, 1901.

Farber, Daniel A. and Suzanna Sherry. "Telling Stories Out of School: An Essay on Legal Narratives." *Stanford Law Review* 45 (April, 1993): 807–55.

Farini, Luigi Carlo. *La diplomazia e la quistione italiana: lettera di Luigi Carlo Farini al signor Guglielmo Gladstone.* Turin, 1856.

Formigoni, Giorgio. *L'Italia dei Cattolici. Fede e nazione del Risorgimento alla Repubblica.* Bologna: Mulino, 1998.

Forti, Giacomo. "Lettera di Giacomo Forti à suoi genitori israeliti per la sua conversione dal giudaismo alla fede cristiana." *Annali delle Scienze Religiose* 18, no. 53 (1844): 3–12.

Fossi, Piero. *La conversione di Alessandro Manzoni.* Florence: La Nuova Italia Editrice: 1974.

Fremantle, Anne., ed. *The Papal Encyclicals in their Historical Context.* New York: New American Library, 1956.

Fubini, Guido. *La condizione giuridica dell'ebraismo italiano.* Florence: La Nuova Italia, 1974.

Furlani, Silvio. *La politica postale di Metternich e l'Italia. Quaderni di storia postale.* Vol. 8. Prato: Istituto di studi storici postali, 1987.

Gambini, Francesco. *Dell'Ebreo possidente.* Turin: Stamperia Pane, 1815.

———. *Della cittadinanza giudaica in Europa.* Turin: Tipografia di G. Pomba, 1834.

Garibaldi, Giuseppe. *I Mille.* Turin: Camilla e Bertolero, 1873.

Garrone, Alessandro Galante, and Franco Della Peruta. *La stampa italiana del Risorgimento.* Edited by V. Castronovo and N. Tranfaglia. Rome: Laterza, 1979.

Gatt-Rutter, John. "When the Killing Had to Stop: Manzoni's Paradigm of Christian Conversion." *The Italianist* 10 (1990): 7–40.

Gellner, Ernest. *Nations and Nationalism.* Oxford: Oxford University Press, 1983.

Ghezzo, Silvana. "Il nome di Maria nel *Nome di Maria* di Alessandro Manzoni." *Otto/Novecento* 4 (1983): 185–93.

Gilman, Sander, and Steven Katz, eds. *Antisemitism in Times of Crisis.* New York: New York University Press, 1991.

Ginzburg, Natalia. *La famiglia Manzoni.* Turin: Einaudi, 1994.

"Gli ebrei si devono rispettare," *Il Povero* January 5, 1848, 402.

Gramsci, Antonio. *Selections from Cultural Writings.* Edited by David Forgacs and Geoffrey Nowell-Smith. Translated by William Boelhower. London: Lawrence and Wishart, 1985.

———. *Quaderni del carcere*, vol. 3. Edited by Valentino Gerratana. Turin: Einaudi, 1975.

———. *Il Risorgimento.* Rome: Editori Riuniti, 1977.

Greenblatt, Stephen. "Invisible Bullets: Renaissance Authority and its Subversion." *Glyph* 8 (1981): 40–61.

———. "Towards a Poetics of Culture." *The New Historicism.* Edited by H. Aram Veeser. London: Routledge, 1990.

Gregg, Joan Young. *Devils, Women and Jews: Reflections of the Other in Medieval Sermon Stories.* Albany: SUNY Press, 1997.

Gunzberg, Lynn. *Strangers at Home: Jews in the Italian Literary Imagination.* Berkeley: University of California Press, 1992.

Hales, E. E. Y. *Revolution and Papacy: 1769–1846.* London: Eyre & Spottiswoode, 1960.

Hawley, John C. "Making Disciples of All Nations," *Historicizing Christian Encounters with the Other.* Edited by John C. Hawley. London: Macmillan, 1998. 1–17.

Hsia, R. Po-Chia. *Trent 1475: Stories of a Ritual Murder Trial.* New Haven: Yale University Press, 1992.

Iannace, Florinda, M. *Conservatorismo cattolico in Antonio Bresciani.* Rome: Trevi editore, 1973.

———. "Silvio Pellico in un inedito di A. Bresciani." *Forum italicum* 4, no. 3 (1970): 364–69.

Ihm, Claudia Carlen, ed. *The Papal Encyclicals, 1740–1878.* Raleigh: The Pierian Press, 1990.

Jacini, Stefano. *Il tramonto del potere temporale nelle relazioni degli ambasciatori austriaci.* Bari: Laterza, 1931.

Jemolo, A. C. *Chiesa e stato in Italia dal Risorgimento ad oggi.* Turin: Einaudi, 1955.

John, Richard R. *Spreading the News: the American Postal System from Franklin to Morse.* Cambridge, MA: Harvard University Press, 1995.

Jussi, Francesco. *Difesa del Padre Pier Gaetano Feletti. Imputato come inquisitore del santo uffizio del ratto del fanciullo Edgardo Mortara davanti al tribunale civile e criminale di prima istanza in Bologna.* Bologna, 1860.

Kalmar, Davidson and Derek J. Penslar, eds. *Orientalism and the Jews.* Waltham, MA: Brandeis University Press, 2005.

Kertzer, David I. *The Kidnapping of Edgardo Mortara.* New York: Vintage, 1998.

———. *The Pope against the Jews.* Knopf: New York, 2001.

Lang, Jessica. "Circulating Bodies: Reading *Charlotte Temple* and Susannah Rowson." Unpublished essay, 2003.

Laras, Giuseppe. "Ansie e speranze degli ebrei di Roma durante il pontificato di Pio IX." *La Rassegna Mensile di Israel* 39, no. 9 (1973): 512–31.

Laurentin, René. *20 janvier 1842, Marie apparaît à Alphonse Ratisbonne*, vols. 1–2. Paris: O.E.I.L., 1991.

"L'Ebreo di Bologna." *L'Armonia della religione collà Civiltà*, October 6, 1858, 923–24.

"L'Ebreo di Bologna e le bombe di Giuseppe Mazzini." *L'armonia della religione colla Civiltà*, August 17, 1858, 755–56.

Leddy, Annette. "The Conversion of Manzoni's L'Innominato or, the Repressed Catholic Consciousness of a Criminal." *Carte Italiane* 2 (1980–81): 27–41.

Legitimo, Gianfranco. "Il padre Bresciani cento anni dopo." *Dialoghi: Rivista Bimestrale di Letteratura Arti Scienze* 10 (1962): 155–70.

"Lettera di Madamigella de Joux de la Chapelle a sua sorella. Per informarla del suo ritorno al seno della Chiesa cattolica, ed esporle i motivi della conversione sua," *Memorie di Religione, Morale e Letteratura* 10 (1826): 435.

Levi, Fabio. "Gli ebrei nella vita economica italiana dell'Ottocento." In *Storia d'Italia. Gli ebrei in Italia. Dall'emancipazione a oggi*, vol. 11.2, edited by Corrado Vivanti, 1171–1210. Turin: Einaudi, 1997.

Lindon, John. "Alessandro Manzoni and the Oxford Movement: His Politics and Conversion in a New English Source." *Journal of Ecclesiastical History* 45, no. 2 (April 1994): 297–318.

Loevinson, Ermanno. "Gli ebrei dello Stato della Chiesa nel periodo del risorgimento politico d'Italia." *Rassegna mensile di Israel* 9 (1934): 159–74.

———. "Gli israeliti della Stato Pontificio e la loro evoluzione politico sociale nel periodo del Risorgimento italiano fino al 1849." *Rassegna Storica del Risorgimento* 4 (1929): 768–803.

Luzzati, Michele, ed. *L'inquisizione e gli ebrei in Italia*. Rome: Laterza, 1994.

Machin, Ian. "British Catholics." In *The Emancipation of Catholics, Jews and Protestants*, edited by Rainer Liedtke and Stephan Wendehorst, 11–32. New York: Manchester University Press: 1999.

Manzoni, Alessandro. *The Betrothed and History of the Column of Infamy*. Edited and translated by D. Forgacs and M. Reynolds. London: J. M. Dent, 1997.

———. *Carteggio di Alessandro Manzoni*, vol. 1. Edited by Giovanni Sforza and Giuseppe Gallavresi. Milan: U. Hoepli, 1912.

———. *Inni Sacri*. Edited by Franco Gavazzeni. Parma: Ugo Guanda Editore, 1997.

———. *Opere*. Edited by Riccardo Bacchelli. Milan: Riccardo Ricciardi Editore, 1953.

———. *Poesie di Alessandro Manzoni prima della conversione*. Edited by Alberto Chiari. Florence: Felice Le Monnier, 1947.

Marchese, Angelo. "Il grande capitolo di Renzo." *Humanitas* 50, no. 1 (1985): 5–14.

Marchione, Margarita. *Pius XII: Architect for Peace*. New York: Paulist Press, 1999.

Marcotti, Giuseppe. *Cronache segrete della polizia toscana*. Firenze, 1898.

Martina, Giacomo. "Ancora sull'allocuzione del 29 aprile e sulla politica vaticana in Italia nel 1848." *Rassegna Storica del Risorgimento* 54, no. 1 (January–March 1967): 40–47.

Masetti Zannini, Gian Ludovico. "Nuovi documenti sul caso Mortara." *Rivista storica della chiesa italiana* 13, no. 2 (1959): 239–79.

Maternini Zotta, Maria Faust. *L'Ente comunitario ebraico: la legislazione negli ultimi due secoli*. Pubblicazioni della facoltà di giurisprudenza della università di Trieste, vol. 27. Milan: Giuffrè Editore, 1983. 60–83.

Menozzi, Daniele. *La chiesa cattolica e la secolarizzazione*. Turin: Einaudi, 1993.

———. "Intorno alle origini del mito della cristianità." *Cristianesimo nella Storia* 5 (1984): 523–62.

Meyersohn, Rolf. "Sociology and Cultural Studies: Some Problems." In *Literary Taste, Culture and Mass Communication: The Sociology of Literature*, vol. 6, edited by Peter Davidson, Rolf Meyersohn, and Edward Shils, 3–22. Teaneck, NJ: Somerset House, 1978.

Miccoli, Giovanni. *I dilemmi e i silenzi di Pio XII. Vaticano, Seconda guerra mondiale e Shoah*. Milan: Rizzoli, 2000.

———. *Fra Mito della Cristianità e secolarizzazione*. Casale Monferrato: Marietti, 1985.

———. "Santa Sede, questione ebraica e anti-Semitismo fra Otto e Novecento." In *Storia d'Italia. Gli ebrei in Italia*, vol. 11.2, edited by Corrado Vivanti 1369–1574. Turin: Einaudi, 1972.

Milano, Attilio. "Battesimi di ebrei a Roma dal Cinquecento all'Ottocento." In *Scritti in Memoria di Enzo Sereni*, edited by Daniel Carpi, Attilio Milano, Umberto Nahon., 153–67. Jerusalem: Fondazione Sally Mayer, 1970.

———. *L'impari lotta della Comunità di Roma contro la Casa dei catecumeni*. Città di Castello: Tip. Unione arti grafiche, 1950.

———. *Storia degli ebrei in Italia*. Turin: Einaudi, 1992.

Mitchell, B. R., ed. *The International Historical Statistics Europe, 1750–1993*. Fourth edition. New York: Stockton, 1998.

Mitchell, W. J. T. *On Narrative*. Chicago: Chicago University Press, 1981.

Moe, Nelson. *The View from Vesuvius: Italian Culture and the Southern Question*. Los Angeles, CA: California University Press, 2001.

Moretti, Franco. *Atlas of the European Novel*. London: Verso, 1999.

Moro, Renato. "L'atteggiamento dei cattolici tra teologia e politica." In *Stato nazionale ed emancipazione ebraica. Atti del convegno Stato nazionale, società civile e minoranze religiose: l'emancipazione degli ebrei in Francia, Germania e Italia tra rigenerazione morale e intoleranza*, edited by F. Sofia and M. Toscano, 305–49. Rome: Bonacci Editore, 1992.

Mosse, George. *The Culture of Western Europe: The Nineteenth and Twentieth Centuries*. Boulder, CO: Westview, 1988.

Nardi, Francesco. *Elementi di diritto ecclesiastico*, vol. 1. Venice: Giovanni Cecchini, 1846.

Navarotto, Adriano. "'L'Affare Mortara' nell incubazione della guerra austro-franco-italiana." *Vita e pensiero* 31 (1940): 269–73.

Nigro, Salvatore. *Il Primo ottocento: l'età napoleonica e il risorgimento*. Rome: Laterza, 1978.

Norsa, Davide. *Pensieri d'un cattolico*. Prato: Guasti, 1850.

"Notizie del giovanetto cristiano Mortara," *L'Armonia della religione collà Civiltà*. October 16, 1858, 959–60.

"Notizie Ecclesiastiche," *L'Araldo* October 12, 1859, 331.

"Notizie ecclesiastiche sulla conversione del Principe d'Anhalt-Coethen, e del Ministro Le Joux." *Memorie di religione di morale e di letteratura* 10 (1826): 203–8.

Pacca, Bartolommeo Cardinal. *Memorie storiche del ministero de' due viaggi in Francia e della prigionia nel Forte di S. Carlo.* Rome: F. Bourlie, 1830.

Paiano, Maria. "Il dibattito sui riflessi dell'anti-Semitismo nella liturgia Cattolica." *Studi Storici* 41, no. 3 (2000): 647–710.

Papke, David Ray, ed. *Narrative and the Legal Discourse.* Liverpool: Deborah Charles Publications, 1991.

Parfitt, Tudor. "The Use of the Jew in Colonial Discourse." In *Orientalism and the Jews,* edited by Ivan Davidson Kalmar and Derek J. Penslar, 51–67. Brandeis University Press, Waltham, MA, 2005.

Passelecq, Georges and Bernard Suchecky. *The Hidden Encyclical of Pius XI.* Translated by Steven Rendall. New York: Harcourt Brace & Co, 1997.

Passerin D'Entrèves, Ettore. *Religione e politica nell'Ottocento europeo.* Edited by Francesco Traniello. Rome: Istituto per la storia del risorgimento italiano, 1993.

Pelczar, G. S. 1910. *Pio IX e il suo pontificato sullo sfondo delle vicende della Chiesa nel sec. XIX,* vol. 2. Turin: Libreria Berruti, 1910.

Peters, Edward. *Inquisition.* New York: The Free Press, 1988.

"Il piccolo neofito Edgardo Mortara," *Civiltà Cattolica* 9, no. 12 (1858): 373–416.

Pickering, Michael. *Stereotyping: The Politics of Representation.* New York: Palgrave, 2001.

Pirri, Piero. *Pio IX e Vittorio Emanuele II dal loro carteggio privato. La Questione Romana, 1856–1864,* vol 1. Rome: Pontificia Università Gregoriana, 1951.

Pistelli Rinaldi, Emma. "Il cosiddetto 'miracolo di san Rocco' nella conversione del Manzoni." *Italianistica* 14, no. 3 (1985): 433–57.

Portier, Lucienne. "La conversion d'Alessandro Manzoni et son refus de la mythologie." *Revue des Etudes Italiennes* 10 (1964): 92–100.

Prieto, Antonio. "La logica della sua conversione." In *Manzoni Pro e Contro,* vol. 3, edited by Giancarlo Vigorelli, 1975–76. Milan: Istituto di propaganda libraria.

Puglisi, Filippo. *L'Arte del Manzoni.* Rome: Edizioni Studium, 1986.

Ragussis, Michael. *Figures of Conversion. "The Jewish Question" and English National Identity.* Durham: Duke University Press, 1995.

Raimondi, Ezio. *Letteratura e identità nazionale.* Milan: Mondadori, 1998.

Rambo, Lewis R. *Understanding Religious Conversion.* New Haven: Yale University Press, 1993.

Riall, Lucy. *The Italian Risorgimento: State, Society and National Unification.* New York: Routledge, 1994.

Riccards, Michael P. *Vicars of Christ. Popes, Power and Politics in the Modern World.* New York: Crossroad Publishing, 1998.

Rignano, I. E. *Sulla Attuale Posizione Giuridica degli Israeliti in Toscana. Brevi Cenni.* Firenze, 1847.

Riva, Massimo. *Malinconie del moderno: Critica dell'incivilmento e disagio della nazionalità nella letteratura italiana del XIX secolo.* Ravenna: Longo Editore, 2001.
Rogeard, A. "La Propriété sous l'Empire." *Pauvre France.* Brussels, 1859.
Romagnani, Gian Paolo. "Italian Protestants." In *The Emancipation of Catholics, Jews and Protestants,* edited by Rainer Liedtke and Stephan Wendehorst, 148–68. New York: Manchester University Press, 1999.
Rosa, Mario. "Tra tolleranza e repressione: Roma e gli ebrei nel '700." *Italia Judaica: Gli ebrei in Italia dalla segregazione alla prima emancipazione.* Atti del II Convegno internazionale, Tel Aviv 15–20 giugno 1986. Rome: Ministero per i beni cultura e ambientali, Ufficio centrale per i beni archivistici, 1989. 81–98.
Roveri, Alessandro. *La Santa Sede tra rivoluzione francese e restaurazione: Il cardinale Consalvi, 1813–1815.* Florence: La Nuova Italia, 1974.
Rubin, Miri. *Gentile Tales: The Narrative Assault on Late Medieval Jews.* New Haven: Yale University Press, 1999.
Rudt de Collenberg, W. H. "Le baptême des juifs à Rome de 1614 à 1798 selon les registres de la 'Casa dei catecumeni.' Troisième partie 1730–1798." *Archivum Historiae Pontificiae* 26 (1988): 119–294.
Ruffini, Francesco. "La 'conversione' del Manzoni." In *Manzoni: Testimonianze di critica e di polemica,* edited by Giorgio Bárberi Squarotti and Marziano Guglielminetti, 39–44. Florence: G. D'Anna, 1973.
Rychlak, Ronald J. *Hitler, the War and the Pope.* Columbus, MS: Genesis, 2000.
Said, Edward. *Orientalism.* New York: Pantheon Books, 1978.
Salvadori, Roberto. *Gli ebrei toscani nell'età della Restaurazione, 1814–1848.* Florence: Centro editoriale Toscano, 1993.
Samaja, Nino. "La Situazione degli ebrei nel periodo del Risorgimento." *Rassegna Mensile d'Israele* 23, nos. 7–9 (July-Sept. 1957): 298–309; 359–71; 414–21.
Sansone, Mario. *Manzoni Francese (1805–1810): Dall'Illuminismo al Romanticismo.* Rome: Laterza, 1993.
Scalvini, Giovita. "Il Cristianesimo antico e nuovo del Manzoni." In *Manzoni Pro e Contro,* vol. 1, edited by Giancarlo Vigorelli, 199–207. Milan: Istituto di propaganda libraria, 1975–1976.
———. *Foscolo, Manzoni,Goethe.* Edited by Mario Marcazzan. Turin: Einaudi, 1948.
Scherillo, Michele, ed. *Manzoni intimo,* vol. 2. Milan: U. Hoepli, 1923.
Segal, Alan F. *Paul the Convert: The Apostolate and Apostasy of Saul the Pharisee.* New Haven: Yale University Press, 1990.
Shapiro, James. *Oberammergau.* Vintage Books: New York, 2000.
———. *Shakespeare and the Jews.* New York: Columbia University Press, 1996.
Shorter, Aylward. *Toward a Theology of Inculturation.* Cassell Publishers: London, 1988.
Siegert, Bernhard. *Relays: Literature as an Epoch of the Postal System.* Translated by Kevin Repp. Stanford: Stanford University Press, 1999.

Singer, Joseph William. "Legal Storytelling: Persuasion." *Michigan Law Review* 87 (August, 1989): 2442–57.
Spadolini, Giovanni. "L'intransigentismo cattolico: dalla *Civiltà Cattolica* al *Sillabo.*" *Rassegna Storica Toscana* 4, no. 1 (1958): 309–32.
Spini, Giorgio. *Risorgimento e protestanti.* Turin: Claudiana, 1998.
Spinazzola, Vittorio. *Il libro per tutti: saggio sui "Promessi Sposi."* Roma: Editori Riuniti, 1983.
Stallybrass, P., and A. White. *The Politics and Poetics of Transgression.* Ithaca, New York: Cornell University Press, 1986.
Edith Stein. "'Il Silenzio Colpevole.'" *Corriere della Sera.* Translated by Brigida Pesce. February 19, 2003, 24.
Stowe, Kenneth. *Alienated Minority: the Jews of Medieval Latin Europe.* Cambridge, MA: Harvard University Press, 1992.
Taparelli, Father Luigi. *Della nazionalità.* Rome, 1847.
———. *Esame critico degli ordini rappresentativi nella società moderna.* Rome, 1854.
Taradel, Ruggero, and Barbara Raggi. *La segregazione amichevole. La 'Civiltà Cattolica e la questione ebraica, 1850–1945.* Rome: Editori Riuniti, 2000.
Tobin, Bruno. *Una patria per gli italiani.* Rome: Laterza, 1998.
Toscano, Mario, ed. *Integrazione e identità. L'esperienza ebraica in Germania e Italia dall'Illuminismo al fascismo.* Milan: FrancoAngeli, 1998.
Trachtenberg, Joshua. *The Devil and the Jews: The Medieval Conception of the Jew and its Relation to Modern Antisemitism.* New Haven: Yale University Press, 1943.
Traniello, Francesco. "Religione, nazione e sovranità nel Risorgimento italiano." *Rivista di Storia e letteratura religiosa* 32 (1992) 326–39.
Traniello, Francesco, and Giorgio Campanini, eds. *Dizionario Storico del Movimento Cattolico.* Genoa: Marietti, 1997.
Tribunale Civile e criminale di prima istanza in Bologna nella causa di Ratto del fanciullo Edgardo Mortara, avvenuto in Bologna il 24 giugno 1858. Per la Curia ed il Fisco Contro Il Padre Pier Gaetano Feletti dell'Ordine dei Predicatori di San Domenico, Inquisitore del Sant'Uffizio in Bologna. Conclusioni Fiscali. Bologna, 1860.
Turi, Gabriele. "Patria e nazione nel linguaggio politico italiano." *Passato e presente* 16, no. 45 (1998): 37–55.
Tusiani, Joseph. "Manzoni's *inni sacri* and *il cinque maggio.* A Translation." *Annali d'Italianistica* 3 (1985): 6–43.
Venosta, Giovanni Visconti. *Ricordi di gioventù.* Milano: Cogliati, 1906.
Ventura, Gioacchino. *Lettere ad un ministro protestante ed altri scritti minori.* Naples, 1860.
Verucci, Guido. *La Chiesa cattolica in Italia dall'Unità a oggi. 1861–1998.* Bari: Laterza, 1999.
Riccardo Verzini, "Il sogno della giustizia non violenta." In *I mondi impossibili: l'utopia*, edited by G. Barberi Squarotti. Turin: Tirrenia Stampatori, 1990. 175–86.

Veuillot, Louis. "Le Parfum de Rome, II." *Oeuvres complètes*, vol. 9. Paris, 1862.

Vicini, Giovanni. *Giovanni Vicini: memorie biografiche e storiche*. Bologna: Zanichelli, 1897.

Volli, Gemma. "Alcune conseguenze benefiche dell'affare Mortara." *Rassegna mensile di Israel* 28 (1962): 309–20.

Wald, Priscilla. *Constituting Americans. Cultural Anxiety and Narrative Form*. Durham, NC: Duke University Press, 1995.

Wales, Brennan. "Conversion in the *Promessi Sposi*—Coincidence and Disposition." *Queensland Dante Review* (1983–1986): 44–48.

Weber, Eugen J. *Peasants into Frenchmen: The Modernization of Rural France, 1870–1914*. Stanford, CA: Stanford University Press, 1976.

Weil, Le Commandant. "Un précédent de l'affaire Mortara." *Revue historique* 137 (1921): 3–20.

Weisberg, Richard. *Poethics: And Other Strategies of Law and Literature*. New York: Columbia University Press, 1992.

———. "Proclaiming Trials as Narratives: Premises and Pretenses." In *Law's Stories: Narrative and Rhetoric in the Law*, edited by Peter Brooks and Paul Gewirtz, 61–83. New Haven: Yale University Press, 1996.

West, Robin. *Narrative, Authority, and the Law*. Ann Arbor: University of Michigan Press, 1993.

Wiseman, Nicholas Cardinal. *Recollections of the Last Four Popes and of Rome in their Times*. New York: Joseph F. Wagner, 1858.

Zickmund, Susan. "Approaching the Radical Other: The Discursive Culture of Cyberhate." In *Virtual Culture: Identity and Communication in Cybersociety*, edited by S. G. Jones, 185–205. London: Sage, 1997.

Zuccotti, Susan. *Under His Very Windows: The Vatican and the Holocaust in Italy*. New Haven: Yale University Press, 2001.

Index

Please note that page numbers appearing in *italics* indicate end notes.

rich archival documentation
possible